At Home In a Strange Land

Andrew Sloane

At Home In a Strange Land

Using the Old Testament in Christian Ethics

HENDRICKSON
PUBLISHERS

At Home in a Strange Land:
Using the Old Testament in Christian Ethics
© 2008 by Hendrickson Publishers, Inc.
P. O. Box 3473
Peabody, Massachusetts 01961-3473

ISBN 978-1-59856-084-8

Printed in the United States of America

First Printing – November 2008

Library of Congress Cataloging-in-Publication Data

Sloane, Andrew.
    At home in a strange land : using the Old Testament in Christian ethics / Andrew Sloane.
       p. cm.
    Includes bibliographical references and indexes.
    ISBN 978-1-59856-084-8 (alk. paper)
    1. Ethics in the Bible. 2. Bible. O.T.–Criticism, interpretation, etc. 3. Christian ethics. I. Title.
    BS1199.E8S56 2008
    241–dc22
                2008026194

To Alison

Charm is deceitful and beauty is fleeting, but a woman who fears Yahweh is to be praised. (Prov 31:30)

TABLE OF CONTENTS

Acknowledgments

THE ACKNOWLEDGMENTS AT THE START of a book are a bit like the thank-you speeches on Oscar night (without, thankfully, all the cameras, sequins, and low-cut gowns): someone you don't know bores you silly by listing a bunch of other people you don't know, ranging from their first-grade teacher to their pedicurist. I won't go to those lengths, but there are a number of people whose help with this book cannot go unacknowledged, so let me at least thank them in lieu of more tangible expressions of gratitude. The editorial staff at Hendrickson, especially Shirley Decker-Lucke and Allan Emery, has been kind and patient in the face of many delays and complications. Thank you both for your patience and your helpful editorial suggestions.

I have profited greatly over many years from the people with whom I have worked in Australia, at Ridley College in Melbourne and at Morling College in Sydney. Thanks are due to them, but especially to Graham Cole, who gave me my first teaching job, apprenticed me in the craft of theological education, and whose example of faithful and careful scholarship challenges and inspires me; to Mike Frost, who prompted me to embark on the project and introduced me to the staff at Hendrickson; and to the Morling College council and its generous provision of sabbatical leave in 2006 which enabled me to work on this and other projects. To my readers, James Clarke, Glen Newman, and Margaret Wilkins: thanks for your generous gift of time and your thoughtful and encouraging responses. These people, and many others, have helped make this a much better book than it would otherwise have been. It may be a hackneyed thing to say, but it is nonetheless true: much of what works in the book is thanks to them; the only things for which I can claim sole responsibility are the defects that remain. I close by acknowledging the love and support of my family: my daughters, Elanor, Laura, and Alexandra, and of course my wife, Alison. Proverbs 31:10 asks, "An excellent wife, who can find?" Well, I have. Her love, companionship, and godliness—and, yes, beauty—are among God's greatest gifts to me. So thanks, Alison. I thank God for the gift of a life shared with you.

ABBREVIATIONS

GENERAL

A.D.	anno Domini
ANE	ancient Near East
AV	Authorized Version
B.C.	before Christ
DNA	deoxyribonucleic acid
ESV	English Standard Version
IVF	in vitro fertilization
OT	Old Testament
NASB	New American Standard Bible
NIV	New International Version
NRSV	New Revised Standard Version
NT	New Testament
RSV	Revised Standard Version
SCNT	somatic cell nuclear transfer

OLD TESTAMENT

Gen	Genesis
Exod	Exodus
Lev	Leviticus
Num	Numbers
Deut	Deuteronomy
Josh	Joshua
Judg	Judges

1–2 Sam	1–2 Samuel
1–2 Kgs	1–2 Kings
1–2 Chr	1–2 Chronicles
Neh	Nehemiah
Esth	Esther
Ps/Pss	Psalms
Prov	Proverbs
Eccl	Ecclesiastes
Song	Song of Songs
Isa	Isaiah
Jer	Jeremiah
Ezek	Ezekiel
Dan	Daniel
Hos	Hosea
Mic	Micah

New Testament

Matt	Matthew
Rom	Romans
1–2 Cor	1–2 Corinthians
Gal	Galatians
Eph	Ephesians
Col	Colossians
1–2 Thess	1–2 Thessalonians
1–2 Tim	1–2 Timothy
Heb	Hebrews
Jas	James
1–2 Pet	1–2 Peter
Rev	Revelation

Introduction

Neglected, Despised, and Abused—The Strange Land of the Old Testament

My daughters have described me as perhaps the ultimate Christian geek. They may be right. After all, I teach at a theological college, training women and men to serve God and the church. That's pretty geeky. What's worse, I teach Old Testament, among other things, and I love it. I love the OT for its rich diversity and surprising, confronting, exhilarating message. I love teaching it because it's a delight and a privilege to try to bring it to life for students, or rather, to allow it to come to life for them. I also love teaching it because my students are often daunted and confused by it, sometimes even intimidated by it, and it gives me almost selfish pleasure to see them engage it, be engaged by it, and come to see that it is, after all, relevant to their lives and ministries. The same applies to preaching from the OT in churches.

Of course, as an "Old Testament professor," I get lots of people asking me questions, not just about what a particular bit of the OT means, but also about how it can be considered Scripture at all and of any value for Christians. In fact, in my experience many people are afraid of or puzzled by the OT, as it is frequently abused (e.g., in apartheid or prosperity theology), seems to say much that is "sub-Christian" (e.g., Deuteronomy's take on warfare, or Ps 137), or is just plain bizarre (e.g., most of the early chapters of the books of Leviticus and Ezekiel). The OT is also a big, sprawling, diverse, and puzzling set of documents with a main story line spanning over fifteen hundred years of history. As a result, it is frequently, even generally, neglected or avoided by Christians. This strikes me as a problem, given that it was the Scripture of Jesus and the earliest churches, the Scripture that 2 Tim 3:16 famously describes as "God-breathed" and given for our moral and spiritual benefit. So, what to do? We seem to be stuck between a rock and a hard place: on the one hand, we claim these texts as our Scripture, and therefore we must read them and seek to understand what God is saying to us by way of them; on the other hand, we are struck by their oddness, even their offensiveness. We are Christians, after all, and the ᴏᴛ is a very strange land.

What most people do, of course, is treat the ᴏᴛ with benign neglect. They say that it's part of their Bible, but they rarely read more than a few favorite bits from Psalms or Proverbs and, if they're feeling brave at Christmas, sections from Isaiah and Micah. And that neglect is found not only in the pews but also in the pulpits. I do occasional snap polls of my students to find out what their pastors have been preaching. Often the results are depressing. Those students whose pastors do preach expository sermons (i.e., a sermon that addresses the contemporary world based on a clear explanation of a passage of Scripture) and sermon series based on a particular book of the Bible rarely hear from the ᴏᴛ more than about a quarter of the time. I have yet to have a class in which at least one student has not heard an expository sermon from the ᴏᴛ in the last year. While in theory many Christians, professional or otherwise, take the ᴏᴛ to be Scripture, mostly they ignore a good deal of it. Others are, perhaps, a little more honest. They don't neglect the ᴏᴛ; they either see it as second-class Scripture, or reject it outright.

Clearly, I don't want to do that myself, nor do I believe that anyone else should. In fact, I fervently believe that the ᴏᴛ is God's word to us. If I may put it bluntly (and rather simplistically), the Scripture that was good enough for Jesus and the authors of the ɴᴛ is good enough for us, or at least it ought to be. But how does that work? We are New, not Old, Testament believers. We do, thank God, have the ɴᴛ and its witness to God's great and glorious work in and through Jesus, who is, we believe, at the heart of the Bible and its story of God's dealings with the world. We are Christians, and so our Bible includes much more than the ᴏᴛ—but it *does* include it.

But, you might argue, the world in which we live is very different from the world of the OT, and we face cultures and circumstances that the human authors of the Bible could not have imagined (of course, this is true also for the NT). Here are a couple of examples. For the last half century or so humans have had the technological ability to destroy life on this planet as we know it and have used some of that technology to devastating effect. Other technology gives us next-to-immediate knowledge of world affairs. We can watch events from the other side of the globe within hours or minutes of their happening, or even as they happen, on television and the Internet. Such technology, of course, was not in view in the Bible, nor could it have been. Given that we live on this side of the cross and not two or three thousand years ago, how does the OT work as Christian Scripture? To address the questions of this book more specifically: How does the OT work as Scripture when we as Christians think about some of the ethical issues that we face? How do we use the OT, a "B.C." text, in Christian ethics without defying either the text or our context, which is, so to speak, both theologically and culturally "A.D."? How do we move from the "then" of the text to the "now" of the world in which we live? And, how do we move from "now" to "then" to gain insight into the decisions that we need to make without imposing our own issues and questions on the Bible? These are some of the questions that I want to tackle in this book.

First, however, I think that it's worth being a bit clearer about the issues and problems and questions that we face, because, I believe, the first step in being at home in the OT is recognizing that it is indeed a "strange land." So here I want to talk about some of the issues that have come up in my teaching and preaching from the OT.

Recently a group of evangelical Christian organizations formed the Micah Network and promoted the Micah Challenge, an attempt to mobilize (evangelical) Christians in advocating for justice on behalf of the poorest and most marginalized people in our global economy. This is a project that I am passionately committed to, one that I see as reflecting God's own passion for justice (see Mic 6:6–8). In early 2006 I was asked to speak about an OT perspective on justice at a training session for people interested in the Micah Challenge. Having spoken on Ps 99, one of many texts that speak of the centrality of justice to the Lord our God and God's purposes for God's people and world, I opened up the session for questions and discussion. The issue that occupied most of our time was how the OT can speak a word of freedom and justice when it specifically allows for, even legislates, slavery. And clearly it does. Exodus 21:2-11 speaks of Hebrew male and female slaves (the NIV translates it "servants," but the Hebrew word clearly includes slaves), the latter possibly acting as either a concubine or wife (Exod 21:7-11). As we will see later, it is important that we distinguish slavery in the OT from that of African slaves in, say, seventeenth-century Europe or America. The details need not detain us here, but it is clear that a master had extensive, though not absolute, power over his slaves (see Exod 21:20-21, 26-27; 23:12; Deut 15:12-18; 23:15-16). Clearly, the OT allows for slavery. How is that consistent with God being just and merciful?

Some years ago I was invited to run a teaching camp over Easter weekend for a local church in Melbourne. The organizers of the camp and I decided that Leviticus would be a good book to look at, partly because of the importance of the sacrificial system for understanding the death of Jesus, and partly, I must confess, because I was pretty sure that no one would have ever studied it before. I had a great time, especially discussing the Day of Atonement (Lev 16) and its application to Jesus' death, and the Year of Jubilee (Lev 25) and its relation to his ministry and resurrection (Luke 4:14-22 in light of Isa 61:1-4). But I thought that it was also important to look at the issue of "clean" and "unclean," especially as it related to people (Lev 11-15), which, of course, raised very big questions for the people at the camp. What are we supposed to do with all that stuff about food and skin diseases (including for buildings [Lev 13:47-58; 14:33-53])? In particular, many of the women (and some of the men) were unsure how to respond to the fact that a woman is unclean for one week every month and makes anyone who touches her similarly unclean (Lev 15:19-24). That seems to be an unfair way to deal with something both unavoidable and natural. Even worse, a woman is also unclean after childbirth, and she is in this state for twice as long if she bears a daughter rather than a son (eighty days compared to forty [Lev 12:1-5]). How is that fair? Isn't it simply misogynistic? Doesn't it reflect a fearful, belittling view of women held by men trying to control them and their place in society? How is that tolerable, let alone useful or relevant, for Christians?

A few years ago I was asked to run an afternoon seminar at a local church in Sydney on Joshua, "holy war," and the Canaanite "genocide." Joshua 10-11 clearly portrays Joshua and the Israelites as exterminating the Canaanite population of the land, and doing so in obedience to the Lord's command (Josh 10:40; 11:15; see also Deut 7). How, I was asked, is this at all consistent with the message of the gospel? How does it square with Jesus and his call to love our enemies? Does it not justify the kind of religiously inspired violence that we have all come to know and loathe? Good questions, particularly in light of the horrific things we've seen in the Serbian "ethnic cleansing" program (perpetrated, we must remember, by Serbian Christians against their Muslim neighbors), the bombing of the World Trade Center, and the ongoing violence in Iraq and Israel/Palestine. We abhor and are appalled by such wanton destruction of human life. Yet, doesn't our own Bible contain similar violence? It even goes so far as to command the death penalty for transgressions such as idolatry, cursing one's parents, adultery, incest, (male) homosexual intercourse, and bestiality (Lev 20:1-16). What are we to do with such violent texts, especially when the violence is commanded by God? Are we even talking about the same God?

Clearly, there are many other issues that I could raise here. Outlining them all would take another whole book, and my aim here is both more than and different from that; in any case, some of these issues will come up as we go along. What I want to do is address these types of questions and "rehabilitate" the OT so that we can use it effectively in our ethical reflection and faithful living. I don't want to pretend that the OT is other than it is—at times exhilarating, at others strange, puzzling, even disturbing. It is a strange land. But it is also, so to speak, our land. For Christians, it is an essential part of the Bible, God's authoritative word, which is meant to govern our lives and shape our thinking. As we deal with its implications for Christian ethics, I will focus on shaping ways of thinking about Scripture and the world rather than giving detailed and specific instruction on current policies and so on. This is in part because the world is constantly changing, and so are the issues; it is also in part because you know your circumstances and the issues that you face better than some academic in Australia could ever hope to do. But it is mostly because the aim of this book is to equip you to use the OT for yourself as you think about what it means to live as a disciple of Jesus in this world. My aim is not to tell you what I think it all means and how I think you should live. Obviously, I won't be able to deal with all the important texts and themes in OT ethics. The OT is too rich and complex to allow me to do that. My goal is to act as a guide on your journey into this strange territory, pointing out key landmarks, noting trouble spots and dangers, seeking to equip you to explore it for yourself and find a home in it.

So, here's the plan. In chapter 1, "Equipment for the Journey," I will begin the discussion by stepping right back from the problems and even the text to look at underlying questions of the nature of the OT, its authority, and how we go about interpreting biblical texts. In the process I will briefly sketch an outline of how I think Christians should approach ethics in general as well as a framework for understanding OT ethics in particular. Chapter 2, "Getting Going," will look at background issues and basic skills that will help you interpret different kinds of OT texts (law, story, prophecy, poetry, wisdom) and provide "worked examples" of interpreting these texts—this is the first step in feeling at home in the OT and knowing how to use it as Scripture. Chapter 3, "Avoiding Pitfalls, Hacking through the Jungle," will return to the issues that I've raised in this chapter in light of our discussion, seeking to present a Christian perspective on these difficult issues and so clearing the ground for the rest of our exploration of the OT. Chapter 4, "Exploring the Territory," will examine two major landmarks in OT ethics—the stories of creation and the fall (Gen 1-3) and the Ten Commandments (Exod 20:1-17; Deut 5:6-21)—and explore some of their contributions to Christian ethics. Finally, chapter 5, "Bringing the Old Testament Home," will seek to bring it all together, framing an overall approach to using the OT in Christian ethics as well as providing two worked examples. One example tackles an issue that confronts us today but is not addressed in Scripture (cloning) to see how the OT can shape our ethical reflection on it. The other example moves from the OT to today, seeking to apply a text that at first glance seems theological rather than ethical (Isa 46) to our contemporary circumstances.

At the end of the book I have provided two annotated bibliographies, which I've called the "Geek Zone" and "Further Travels in the Geek Zone," containing what I see as the most useful or important works on the questions explored in this study. It will give you a start on your further reading if, like me, you get captured by the adventure of reading the ᴏᴛ. I trust that this book will help you, if not to find the ᴏᴛ less strange, at least to feel at home in that strange land. So, let's get on with the journey.

CHAPTER 1

EQUIPMENT FOR THE JOURNEY

WHEN OUR DAUGHTERS WERE LITTLE we lived for six years in Melbourne, on the southeastern tip of Australia, but our families lived in Sydney, over five hundred miles to the north. So every year, for six years, we would make the trip to Sydney to have Christmas with the family—a twelve-hour car ride in the middle of an Australian summer, with three daughters crammed into the back seat, and then twelve hours back again. As much as they loved their grandparents, every year at least one of the girls (and sometimes my wife) would ask, "Do we have to go?" And yes, we did. Every year. These car trips are not, I must say, among my fondest memories. These were trips to be survived and endured, not enjoyed. Survival, in fact, was the best that we could hope for. What made survival possible for me and my wife (and for our kids) was careful planning. We made sure that we were well equipped for the journey. We had all our stops mapped out, snacks and little presents to give out every hour, story tapes to play, strategies for ignoring "Are we there yet?," and on and on. And every year we got there and back again safely, family intact. It was all about preparation, making sure that we knew where we were going, how we were going to get there, and what we would need along the way. It's the same for our journey to the strange land of the OT. That's what this chapter is about. I will give you a map of the territory (a framework for understanding the OT and its ethics) and say something about how to get there (look at basic issues in interpreting the Bible). But first, I should deal with my daughters' question, "Do we have to go?"

Many Christians would answer, "No, we don't." In fact, they would say we that shouldn't, that the OT is too strange, its ethics too far from us and our circumstances, too contaminated by violence and misogyny, to be of any benefit. And after all, they might add, we are Christians, and Christ is the end of the law (Rom 10:4). A second group would disagree vehemently, arguing that the OT is God's word, and that is all that matters: "God said it, I believe it, that settles it." Unless Jesus or the apostles have told us otherwise, everything in the OT Scriptures is binding on us as Christians. A third group takes a mediating position, maintaining that although the OT is Christian Scripture, we need to think carefully about what it meant then and how we use it now. Yes, this is a journey we need to go on, but it's a more complicated one than some might think. (I guess it's fairly obvious which is my view.) Clearly, these three views differ on whether this is a journey that we should undertake and, if it is, what route we should take. So, before we head off on our journey, let's first make sure that we have to go and think a bit about how we might get there.

THE MORAL AUTHORITY OF THE OLD TESTAMENT

The idea that the OT has no bearing on Christians, that the God of the OT is not really the same God as the God and Father of our Lord Jesus Christ, has a long pedigree going back to the second century A.D. The Christian theologian Marcion believed that the God of the OT was an inconsistent, violent, repressive being. While acknowledging the creator god, Marcion believed that this god did a poor job of creating the world, and that the fractured nature of current reality reflected the nature of this god. He also saw this god as harsh and judgmental, as imposing contradictory and burdensome rules on people and ruthlessly punishing them for any breaking of the rules. Marcion's solution was to propose a radical distinction between Yahweh, the creator and lawgiver of the OT, and the one true God revealed in the person of Christ. Christ, in fact, was seen as the one who redeemed us from the power of the second-class OT god and showed us a different God, a God of mercy and grace. As a result, Marcion and his followers rejected the OT outright (along with most of the NT, other than some of Paul's letters and his own version of Luke). According to Marcion, the OT had no role to play in Christian life and faith. Some of this may sound familiar; it certainly is echoed in many comments that I hear today about the OT and its relation to Jesus and the NT. It is a view, however, that was rejected by the early church, which excommunicated Marcion for his teachings.

Marcion's views have reappeared periodically in Christian history and are reflected, in my view, in the work of the eighteenth-century German theologian Friedrich Schleiermacher and his followers. Admittedly, Schleiermacher was not an avowed Marcionite (as those who accept Marcion's teachings are known). However, he very clearly distinguished Christian faith and theology from anything related to Judaism, including its Scriptures. His reasoning was careful and intricate, but the details need not detain us here. What is clear is that for Schleiermacher, the proper subject of Christian theology (and so ethics) is Christian faith and experience, as distinct from any other religion. That, in turn, meant that he rejected not only all OT Scriptures as an authority for Christian faith and theology but also anything in the NT that merely reflected Jewish (i.e., OT) ideas. It was, after all, only what was distinctly Christian that was relevant for Christian theology and ethics.

Others take a radically different line. For them, the authority granted to the OT by Jesus and the authors of the NT means that it must be authoritative for us. If it was God's word then, it is God's word now, and only the author has the right to change it, only the lawgiver is entitled to bring in a new law. Jesus himself stated very clearly that he came not to abolish but rather to fulfill the law (Matt 5:17-19). This means that the only OT commands that are not binding on us are those specifically superseded in the NT. Thus, for instance, we are no longer bound by the food laws outlined in the OT (e.g., Lev 11), since Jesus has rendered all foods clean (Mark 7:1-23; cf. Acts 10); we no longer have to sacrifice animals (e.g., Lev 1), since Jesus' once-for-all sacrifice has made the old sacrificial system obsolete (Heb 7-10). Other OT laws, however, are fully binding and are to govern a Christian's conscience and practice.

The theonomist (or Christian Restoration) movement is a current example of this line of thinking. Theonomists argue that the law of God ought to be the law of the land. Old Testament law, except where clearly negated by later NT teaching, ought to be the basis of our civil and criminal law. Thus, adultery, homosexual practice, and so on ought not just be considered morally wrong; they ought to be illegal. Furthermore, OT law gives us the basis not only of legislation but also of punishment, including capital punishment where relevant. So, for instance, certain sexual crimes ought to be punishable by death (although blasphemy should not, given theonomist belief in the NT's teaching of freedom of religious conscience). Here I need to stress that theonomists do not seek to impose this law on a reluctant populace; rather, they seek to bring people to faith in Christ who will then voluntarily adopt the theonomic ideal. Nonetheless, according to theonomists, we should not just travel to the strange land of the OT; we ought to take up residence there.

Theonomic Reformed Approach to Law and Gospel

God's holy and good law is never wrong in what it demands. It is "perfect" (Deut. 32:4; Ps. 19:7; James 1:25), just like the Lawgiver himself (Matt. 5:48). . . . Two premises about the law of God are thus abundantly clear if we want to be faithful to the infallible testimony of Scripture: (1) The law of God is *good* in what it demands, being what is natural to the Creator-creature relationship. (2) The demands of God's law are *universal* in their character and application, not confined in validity to Old Testament Israel. . . . In short, it is the civil magistrate's proper function and duty to obey the Scripture's dictates regarding crime and its punishment. . . . The Bible stands squarely against the personally chosen starting point of those who recoil from the penal sanctions of God's law. The Word of God insists that "the law is good" (1 Tim. 1:8-10). According to its infallible teaching, it is necessary to execute civil penalties against criminal behavior (Prov. 20:2, 8; 1 Pet. 2:14), and to do so without exception or mercy (Deut. 19:13, 21; 25:12).[1]

Both of these views are, however, fatally flawed. The first, which we could call the "total rejection" viewpoint, is difficult to reconcile with what NT authors say and how they say it. For them the OT clearly functioned as Scripture, as God's authoritative word, as can

---

[1] Gregory L. Bahnsen, "The Theonomic Reformed Approach to Law and Gospel," in *The Law, the Gospel, and the Modern Christian: Five Views* (ed. Wayne G. Strickland; Grand Rapids: Zondervan, 1993), 109, 112, 128, 133.

be seen in, for instance, the frequency with which Paul quotes the OT in Romans. The second viewpoint, which we could call "total acceptance," also fails to do justice to the way in which NT authors used the OT, as well as how the law worked in the OT itself (we will see more on this later).

Here it is worth noting that although NT writers refer frequently to the OT, they never speak of it as binding on governments or use OT law as the basis for new forms of government. Paul, for instance, would have had a perfect opportunity to do so in Rom 13; it is striking that he doesn't. Whatever role the OT plays in Christian ethics, there is no evidence that NT authors saw OT law as binding on the state. Furthermore, Paul seemed to see Christians as free from the constraints of the law so as to be bound to a deeper obedience to God in the power of the Spirit (e.g., Gal 5:1-15). That, surely, rules out all forms of legalism. There are other points of view that, though less extreme, cluster around the poles of total rejection of the OT as a source of Christian ethics (e.g., classical dispensational theologies) or total acceptance (e.g., some, more legalistic, versions of Seventh Day Adventist tradition). In my view, they are subject to criticisms similar to the ones that I have outlined here. So, we should neither abandon the journey (total rejection of the OT) nor seek to emigrate (total acceptance); rather, we should prepare to visit this strange land. Shortly, we will look at what we should do when we get there; for now, however, we need to think about the journey itself. It is time to think about the task of biblical interpretation and related ideas regarding the nature of Scripture.

HERMENEUTICS: HOW DO WE INTERPRET THE BIBLE?

The issues that we have looked at so far are, broadly speaking, issues of hermeneutics. "Hermeneutics" is one of those words that "insiders" in the game of biblical studies like to bandy around and that completely mystify "outsiders." Perhaps that's the point of some of the jargon that we use. Let me demystify the word. Hermeneutics, simply put, is the task of understanding how people communicate and discern meaning (especially in texts). Admittedly, what most of us are concerned with is practical exegesis–getting the meaning out of a text by reading a passage and understanding it. Hermeneutics of Scripture is a theoretical discipline but one closely related to the practicalities of reading and interpreting texts. In fact, I suggest, all interpretation assumes a hermeneutic, be it explicit or implicit. Hermeneutics guides what questions you put to a text, what answers you think it can give, and so on. Theory shapes practice (and vice versa).

But, you might say, surely we can do without hermeneutics. You've been reading your Bible for years and only just heard the word. On the other hand, you might say that looking into hermeneutics means that you've been doing it all wrong, that what you've been doing with the Bible is naïve and illegitimate. Or you might feel that you need to have a university degree to read your Bible correctly. Some writers in the field certainly seem to imply that without a lot of specialized knowledge and access to tools of biblical criticism, our readings of Scripture are questionable at best. I am not one of them (I am neither a hermeneutician nor the son of a hermeneutician [apologies to Amos 7:14]). As I see it, hermeneutics is not about throwing away everything you already know and all you currently do; rather, hermeneutics is about seeking to understand how and why your current method and practice work and perhaps learning to improve upon them.

Let me draw an analogy: the relationship between hermeneutics and interpreting a text is like the relationship between (civil) engineering and building a bridge. Bridges can be built by people who have never studied engineering, and frequently they have been—what's more, these bridges stay up. People learn what to do by a process of trial and error (if it collapses, clearly you need to try something different) and by being taught by others who knew what they were doing (this one fell, and that one stayed up, so do it that way). The problem is that some designs work only in particular circumstances: a simple arched bridge made of stone may work over a stream; you can even use a series of arches to cross a large river. This method won't work, however, if you want to cross Sydney Harbor. For that, you need a completely new kind of bridge. Engineering helps you know not only what design to use and where—experience can do that—but also why a particular design works. This means that if you are faced with a problem that you or your teachers haven't encountered before, you can go back to first principles and figure out a solution. It can even help you improve on an old design, eliminating faults and streamlining the design. So it is with hermeneutics. People can and do read their Bibles and understand them without ever having studied hermeneutics or even knowing the word. (You are now among the blessed elite who know the term and what it means!) Knowing a little about hermeneutics can help you understand how and why particular interpretations work and give you skills to deal with texts and issues that you have not encountered before and ones that you have not adequately dealt with in the past.

I admit that hermeneutics can get fairly involved, given the nature of some of the issues that it has to deal with. But engineering can get fairly complicated too. My engineering friends at university used to regularly curse something called "statics," a mind-bending subject dealing with the rules governing the forces producing an equilibrium between material bodies way beyond the capabilities of a mere medical student such as I was at the time. Hermeneutics looks at issues related to the nature of meaning: where it resides (if anywhere); whether it is fixed and, if so, how and by whom; whether it is created in the interpretive process or inscribed by authors and discovered by readers; how the things that we already believe (our presuppositions) influence both how we read texts and what meaning we find there. We'll need to look at some of these issues as we go along; others we can happily ignore.

Nonetheless, hermeneutics is an important matter for us to consider, given that it deals with something central to Christian life and faith: reading the Bible. There are many legitimate ways that we as Christians use the Bible. We use it in our worship services, shaping our communities and their underlying values; we use it to shape our prayers and our imaginations; we use it for guidance; we allow God's Spirit to use it to challenge and enrich us. The philosopher Nicholas Wolterstorff has argued that one of the most important things we do with the Bible (something, I suggest, that informs or should inform most of our other uses of the Bible) is to read it for what he calls "divine discourse"; that is, we read the Bible so as to understand what God is saying to us by way of it. That, I suggest, is one thing that lies behind our calling the Bible "God's word." But now things get a little bit complicated, for the Bible doesn't come to us as a word from on high, untouched by human hands (or lips); rather, the Bible is God's word to us through human words. That means two things: first, we need to understand what the human authors were saying; second, we then have to understand what God was and is saying through them. We will look at each of these in turn.

When looking at the role of the human author, we should recall what texts are and why people write them. Texts are linguistic objects, produced by persons in particular contexts, addressed to other persons in order to achieve particular purposes. Let me unpack that. Texts are particular instances of human use of language; they are a species of communication. People use language with particular purposes in mind, generally involving other people and their actions or beliefs. Even if the purpose is simply to entertain, language has a point, a personal purpose. People *do things* with words. Generally, for these purposes to be achieved, the language needs to successfully communicate; messages need to be received as well as sent. But also, texts are different from other kinds of communication: they are not just language; they also are objects. I can pick up my copy of Margaret Atwood's *The Handmaid's Tale* and look at it, read it, give it to my daughter, and so on. (That is true even with electronic texts. They may not have the same physical presence that a book has, but somewhere electrons are configured in such a way as to produce words on a screen. They are, so to speak, virtual objects.) What does the idea of texts as linguistic objects mean for the task of biblical interpretation?

We need to keep in mind that the Bible is a text or, more properly speaking, a coherent collection of texts. This collection of texts was produced by persons (including God) in particular contexts and was addressed to other persons (again, including God) in order to achieve particular purposes. These purposes include promises (e.g., Gen 12; John 14), warnings (e.g., Deut 8; Heb 5:11–6:12), relationships (e.g., Exod 19:5-6; John 21:25), praises (e.g., Pss 146–150; Eph 1:3-14), instructions (e.g., Deut 6; 1 Thess 4:13-5:11), and truth claims (e.g., Isa 44:9-20; Acts 2:14-36). All these are things that people did with these words. Now, you may be puzzled by the idea that the Bible speaks to God. Is it not, after all, God's word to us? Is it not God speaking to us? Yes it is. But it is also a record of human beings speaking to God. Think, for instance, of Psalms, or large sections of Job, or important bits of Paul's letters, or, for that matter, Jesus' own prayers in John 17. All of these passages are addressed to God. Is that not what prayer is about? They are, nonetheless, God's words to us, for they are prayers that God has endorsed for our use. These are prayers to which, if you like, God has already said, "Amen"; they are models for our praying. These observations have interesting implications for our understanding of the Bible and its authority.

As we turn to the question of biblical interpretation, we must remember these three key aspects of communication: the text, the author, and the reader. The first aspect is obvious: if we seek to understand what someone is saying by way of a text, we must attend to the text. That is to say, we must seek to understand the text, how it has been put together, how language is being used, what kind of argument, metaphor, or story is put forward and how. We do this in order to understand the author's intention; nonetheless, the text itself and its literary features are primary, as they are the primary way we can come to grasp authorial intentions. The first, most important (and obvious) step in the process is to read the text, to do so carefully, and, if it's an important text or one that you are struggling to grasp, to do so repeatedly. But here some background knowledge is often helpful because texts, including biblical texts, are created by persons in the context of a particular culture and language, according to conventions of language and communication that they shared with their original readers. We need to understand the ways in which language is used, arguments are constructed, narrative unfolds, metaphors are used, and so on if we are to understand the text and so grasp the author's meaning. Sometimes we either skip this step or assume that the words are being used the way we would use them, when that may not be the case. And this may create problems where there are none. For instance, in Exod 33:11 Moses is described as "speaking face to face" with God; yet a little later in the same chapter he is told that no one can see God's face and live (Exod 33:20-23). So, does he see God's face or doesn't he? In this instance we need to realize that "speaking face to face" is a metaphor, an image of the kind of intimate relationship and direct communication that Moses enjoyed with the Lord. Moses has that kind of relationship, almost unique in the OT, but even he cannot see the unveiled glory of God. So, then, understanding the text as a linguistic object is a key dimension of biblical interpretation.

Texts are, however, produced to communicate, which means that the people who produced them had intentions that the texts were created to convey to other people. This is true no matter whether the text is the work of a single individual (like, say, the books of Jonah, Esther, and Galatians) or of many authors (like, say, Proverbs, which specifies a number of collections, and Luke, who specifically states that he drew on the memories of others and records of the words and actions of Jesus). The intentions that the authors and collectors had for the texts that they produced are crucial to understanding the text, but they must be understood properly. The notion of "intention" has come under fire in some philosophical and theological circles, in part because of romantic failures and excesses. An older school of interpretation spoke of "understanding the mind of the author"—sometimes even better than the author understood his or her own mind! This has been rightly criticized, for we have no access to the mind of the author other than by way of the text; another person's internal states of mind are closed to us. Furthermore, we know that we don't always say what we mean or mean what we say, and more importantly, we have no access to the author to check up on our conclusions. There is, then, a certain "distance" between the author and the text, a distance made all the greater by the very fact that these individual texts are now part of the canon of Scripture—that set of texts recognized to be unlike all other texts, being God's word. This gives them new and broader contexts, and others' intentions (such as later editors of some biblical texts and those responsible for larger collections within Scripture) may also be expressed through the original authors' words. Still, texts are not cut off from their original contexts or authors, as if they were a kite with no string. The authors' intentions are expressed in the linguistic and literary "codes" of the text and are to guide us in our interpretation.

Here we see the crucial connection between context, text, and intention. Knowing the context of writing, including the ways in which language was used and texts were written, gives us clues as to what the text's "code" means, what intentions have become public in this act of communication. So, for instance, if we read the words "Once upon a time" at the start of a book, we know that we are reading a story, and usually a story of a particular kind, a fairytale. This literary code tells us that, except in unusual circumstances (such as an ironic retelling of someone's history), the story is not to be taken as a description of events in the world. If someone were to criticize a telling of "Goldilocks and the Three Bears" because bears don't eat porridge, sit in chairs, or sleep in beds, we would say that the critic simply got it wrong. The teller of the story may be making a point about irresponsible, selfish behavior but certainly is not making claims about animal behavior. In the same way, Jesus often introduces a parable by simply talking about a certain man or woman, as in, for instance, the so-called parable of the Good Samaritan (Luke 10:30–37). Jesus is making a number of points in the parable, most particularly challenging the "expert in the law" to reconfigure his moral universe; Jesus is not making historical claims about events on the Jerusalem-to-Jericho road (nor, for that matter, is Luke). Other times, a certain set of words carries with it very clear implications and allows the author to make clear claims of intent. So, for instance, the prophetic messenger formula "Thus says the LORD" or "The word of the LORD came to . . ." clearly functions as a way of authorizing the speaker and the speaker's words as an instance of divine communication.

Understanding the author's likely historical context is also often important in understanding intention. Let me give two examples, beginning with the first commandment's demand that we have "no other gods" but Yahweh, the Lord (Exod 20:3; Deut 5:7). Later texts make it plain that God is the one true God, and that all other claims to divinity are simply false (see, e.g., Deut 32:16–18, 21; Isa 44; Ps 96:5). That is not something that Israel had grasped, however, as is apparent both in the incident involving the golden calf and in Israel's behavior during the period of the judges (Exod 32; Judg 2:11–23). The commandment, then, does not make any claims about the (non)existence of other gods; it is a clear and unambiguous call to sole allegiance. Yahweh is our God, and Yahweh alone. So too, when we are dealing with an unfamiliar type of text, it can be important to look at the cultural context of similar texts in order to understand both the literary conventions of the time and the likely purposes to which someone might put such a text. Indeed, observing the differences between biblical texts and texts written at about the same time by Israel's neighbors can be most revealing. This is particularly clear in the creation account in Gen 1:1–2:3. There were many stories and poems dealing with the creation of the world in OT times. Many of them describe the creation of the world as the result of a bloody and violent conflict between competing groups of gods, some of whom persist as potential threats to the stability of the cosmos. Although dim echoes of the language of these myths can be found in Gen 1:1–2:3 (the "deep" in Gen 1:2; "great creatures of the sea" in Gen 1:21), the very patterns of the account indicate that the author was telling us that the world is not a chaotic place, subject to the whim of competing gods, but rather is the purposeful product of the one true and sovereign God.

So we see that text and context are important and give us keys to understanding the author's intention, allowing us to better grasp the meaning being conveyed by the author to other persons by way of the text. But, as we have already seen, this meaning must be recovered in the act of reading or interpretation, for we must grasp the meaning, we must understand the text and its context, and so on. There is, then, an important role for the reader in discerning or discovering meaning, but this doesn't mean that readers create meaning, as some recent writers have supposed. Their focus on readers and the act of reading can, however, help us to understand the ways in which we discern meaning. One of the most important issues here is in the way in which our presuppositions bring out, obscure, or distort the text's meaning. These presuppositions are legion, including things that we currently believe about God, the world, the Bible, and so on; our assumptions about how we ought to read the Bible; our theological commitments; and our patterns and habits of interpretation. These patterns and habits are nurtured by traditions of interpretation; that is, we are not alone in the way we approach the text, but rather we were introduced to a way of reading Scripture by those who nurtured us in the faith. And they too were "inducted" into patterns of Bible reading, many of which have a long and rich tradition. The thing about these traditions—established patterns of reading—is not that they are somehow wrong in themselves. Indeed, without them, it is hard to see how the business of reading Scripture can get off the ground. It is interesting to note that just before the famous words about the inspiration of Scripture in 2 Tim 3:16 (speaking, of course, about the OT in the first instance), Timothy is reminded of how he was instructed in the faith, including his knowing the Scriptures from infancy. Part of his training for the ministry of the gospel in Ephesus involved Timothy's coming to know the Scriptures and, I suggest, his being trained to read them. These patterns of Bible reading are essential in our seeing the meaning of the text (or, to be more precise, the author's meaning conveyed by way of the text). These traditions are essential in unveiling meaning, and they do so in characteristic ways. Being partial and flawed, however, they also tend to veil meaning in characteristic ways. In order to be responsible readers and to get a better grasp on the text, we need to critically engage our traditions and faith communities to try to discern ways in which they accent and distort meaning. In my view, some of the most fruitful challenges to traditional readings of Scripture have come from those who are alert to the way our faith communities have marginalized and excluded women and ignored the plight of the poor.

This brings me to my final point about hermeneutics. We need to realize that readers have interests, intentions, and purposes as much as do authors. And our interests and purposes are distorted by sin. The mere fact that we are reading the Bible does not immunize us against the distorting and destructive effects of sin. Indeed, as Jeremiah and Jesus both experienced in their encounters with the religious elites in Jerusalem, having and reading the Scriptures can be used to mask our sinful self-interest. Sin can, in fact, become so much a part of an interpretive system that we become blind to our own sin and the way it distorts our Bible reading. This has been tragically evident in some Reformed Christians' support of apartheid in South Africa and the widespread championing of slavery among evangelicals in the eighteenth and nineteenth centuries (people such as John Newton were not representative of all evangelicals in their opposition to the slave trade). The problem is not, we must accept, safely "out there": we are all too prone to manipulating Scripture for our own ends. Indeed, I suggest that a healthy dose of self-directed suspicion ought to govern our reading of the Bible. We constantly need to consider whether our conclusions on a particular passage and its implications may in fact be driven by self-interest rather than by faith. Here, I suggest, exposing ourselves to readings from other perspectives is going to be painfully useful.

But the news isn't all bad, for although we are influenced by sin, we are also people of faith in whom the Spirit is at work, leading us into truth. So, although what's called the "hermeneutics of suspicion" can play an important role in unmasking distorted readings, we must also exercise the "hermeneutics of faith," for our commitment to God and God's purposes has an important impact upon our ability to perceive certain things in the text. For instance, our recognition that God is consistent and faithful helps us to recognize in the texts a consistency of character and purpose in the midst of both the difficulties and diversity that exist in the Bible. This is an instance of the hermeneutics of faith rather than an imposition on the texts as some have supposed, as will become evident when we look at some of the "problem passages" in the OT. The judicious use of both suspicion and faith is one way that the Spirit shapes us and our reading of Scripture, bringing our reading of the text and our responses to it more in line with the author's intention. In this respect, we could argue that the ultimate author of the text assists us in our reading. We might even say that if texts are "distanced" from us as objects, they can be brought near again by the work of the Spirit of God, their ever-present author. Furthermore, the divine author desires not simply that we understand these texts, but also that we live by them: we are to be doers, not just readers, of the word. The aim, then, of our reading is that the purposes that God had in authoring this text might be achieved also in and through us. We will see more on that shortly.

HERMENEUTICS AND THE BIBLE AS GOD'S WORD

This brings us to another issue: the Bible is not just human words; it is also the word of God. Here we should be more precise. As Wolterstorff reminds us, this claim is properly made of the Bible as a whole: it alone is God's complete word to us—especially, I might add, in light of God's final word in Jesus. When we come to a particular passage of the Bible, we seek to understand what God says to us from that portion of the whole of Scripture. Three things are worth noting here. First, each passage is part of the whole of God's word to us and must be interpreted in light of the total picture. Second, each part nonetheless also contributes to the meaning of the whole, and no part of it is dispensable; it's not as if we now have the latest model so we can trade in the OT as we might an old car. Third, what God says through a particular portion of Scripture is said by way of the human author's communicative act. Let's look at each of these three, in reverse order.

THE DIVINE THROUGH THE HUMAN

We have already looked at how texts work as communication. As Christians, we claim that the Bible is also communication from God to human beings. However, in communicating to us, God does not somehow bypass or short-circuit the element of person-to-person communication. As Christians, we do not believe that Scripture fell out of heaven or was directly dictated to human recipients in such a way that no trace of the human author was left on it. Rather, we believe that God uses meaning imbued by human authors as the vehicle for God's own communication: God did, in the past, speak through the prophets (Heb 1:1). What the author said by way of the text is what God says. Sometimes that message is fairly clear, as in the case of God speaking to Israel through Moses at Sinai, or Ezekiel speaking God's words to Jerusalem in the sixth century B.C. There, it would seem, God used individuals as divine spokesmen. This is not to say that God ignored their interests and backgrounds. Ezekiel, for instance, clearly shows his priestly background and interests in both the content and form of his message (e.g., Ezek 40–48). Nonetheless, these words are directly authorized by God.

At other times the relationship between a biblical text and its authorization by God is not so clear. The book of Proverbs, for instance, is made up of numerous individual sayings and some longer poems from a number of sources, all of them the result of reflections of the wise on the ways of the world. There is no hint in the text that these words were directly given to the wise by God, nor, indeed, is that claim made in much of the Bible. What seems to have happened is that sayings were composed, used, gathered, found to be useful, placed in larger collections, and then given an introduction and conclusion to make the book of Proverbs as we know it. A similar process took place with Psalms. Other books are the result of systematic presentations of stories of the past (Judges through Kings, the Gospels), a person's reflections on life (Ecclesiastes and, to an extent, Job), personal correspondence (Paul's letters), and so on. Scripture, as we will see, contains many kinds of literature, each produced in different ways. Even so, all of this is God's word, and, I would add, all of these words are God's words and the means of God's communication with God's people then and now.

I suggest that we see God as superintending the complex processes by which the human words of Scripture were produced ("inspiration," if you like) and endorsing the end result as God's own words. This is what Wolterstorff calls "appropriated discourse" (trust a philosopher!). By this he means that God takes these words and makes them God's own, just as we do from time to time with other people's words. That's why people learn poetry or the words of songs. If I wanted to warn you about the dangers of unthinking suburban conformity, I might play for you the Radiohead song "No Surprises"; if I wanted to alert you to the dangers of mindless capitalism, I might (with a warning about its language) play for you Pink Floyd's "Money." That, I suggest, is what God does with Scripture, with the added element that God both controls the various complex processes of production and endorses the end result. God says what the writers said.

THE SUM OF THE PARTS

Furthermore, each portion of Scripture is used by God to contribute to a complex whole. This largely follows from what I've just said, with the added claim that God doesn't "move on." Sometimes we find that words that once spoke for us no longer do so. We may find, as I have done with Joy Division's songs, that they no longer say what we want to say. As Christians, we don't want to say that about God and the Bible, nor do we need to. God hasn't moved on: all Scripture is God-breathed, not just the new bits. But the different portions of Scripture don't all say the same thing. You see, the world is too complex to be captured by one individual point of view, as is the reality of God and God's work in the world. That's one reason why we need the full diversity of Scripture, including puzzling and disturbing bits (like Ecclesiastes) and seemingly antiquated and irrelevant bits (such as Leviticus [on which I'll say more later]). Ecclesiastes tells us that when we think about the world, it often doesn't seem to make sense, that God's ways in the world are strange and at times inexplicable, and people don't always get what they deserve. Pessimistic? I don't think so. It's a refreshing realization that faith doesn't dissolve all our problems and answer all our questions. But then, we knew that, didn't we? So we need all that God has said, all parts of the Scripture, in order to get the complete meaning.

THE BIG PICTURE

However, we also need to see each portion of the Scripture in light of the big picture. The idea that each passage of Scripture must be interpreted in light of the whole is hardly a radically new one. If you enjoyed or endured Sunday school (I did neither for long, coming from a non-Christian family), I expect that this is old news to you. But then, I expect that most engineers knew before they went to university that all the pylons need to be properly connected to the bridge's span and able to bear sufficient weight if the bridge is to stay up and do its job. Some things are obvious, but still they are worth exploring to understand why they are so clearly true and worth remembering. And this fact is well worth keeping in mind. For instance, no matter how some particular texts might be read, how long would Christian support of the slave trade or discrimination based on gender or ethnicity have survived if we had taken seriously Jesus' radical welcome of the unwelcome and Paul's assertion that in Christ there is no Jew or Greek, slave or free, male and female (Gal 3:28)? Not very long, I think. Anyway, let's think about this a bit more.

Let's go back for a moment to the idea of texts as things that people use to communicate to others. That, of course, is precisely what we believe that the Bible is: something that the personal, trinitarian God uses to communicate with people. When we listen to others to find out what they have to say, we try to listen to everything that they say, as well as how they say it. Journalists and lawyers (and people in the midst of an argument) may do otherwise, and that's because, in general, they are interested in making their own points rather than understanding those of others. Nonetheless, we all have had the experience of someone taking our words out of context or jumping to conclusions before we've finished what we have to say. And we get angry because it means that the other person isn't really listening to us, that they are not really letting us communicate with them. Parents and their teen-age children know this all too well. So it is with the Bible. What we need to do is, so to speak, allow God to finish what God is saying and then go back and look at a particular thing that God said. That is, the ultimate context for our interpretation of a particular passage is not simply its original literary and historical context but rather the context of the whole of Scripture. The key to our understanding this "whole Bible" context is coming to grips with the biblical story.

The story begins with God, the triune God, who exists in relationship as Father, Son, and Spirit. God created the universe and all that is in it, with the result that it reflects God's own character: the wonderful and rich order of the universe is a reflection of God's own glory and the fact that relationships are central to God's own being means that relationships are also central to creation. This creation was good; it worked the way God intended it to work. God created humans in God's own image and likeness, in a particular pattern of relationship with God, each other, and the world. This is, in fact, a key part of how God ordered the universe: God created human beings as part of creation, but also as those given responsibility to help run it. This call to loving dominion over the earth, best understood as servant kingship, is essential to God's purposes for both us and the world. From the beginning, then, humans are social beings who are called to live in God's world as God's people. However, as we are all too aware, the world that we live in is "not the way it's supposed to be," nor are we. For sin entered the picture. Whatever the "origins of evil" might be, humanity used its God-given freedom-in-responsibility, including the freedom of interpersonal relationships, in both neglect and defiance of God's good purposes.

The God who made the world and humanity did so with certain purposes in mind, and God will not allow these purposes ultimately to be frustrated. So God "enters into" human affairs in judgment and grace in order to bring these ends to pass. Central to this story in the ot is the election of Abraham, and so of the nation Israel. By this choice, God's saving acts of power, and particularly the covenant that God makes with Israel, God brings into being a new community. This new community is meant to reflect the character of God and God's rule and thus to live in a manner that aligns with God's creative purposes. Israel's history, however, demonstrates their failure to "live as the people of God," despite God's acts of grace and judgment in their history.

Once more, God's purposes will not be thwarted, so God acts in a radically new way in the incarnation and ministry of the Son, Jesus Christ. The history of God and the world finds its goal in the life and ministry of Jesus the Messiah. In the Gospels we see the Son of God "enfleshed," dwelling bodily among us. Jesus is true God and true human and thus reveals to us the character of God, ideal humanity, and God's pattern of relationships. He is the embodiment of the truth of God and God's purposes (e.g., John 14:6). Through his death and resurrection he pays the penalty for us and restores our broken relationships with God, each other, and the created order. All of this is in anticipation of the end of the story. The end of this history is a new beginning in which God's purposes for humanity and the world are achieved. In this final state the creation itself will be transformed, and so will we: sin will no longer be a factor in human existence; we will be remade in the image of the Son. This new creation both awaits us at the end of history and is at work in us now. Through God's great and gracious action in Jesus and the work of the Holy Spirit the kingdom of God has become a force in human history, and the church plays a crucial role in this phase of the story. The church is a new community, created by Jesus and his Spirit, and its members are called to live out the (re)new(ed) pattern of relationships of the kingdom of God and so act as agents of God's rule in the world. God's kingly rule, which will be fully and finally manifest at the end of human history, is now at work in the church, which is called to be a key instrument by which God achieves these kingly purposes.

This is the story of God and the world, a story that lies at the heart of Scripture and the unity and diversity that it displays. This story is outlined, reflected on, engaged with, sung about, agonized over, disputed, celebrated, mourned, anticipated, longed for, and worked out by the people of God in many and various ways in the writings of the OT and the NT. Not all of that literature takes the shape of a narrative, although, clearly, crucial components do. But for all their diversity, these Scriptures can be related to the story without violating the integrity of either the OT or the NT, or of the different kinds of text that we find within them. A key way of doing this is to relate the story to the idea of *shalom*. Although this Hebrew word is used in various ways in the OT (as is the corresponding Greek word, *eirēnē*, in the NT), it can be understood to capture the main theme of the biblical story.

Shalom is a picture of community, of life in relationships, in which things are as they are supposed to be. Humans live in harmony and delight with God, each other, and the world. In *shalom* people live lives characterized by love, justice, and faithfulness. The Bible brings that story to us and invites us to make it our own. The Torah tells us of *shalom* created, disrupted, re-created, and embodied (more or less) in the life of Israel. The prophets and prophetic history tell us of God's ideal of *shalom* being neglected and perverted by God's rescued people and of the horrendous consequences that result, but they also tell us of the promise of a future of *shalom* beyond the death of judgment and exile. Psalms and other books reflect on this story, helping us to see its riches as well as forcing us to confront the delights, puzzles, and pain of human existence in a world created (and redeemed) by God but marred by sin. The Gospels tell us of the wonderful new thing that God does. The Father sends the Son—who lives a life of *shalom* in the power of the Spirit, is executed, and is raised from the dead—that we might be restored to God the Father and enabled by that same Spirit to live lives that glorify him. In this way we ought to reflect God's own character as made so clearly known in the person of Jesus. The Book of Acts shows us how the Spirit shapes a new community of *shalom;* the letters of Paul and others reflect on the wonders of the story of Jesus and call upon the new communities that comprise the church to be identified and shaped by that story. Revelation, for all its complexities and obscurities, proclaims that the crucified and resurrected Jesus is the Lord of history and will bring it to completion in the new heavens and earth. It reveals a new creation in which *shalom* finds its perfection in a new community, perfectly conformed to the will of God, in perfect relationship with God, within itself, and with the world remade.

THE OLD TESTAMENT AND THE SHAPE
OF CHRISTIAN ETHICS

All this has bearing on the last of the overtly theoretical issues that I want to address: the nature of Christian ethics and the role that the OT plays in it. I suggest that our ethics are, although they have points of contact with general, secular ethics, uniquely Christian, meaning they are shaped by the gospel, the great story of God and the world that lies at the heart of our faith. As such, our ethics necessarily have a narrative shape: when we want to identify God, ourselves, the nature of reality, and the content of our calling in God's world, we need to tell a story. It is that story which identifies God for us and tells us who we are, what this world is, and what we are doing here. That story, as we have seen, focuses on God and God's actions in the world, in particular in the person of Jesus: it is a theocentric (God-centered) and, ultimately, christocentric (Christ-centered) story, and so Christian ethics is theocentric and christocentric by its very nature. It is also personalist and relational; that is to say, it focuses on people and relationships, as indeed do the Christian story and a Christian view of life and the world. Although rules and principles have a role to play in Christian ethics, then, they are not central, but persons and relationships are, particularly the pattern of relationships that we call *shalom* and that we see uniquely embodied in and enabled by Jesus. The OT, of course, plays a vital role in that story and thus plays a crucial role in Christian ethics.

Of course the OT story has different emphases and a different focus from the NT, for although it anticipates the coming kingdom of God, the fulfillment of God's purposes for Israel and the world, and the Messiah as a key agent of God's rule, these realities await the NT. Thus, looked at in its own right (a first and necessary step, as we've seen, in reading the OT as Christian Scripture), OT ethics has its own unique shape. Christopher Wright has outlined what is, in my view, the best framework for understanding the OT in Christian ethics. Wright's framework has three key "angles," as he calls them: God, Israel, and the land, or the theological, social, and economic angles. Old Testament ethics, he rightly notes, is always theological and God-centered. As such, ethics is seen as a response to God's grace, which motivates, shapes, and enables the action of the people of God. Old Testament ethics is also addressed primarily to Israel as a community and seeks to shape them as the people of God–God's primary answer to the problem of human sin. As such, Israel is called to model God's purposes to a watching world; they are, in Wright's terminology, a "paradigm" of God's purposes for human community as a whole. God's people are called to live in God's land, which has a key theological and economic role to play in terms of their covenant relationship with God and the means of production. Israel was, after all, an agrarian community for most of its existence and so was dependent on the land and its agricultural produce for its ongoing existence. In that economic and theological context the land is both a gift from God and a task, and the nature of the gift and the task has important implications for OT ethics. The land was given to all Israel and was to be divided in such a way that all Israelites, no matter how poor, had access to the land, the primary means of production. Justice was a key concern from both the social and the economic angles, so that it comes to dominate OT ethical vision. This vision focuses, then, on a particular picture of persons in social relationship, a focus that we need to maintain in our ethical reflection on the OT. Wright also helpfully reminds us that as we read the text, we need to ask questions about the "function" of this text theologically, socially, economically, and, I would add, relationally.

This properly personal perspective (focusing on persons-in-relationship) ought to govern our reading of the whole Bible. Its primary message is not propositional but rather personal and relational; so too are its individual texts. That is, they present us with a picture of God and the world, the community of faith that God has brought into being, and God's purposes for us and the world. We ought to read Scripture, then, asking what its theological and relational message is. How does a particular text portray God's person, character, and actions, and what does that mean? How does it portray human beings, God's purposes, human community, the consequences of human actions, and so on, and what does that mean? We are to look for the theological and ethical function of the text. How would it have shaped its original audience, their beliefs and behavior? How do we then understand those purposes in light of the bigger picture of the story of God and the world, especially as it focuses on Christ? How can we see the same functions achieved in and through us?

A similarly relational pattern ought to control our broader view of Christian ethics. There has been a lot of debate in ethical theory about the role of rules, consequences, and character. Some suggest that our main (or sole) concern should be the rules or principles that apply to a particular case; others say that our main (or sole) concern should be the consequences of our actions; still others claim that our main (or sole) concern should be the virtues that ought to govern us and our behavior. A biblical personalist perspective says yes (and no) to all of these approaches. It says yes in that they all capture something important about persons and relationships; it says no in that none of them are primary, for that role belongs to persons and relationships. This means that when we are examining particular questions or situations, we can and should examine the principles and consequences and virtues at stake; however, we need to see them as three dimensions of the primary ethical reality, which is persons-in-relationship. That prompts us to ask three sets of questions as we come to analyze ethical issues. What rules or (more commonly) principles are at stake, and how do they fit with key themes of the gospel? What are the consequences of the action or policy, and how does it fit with the ultimate end, the coming kingdom of *shalom?* What kinds of persons would do this, and what kinds of persons (or institutions for larger policies) would be produced by them? Former colleagues of mine call this the AAA or CCC method of looking at principles, possibilities, and persons: Action, Aftermath, Agent, or Command, Consequences, Character. The AAA or CCC (or PPP, for that matter: Principles, Possibilities, Persons) gives us a helpful way of incorporating a wide range of considerations into our ethical analysis, all subordinated to an overarching relational framework.

All of this is, of course, done in the context of a larger moral vision shaped by the story of Scripture and governed by the overarching theme of God's work in the world creating, restoring, maintaining, and, ultimately, re-creating *shalom.* A key concern for Christian ethics, then, should be the shaping of lives and communities that are nourished by that vision, that story. A number of writers in Christian ethics have reminded us that the moral life is less a matter of crisis decision-making (the "moral dilemma" approach to ethics) than a pattern or texture of living. It is more about shaping moral agents who live out of gospel-formed habits than about instructing us so that we can make good decisions when we are surprised by crises. A gospel-shaped person, one whose life is molded by the Christian story and supported by Christian communities, will, in the main, know how to act without agonized deliberation in a crisis. We become the kind of people for whom cheating on our spouse or our tax return is literally unthinkable. Nonetheless, there will be times when we are confronted with something that we haven't thought about before, something that the community hasn't specifically shaped us for. When that happens, this same story provides us with resources, both to analyze the situation and our possible responses and to give content to our decision making (and the forming of new habits of thought and action)–the AAA or CCC or PPP analysis and the story of *shalom*.

So, then, now we are equipped for our journey. We've looked at the nature of the Bible and how we interpret it, as well as some underlying issues of interpretation (hermeneutics). We have looked at the overarching coherence of the Bible as God's word to God's people, and we've explored the nature of the biblical story of God and the world and how that informs our reading of the Bible as a whole as well as individual texts within it. We've looked at the way this story holds together in a vision of persons-in-relationship, the vision of *shalom*, which shapes both our understanding of ethics and our analysis of particular problems and also shapes us as moral agents and members of moral communities. With that in hand, I think we're ready to begin the journey into the strange land of the ot.

CHAPTER 2

GETTING GOING

AUSSIE BLOKES (FOR THE UNINITIATED, Australian men) love working with their hands: changing the oil in the car, adding a deck to the house. I suspect that the love of fixing and building things is generally true of men everywhere. One of the archetypal images of Australian suburban life is the bloke in his shed. It's his retreat, his safe place, a place where he can build things, fix things, have a mate over and play with boys' toys. A bloke in his shed getting his hands dirty—there's an image of Australia (and a bit more realistic than kangaroo chasing or crocodile hunting). A mate of mine is very good at it. I've known James (his real name, as he needs no protection) for over twenty-five years, and for over twenty-five years I've been impressed at his skill. His projects range from cutting out and patching up the rust in his car, to building bookshelves and beds for his kids, to completely renovating the bathroom, literally from floor to ceiling. He's amazing, and I stand in awe of him and his shed. But I'm not a typical Aussie bloke. I can't build things—at least, not things that stay up. I've tried all kinds of things, but it just doesn't work. For the twenty-five years that I've been impressed with James's skill, he's been (rightly) disdainful of mine. If a job is more complicated than changing a tire or a light bulb, I'm not your man. I think the problem is twofold: you need to know what you're doing, to have some plan and understand how it works; and you need to have some basic skills. I have no skills, and when it comes to the whole "handyman" thing, I'm clueless. I'm one of the very few blokes I know who doesn't have a shed, or even a workbench in the garage. What would be the point? In fact, it would be positively dangerous.

This doesn't mean that I don't like doing things with my hands. I do, but my domain is not the shed; it's the kitchen. I love cooking and, if my friends (and kids) are to be believed, I'm almost as good in the kitchen as I am bad in the shed. And the reason is that I have some idea of what I'm doing and, thanks in part to my mom, decent basic skills. I have well over a dozen recipe books, all of which I use. Cooking curries is probably my forte–Indian and Thai are my favorites, but I'll range all through South and Southeast Asia– and I'm glad to say that I've inducted my daughters into the fine art of making and enjoying a good curry. There are certain things you need to get right in cooking a curry, especially Indian curry. You need to take time, slowly sautéing the onion with the garlic (and generally ginger) until it's soft and golden and wonderfully aromatic. You need the right spices, freshly ground (sometimes roasted and ground) and put in at the right time, allowing the flavors to meld and permeate the other ingredients. And, if at all possible, you need to leave it a day or three in the fridge to allow the flavors to mature. I can't build a bookshelf, but I can cook a curry, because I know how they work, and I have some basic skills. And once you've got that, you can cook pretty much anything, no matter how new and unfamiliar.

One year, when my wife and I were celebrating our wedding anniversary, we went not to an Indian restaurant, but to a French one. It was fabulous. One of the dishes that I had was rabbit casseroled in white wine and mustard and served with buttered rice. It was gorgeous. The rich, gamey flavor of the rabbit was beautifully complemented by the sauce, which infused every morsel. My mouth waters at the memory. I'd never had anything like it before, and certainly I wanted it again, but I didn't want to have to go out to a (costly) French restaurant every time the urge hit. So, I decided to have a go at making it for myself. On this occasion my cookbooks let me down. Sure, there were recipes for rabbit, but nothing like what I wanted. So, I had a look on the Internet. Again, there was nothing exactly like what I was after. However, there was something a little bit like it. So, I looked at the recipe, thought about what I'd had in the restaurant, reflected on casseroles and rabbits and how to cook them, and devised my own recipe. And it worked. The casserole was great–so good, in fact, that I made it for my next dinner party. I knew what I was doing, I had some basic skills, and I used them. That's all it took.

Rabbit Casserole with Mustard and White Wine

Ingredients

    1 medium onion
    1 clove garlic
    2 rabbits, approximately 3 pounds total, jointed
    2 tablespoons vegetable oil
    2 tablespoons butter
    2-3 sprigs each parsley and thyme (or lemon thyme)
    1¼ cups dry white wine (e.g., Chardonnay)
    1¾ cups chicken broth
    2 tablespoons Dijon mustard

Method

Preheat oven to 350°F. Finely chop the onion. Pat rabbit pieces dry and coat in seasoned flour. In a deep oven/stovetop casserole (a Le Creusset casserole dish is ideal) heat the oil and half the butter over moderate heat until hot but not smoking, and brown rabbit pieces. When rabbit is browned, transfer it to a large bowl.

Add the rest of the butter to the pan and sauté the onion and garlic over moderately low heat, stirring, until soft and golden. Add wine and boil for 3-5 minutes, then add stock and boil for a further 5-10 minutes, until the liquid is reduced by about half. Add larger pieces of rabbit (legs, saddle) to dish and cover. Cook in moderate oven for about 45 minutes. Add the herbs and the rest of the rabbit, including liver and kidneys. Cook for a further hour (plus or minus), until the rabbit is perfectly tender.

Transfer the rabbit to a large ovenproof bowl and keep it warm in the oven. If necessary, reduce sauce. In a small bowl whisk together 1/4 cup sauce and the mustard and whisk mixture into sauce. Add salt and pepper to taste. Return rabbit to casserole dish and return to oven for 10-15 minutes, or until ready to serve. Serve with buttered rice, steamed vegetables, and either chardonnay or pinot noir.

Makes 4-6 servings

It's the same with reading the Bible. You need to know how texts work and to develop a few basic skills. Once you've done that, you can try your hand at pretty much anything in the Bible. Of course, for some things you'll need a little help. After all, I still turn to recipe books, and there are some things in the kitchen that I've not quite mastered (soufflé I can do; baked custard, not—I leave that to my one of my daughters). In this chapter I aim to deepen your knowledge of how texts work and to sharpen your basic skills of Bible reading. For this, we'll need to work on the skills of "exegesis," or getting the meaning out of a text. We'll also need to work on the skill—more an art than a process—of bringing the text to bear on the world in which we live. This often is seen as the application of exegesis; I prefer to see it as a necessary part of the hermeneutical process in which God grasps us and shapes us by God's word.

In the preceding chapter I talked about the text as the bearer of the author's meaning, and how there are particular ways of communicating—particular conventions of language and so on—which people in various cultures use to communicate. As a result, if we want to understand the text, we need to analyze it as literature. However, there are, as we know, different kinds of literature, which need to be read differently. We read the financial pages of the newspaper for advice about what to do with our money. We read a recipe to learn or recall how to cook the classic curry dish Rogan Josh. We read an overdue electricity bill (with dismay) to learn what we've done wrong and how to fix it. We read a letter from a friend to find out what's going on in his or her life and so maintain a valued relationship. We read novels to be entertained, poetry to be challenged or delighted, newspapers to be informed, textbooks and manuals to be instructed, books of quotations to get just the right words, and on and on. We read them differently, knowing that they have been written with different conventions— no one expects the brilliant linguistic creativity of fine poetry in a computer instruction manual—and with different purposes. One of the skills that we acquire in learning to read is how to grasp the difference between these different kinds of texts and the way we read them. So it is with the Bible. We find many different kinds of literature in the OT, and they have been written with different aims and different techniques. Understanding these aims and techniques is the goal of what can be called "genre analysis." This is a crucial element in literary analysis that also involves looking at the structure of the text (how the narrative or argument develops), how it relates to its context, whether there are words or ideas that control the thought of the text, and so on.

However, knowing, as we now do, a little about hermeneutics, we know that grasping how the text is put together is only part of the story. We also need to have some idea of what purposes the writer might have had and what issues he or she may have been addressing in the audience. To make an obvious point, it is unlikely that someone living in a Bronze Age rural community would speak about the problem of twenty-first-century urban sprawl and its environmental consequences. We might be able to appropriate and apply to this issue something that they said (as we'll see in a later chapter), but we will need to work on it. First, we will need to do some historical work in order to understand the context of the text and so grasp the issues that the writer is addressing. Second, we also need to be self-aware. We are, quite reasonably, interested in urban sprawl and its implications, but we need to make sure that this interest doesn't distort our reading of the text. Now, I could deal with these things abstractly (the way we looked at hermeneutics in the preceding chapter), but I think that it would be more interesting and useful if we looked at some of the different "genres" (kinds of text) that we find in the OT. So, let's get going, looking first at the genre, "law," or *torah*.

LAW (TORAH): LEVITICUS 19:9-10

When we think about the OT and ethics, one of the first things that comes to mind is the law, so we'll begin there. Before we get to our text, however, there are a few preliminary things to sort out. First, I'd like to be picky about words. We tend to refer to texts like the one we're about to examine as "law"; in fact, that's how the Hebrew term *torah* is often translated by modern readers and it has become a traditional way of talking about Genesis through to Deuteronomy. For modern readers the term "law" brings with it all kinds of thoughts and feelings, many of which not only are foreign to the texts but also distort how we see them. When I mention law, people commonly react with words such as "rules," "do this, don't do that," "dead letter," "demand," "burden," "punishment," and so on. And that's fair enough, for our English word "law" comes with those associations. Not so, however, the Hebrew word. The word *torah* can be used to refer specifically to the commandments, as is the case for the ritual instructions in Leviticus where *torah* is generally used, normally translated by the NIV as "regulation" (e.g., Lev 6:2, 7, 18). However, it is much more frequently used in the sense of "teaching" or "instruction," as is clearly the case in Ps 78:1, where the NIV and the NRSV translate *torah* as "teaching" (see also Pss 19; 119). Indeed, that is the predominant use in Exodus through Deuteronomy, four of the books that are called the Torah in the Hebrew Bible.

Deuteronomy is a case in point. The book opens by setting the scene and having Moses "expound this law [*torah*]" (Deut 1:5) in a series of speeches to Israel. Moses's first speech, however, contains no rules or regulations; it consists entirely of a recitation of Israel's history, or, more properly, of Yahweh's great and gracious acts on their behalf and their past response. The regulations don't start until Moses's second (and longest) speech, and even there much of it is more exhortation to action than specific rules for their behavior. Yet, the book tells us, this is part of the Torah that Moses began to expound on the borders of the promised land. What is true of Deuteronomy is true of the Torah as a whole. As you read Genesis through Deuteronomy (the Law or Torah), you will find many more stories than rules. Genesis, of course, has no legislation (except perhaps Gen 9:4-6; 17:9-14; and, some would say, 2:17), consisting as it does almost entirely of narratives and family trees. The first half of Exodus is narrative, as is the bulk of Numbers. Leviticus contains the most legal material of any book in the Torah, a large proportion of it relating to matters of worship. Clearly, Torah is more than a bunch of rules and regulations.

The story is important for other reasons as well: most importantly, it sets the scene. When we do finally come to the legal material in Exodus (and Leviticus and Deuteronomy), we have already heard the story of God's work in the world and, in Exodus in particular, of God's actions on behalf of Israel. And that story, while it is a story of judgment, is primarily one of grace. This is crucial. One of the most common mistakes that people make is thinking of the law as a set of demands that Israel must keep in order to be in relationship with God; they see Israel's relationship with God as a matter of works and not grace. They couldn't be more wrong. Let's think for a moment of the familiar story of the exodus. There we see Israel in Egypt, suffering at the hands of an oppressive imperial regime. They cry out to God, and God hears and responds and initiates a chain of events that will lead them to freedom. But note this: God saves them before giving them the law. Grace precedes instruction. The only motivation that Exodus gives us for God's action is found in Exod 2:23-25. Yahweh hears Israel's cry, remembers the covenant with their ancestors, and is concerned about them. Yahweh is a faithful God, a compassionate God, a God who acts with gracious, saving initiative.

This is of more than academic interest, of course, for it shapes our whole way of approaching and understanding OT law. Law is not the way Israel establishes relationship with God or earns God's favor. God shows them favor on the basis of grace and faithfulness; the relationship is established by Yahweh in an act of undeserved favor. Having become the people of God, Israel is now called, through Yahweh's Torah instruction, to live as the people of God. This is their grateful and loving response to their gracious and loving God. Their response, as encoded in Torah, is shaped by God's own character and the nature of God's saving action on their behalf (Deut 5:12-15; 10:17-19). Further, when we place this part of the story in the context of the whole, we see that this choice of Israel and God's action on behalf of a particular people are not at the expense of a concern for the world; it is for the sake of the world. This particular action is in fulfillment of the promises that God made to Abraham, promises made in the context of the utter and hopeless sinfulness of humanity. These promises and the story that they shape, which Israel now bears, are God's answer to the plight of the world. That is what motivates Yahweh to call Israel to be Yahweh's own unique people: Yahweh was, is, and always will be a "missional" God (see Exod 19:5-6). "Law," then, is too misleading a term for us to use. In my discussion of this material, then, I will talk about *torah* as God's "instruction," not "law."

Another thing to note is the variety of material that we find in the Torah, including, as we've seen, narrative and laws. There is also genealogy (family tree), song (e.g., Exod 15; Deut 32), and poetry (Gen 49; Num 23-24). Moreover, there is much variety within the legal material. For instance, Exod 21-23 is quite different from the Decalogue (Ten Commandments [literally, "Ten Words," from the Greek translation of the Hebrew term for them]; Exod 20:1-17; Deut 5:6-21), which precedes it. In contrast to the Decalogue, which issues unqualified commands without penalties being specified, the book of the covenant (as Exod 21-23 is called) consists mostly of "casuistic law," or "case law." In general it deals with specific circumstances, such as those outlined in Exod 22:1-6 in relation to theft, noting various possibilities and how the people should respond in each case, including specific punishments and penalties. Similar case law is found in Lev 17-26 (especially chs. 18-19) and in Deut 12-26 (especially chs. 22-24). In those sections, however, there are also clear commands, often with a clear penalty, known as "apodictic law"—absolute dictates, if you will (such as Exod 21:15-17; 22:18-20). Sometimes, however, these laws do not prescribe a penalty but rather state a motivation for action, either positive (such as the rescue in Exod 22:21) or negative (such as the threat of retribution in Exod 22:22-24, where, again, the exodus is remembered in the language of God "hearing their cry," but this time it is remembered in judgment against rather than for an Israelite). When working to interpret a particular text in the Torah, it is important to take its genre into account, including variations within a larger category.

We should also note the historical and cultural context of the text. Obviously it's important to remember where in the larger story a particular text falls when trying to interpret it. It matters, for instance, that Abraham marries his half-sister *before* Lev 18:9 is given (see Gen 20); whatever Abraham's faults in this puzzling story (which are many), breaking the law against incest doesn't seem to be counted among them. The cultural context is important here as well, for it seems that ancient Near Eastern (hereafter, "ANE") culture allowed for marriages between close relatives that are prohibited by both OT law (such as Lev 18) and most modern law. Other material in Torah is radically different from existing ANE laws. For instance, one significant body of law from ancient Mesopotamia sheds fascinating light on the very different social vision embodied in OT legal codes. The Code of Hammurabi (late eighteenth–early seventeenth century B.C.), while having much in common with OT law, also differs significantly from it. It shares, in other words, a similar cultural context with the OT, but also demonstrates a divergent ethical vision from it.

The Code of Hammurabi

3: If a seignior came forward with false testimony in a case, and has not proved the word which he spoke, if that case was a case involving life, that seignior shall be put to death. [Note the similarities to and subtle differences from Deut 19:15-21.]

15: If a seignior has helped either a male slave of the state or a female slave of the state or a male slave of a private citizen or a female slave of a private citizen to escape through the city-gate, he shall be put to death.

16: If a seignior has harbored in his house either a fugitive male or female slave belonging to the state or to a private citizen and has not brought him forth at the summons of the police, that householder shall be put to death. [Note the striking contrast with Deut 23:15-16.]

209: If a seignior struck a(nother) seignior's daughter and has caused her to have a miscarriage, he shall pay ten shekels of silver for her fetus.

210: If that woman has died, they shall put his daughter to death.

211: If by a blow he has caused a commoner's daughter to have a miscarriage, he shall pay five shekels of silver.

212: If that woman has died, he shall pay one-half mina of silver.[1]

For instance, the Code of Hammurabi specifically prohibits the harboring of runaway slaves, whereas Deuteronomy commands it on the basis of God's own action on Israel's behalf (Deut 23:15-16 [which I will discuss in chapter 3]). The Code of Hammurabi also

---

[1] Theophile J. Meek, "The Code of Hammurabi," in *Ancient Near Eastern Texts Relating to the Old Testament* (ed. J. B. Pritchard; 2d ed.; Princeton, N.J.: Princeton University Press, 1955), 163-80 [additions in square brackets are the author's].

distinguishes between how important and unimportant people are treated, and who pays the price of a capital crime. If an important person (seignior) kills the daughter of an unimportant one (commoner), then the killer may have to pay a fine; however, if she is the daughter of another important person (seignior), then the killer's daughter can be put to death (see #209-211). Similar penalties apply to an incompetent or negligent builder (see #229-230). Now, many of us have problems with the death penalty per se. The distinctive application of the death penalty in OT legal codes shows, among other things, an equality of offenders and offenses established on the basis of the inherent value in the eyes of God of all human beings regardless of social standing, and that the one who offends is the one who should die (see Num 35:30; Deut 24:16). That, among a number of other features of OT law codes, suggests to me that it functions to shape a moral vision, arising out of God's own character, aimed at expressing God's will and purposes for human community in the world.

That fundamental purpose, as we will see, is reflected in the specific "law" that we will examine as our case in point, Lev 19:9-10. Literally the text says, "When you harvest the harvest of your field, do not finish the corners [or "sides"] and do not glean [or "gather"] the gleaning [or "gathering"] of your harvest. Do not thoroughly strip your vineyard and do not glean [or "gather"] the broken-off bits of your vineyard—leave them for the poor and the sojourner. I am Yahweh." This may, at first glance, seem an unpromising candidate for ethical reflection, since few of us have fields or vineyards, and even if we did, what on earth is "gleaning"? But bear with me, and I think you'll find it both interesting and ethically challenging. Let's look first at the law itself, before placing it in its context in Leviticus in order to gain an understanding of its ethical and theological function. First, while this has some of the features of case law, it also has features of apodictic law (absolute dictates): it speaks of the specifics of how Israelites are to harvest their crops, but it gives very general instructions, with no particulars, and the motivation for following the law is the identity of Yahweh. It instructs Israel, as the people of Yahweh, in how they are to provide for the poor and the sojourners (or "aliens" [NIV]) from its regular harvest. The intent of the instruction is clear: it is for the benefit of the poor and the sojourner, to provide for the needs of those who have little or no access to the land. But to understand that purpose, we need to grasp the significance of the land for Israel, both theologically and economically, as well as the nature of the poor and sojourners.

In the OT the land has enormous theological significance. It is one of the foundational promises given to the ancestors in Genesis and was seen as one of the chief benefits that Israel received from Yahweh (Gen 12; 15; 26; 28). Throughout the Torah instruction it is identified as the land that God promised to Abraham, Isaac, and Jacob; Yahweh gives Israel the land as an act of grace and of faithfulness to those promises (Exod 3; Lev 26; Num 13; Deut 7; 9). It is a good land, as is seen in the common phrase "a land flowing with milk and honey," symbolizing its lush pasture and abundant natural resources (see also Deut 8). This good land is Yahweh's gift, yet it is also a task entrusted to Israel, both to take it and to keep it. It is also, in fact, the land of obedience. It is the place where Israel is called to remember and obey (Deut 8) and the place that it will keep only on condition of obedience (Lev 26; Deut 9; 28; 30). Furthermore, it is given as an inheritance to each clan—hence the tribal divisions (Num 34; Josh 13-21)—as well as each family within the larger tribal networks.

The issue of inheritance is crucial in Israel both theologically and socially. Land could not be sold in perpetuity (except in cities, where it didn't matter so much economically). If it was sold as an emergency measure to cover a debt that could not otherwise be paid, it was "sold" only for a limited period and was to revert to its original "owners" after a Sabbath of Sabbath years in the Year of Jubilee (Lev 25). Indeed, it was Yahweh's land and was merely entrusted to Israel; they were, so to speak, temporary leaseholders of Yahweh's property (Lev 25:23). It was entrusted to them so that they could live, as a nation, as the people of God, and it would be taken from them in the event that they failed to do so (Lev 26; Deut 28; 30). The notion of "inalienable" property rights, then, is doubly foreign to the OT: first, the land is Yahweh's, and Yahweh is the only one with inalienable rights over it; second, the land is entrusted to Israel to use for Yahweh's purposes. Yahweh's purposes, especially Yahweh's intentions for the nature of the community they are called to be in the land, take precedence over property rights. This brings us to the role of the land in Israel's economy.

Economically, the land played a vital role in Israel's life. Israel was, like most ancient societies, a subsistence agrarian culture—that is, one in which most people are farmers and depend on the land for their survival and (occasional) prosperity. This is foreign to most of us who live in "developed" nations, where land's major purpose is to be built on, either for housing or industry. If we have a garden, it is primarily for recreational use; our survival doesn't depend on it. Our livelihood generally is not tied to our land. For us, having or not having land generally is optional. This was not so for ancient Israelites. For them, like most rural people throughout most of human history (including today, especially in so-called developing countries), access to the land was, quite literally, a matter of life and death. To have access to the land meant being able to grow crops that would enable the family's survival and, in a good year, perhaps have a little to be put away to guard against the next bad year (which inevitably would come). This brings us to the poor and the sojourners. The poor (most likely) and the sojourners (most definitely) did not have access to the land by rights. While "the poor" often functions in a general sense in the OT, here it probably refers to those who had to "sell" (better, "lease out") their ancestral land due to economic hardship. During that time the land was another's to use. The sojourners, on the other hand, are non-Israelites who lived within Israelite territory, often as laborers for those with larger estates. As non-Israelites, they were not permitted to own land; they had no inheritance in Israel. They had no portion of land to call their own and so were in a marginal and perilous state; they were, in fact, at risk of being totally excluded from Israel's economic system.

Laws like Lev 19:9-10 aimed to ensure that the poor and the sojourners would not be excluded from Israel's economic system. Rather, the land, entrusted to Israel by Yahweh, would be used for the benefit of all and in a way that reflects Yahweh's character. They aim to ensure that the economic function of the land in Israel's national life matched its theological function in God's purposes. In that regard, it is worth noting what Lev 19:9-10 includes. This instruction covers Israel's fields, where they grow staples (such as grain), but also their vineyards. The provision of grain is clear enough: this provides for the feeding of the poor (the parallel text in Deut 24:19-22 also specifies olives—olives and their oil were essential in Israel both for food and lighting). But Leviticus goes beyond providing the bare necessities, including the product of the vineyards (as does Deuteronomy), which means that the poor in ancient Israel were also to be provided the relative "luxury" of wine. This is more than a miserly provision to keep them alive; it is to enable them to enjoy life in community. This provision must be seen neither as a favor granted to the poor and marginalized nor as passive welfare. It is a right granted to them by Yahweh, the land-holder's landlord, and so is not a matter of condescending largesse on behalf of the wealthy. But equally, this is not a provision that reinforces powerlessness and passivity in the face of adversity; the poor still need to do the work of gleaning, or gathering, the crop.

This, then, is an important text socially and economically, as well as theologically. Its theological significance is seen not just in relation to the land but also in relation to the closing words, "I am Yahweh your God." Those few words (three in Hebrew) tie this in-struction both to the character of God and Israel's call to be God's special (holy) people. "I am Yahweh your God" reminds them of God's character as rescuer, as the one who delivers the poor and needy—foreigners in a foreign system—from bondage and brings them into freedom and a new identity (made explicit in Lev 19:36). This law reflects the character of God, and it calls Israel to reflect that same character. That, in turn, reminds them of their special relationship with God and its consequences for their lives as God's new community. That is particularly clear in light of the "head-line" statement at the start of the chapter, "Be holy because I, Yah-weh your God, am holy" (Lev 19:1), which governs the rest of the chapter. Indeed, the shorter statement "I am Yahweh (your God)"— which recurs throughout the chapter (Lev 19:3, 4, 10, 12, 14, 16, 18, 25, 28, 30, 31, 32, 34, 36, 37)—serves as a reminder of that overarching call. All that follows in Lev 19—be it related to parents and Sabbath (v. 3); worship and sacrifices (vv. 4-8); or prohibitions against theft; deceit; fraudulent, cruel, and unjust behavior; and even malice and revenge (vv. 11-18)—is covered by the call to be holy and is an expression of it. So is this instruction.

This instruction is, in fact, part of a larger block of teaching (Lev 17-26) that focuses on holiness in all areas of life (so it is often called the Holiness Code)—and I mean *all* areas of life, not just the "religious" ones, as we tend to think when we hear the word "holiness" (if we are not, indeed, turned off with images of self-righteous, insular piety). The instructions in the Holiness Code in Lev 17-26 cover sacrifices and ritual concerns (ch. 17), sexual conduct (ch. 18), various matters (ch. 19), capital offenses (ch. 20), priests and related "religious" matters (chs. 21-24), the years of Sabbath and Jubilee (ch. 25), and promises and warnings related to covenant obedience or disobedience (ch. 26). That concern with holiness, and its all-embracing character, is vital for understanding both this law and the nature of the people of God.

We will look at these ideas more in a later chapter; for now, we need to realize that holiness primarily means being called apart from the ordinary and the way of life associated with it into a special relationship with God and a way of life associated with that relationship, one that has implications for all of life and every relationship. Holiness, then, is reflected in the just and merciful ordering of society and provision for the needs of the poor and excluded that enables them to keep their dignity and responsibility as members of the community. This is what it means for Israel to be holy. Holiness is manifested when they act as a just and merciful community that not only includes the poor and marginalized in its economic life but also grants them joy and dignity. The poor are entitled to provision, but they are responsible to glean it for themselves. The marginalized are entitled to the grain and oil that they need to survive but also to the wine that allows them to celebrate. That kind of holiness, expressed as it is in this instruction on agricultural economics, has a lot to say to contemporary Christians.

Israel is called to a holiness that imitates God's own inclusive generosity to the poor and the marginalized. This powerful vision of community, seen at work in the story of Ruth (a story built into the story of David and thus of Jesus, the Messiah [see Ruth 4:13-22]), shapes a radically different understanding of property and community than the one that prevails in Western "free market" democracies. This vision is important for us as Christians, especially as we see that concern for the marginalized and impoverished in the person of Jesus, the descendant of Ruth. In this vision, "private" property is not for acquisitive purposes, nor is use of it driven by an overriding concern for the profit motive. It is not even, primarily, private property; it is a trust granted to us to be used as Yahweh's people, in line with Yahweh's purposes, purposes of justice and compassion. That is the kind of community that Yahweh, the God and Father of our Lord Jesus Christ, calls us to be (seen in, for instance, the picture of the early Christian community in Acts 2; 4). That is the kind of community shaped by this text.

As we think about how we as Christians use this text in our ethics, there are many specific programs that we could reference that embody the "principles" of this text. For instance, microcredit schemes in the majority world have powerfully transformed the lives of individuals and communities through the release of seemingly insignificant sums (generally considerably less than five hundred dollars) to enable the poor to develop small businesses, generating income that transforms their families and often their communities as a whole. Or we could look at the issue of how we ensure that people's sustenance rights are met; those things to which all people are entitled that enable them to function effectively in community, such as clean air, food, water, basic health care, education, and housing.

A Case Study of Microenterprise

Microcredit is often used to start up a small business. Here is an example from Bangladesh, the "home" of microfinance.

Twelve years ago Abdhul Mannan was an illiterate day laborer, struggling to provide enough money to feed his wife and two sons. He was often in debt to the village moneylender—a common problem in rural Bangladesh. Today, through the work of the Garo Baptist Convention Participatory Health Care Program, he can read and write, owns his own land, and runs a recycling business. Both of his children attend school and have a promising future.

This has been possible through a microcredit group in his village (of which Abdhul is now chairman). Abdhul used his first loan to buy land, on which he grows vegetables to feed his family and to sell at the market. His second loan enabled him to start a recycling business. Abdul collects rubbish from his district—tires, metal, paper—and sells it to large companies that use recycled products. This business not only is good for his family financially but also benefits the community and the environment.

Abdhul's group hopes to save up enough money (Tk 200,000 = $4,050) to purchase a diesel water pump so that they can irrigate their fields more easily. This will enable them to increase the quantity and range of vegetables they grow.[2]

A lot could be said about these things, but I will not say it, and this for reasons other than my own lack of economic expertise: first, in the highly politicized world of social policy each suggestion would be contested by someone; second, in our rapidly changing social world each suggestion would be overtaken and outmoded by social change. More significant, however, is the nature and function of the biblical text we have been studying. It is not so much about encoding a particular social rule or policy as it is about shaping a particular kind of moral community. While, as we will see, the nature and implications of holiness are radically different for us who are called into relationship with God in Christ—as are the social and economic systems of ancient Israel and those of our contemporary global economy—the call to imitate God and God's merciful justice is reiterated and reinforced in our call to live as the people of God, whatever our social and economic environment (Matt 5:43-6:4; Jas 2). Holiness is seen in a community whose members hold lightly to possessions, knowing that these are entrusted to them for the benefit of others. Holiness is seen in the recognition that others' interests in survival override our interests in our property and its produce; that this provision is a right to which they are entitled, not a matter of generosity or largesse on our part; and that the poor must be granted dignity and responsibility. That is the vision of life in community that this text projects for us. That is the vision that challenges our self-interested, self-indulgent use of property, calling us to the kind of generous liberality that God displays. That is a vision that has the power to transform our church communities, our societies and economies, and the world economic system. So much for this unpromising textual candidate for ethical reflection!

---

[2] This case study is adapted from TEAR Australia, *Target* 2005, no. 4. The full article can be found at http://www.tear.org.au/resources/target/054. Used by permission.

NARRATIVE: 2 SAMUEL 11-12

Humans live by stories. Our identity, our values, our commitments, and our futures are shaped by stories. That, I suspect, is one of the reasons for the abiding popularity of OT stories in Sunday schools; they have shaped generations of Christians and their imaginations. The problem is that we often leave the stories behind when we graduate from Sunday school, seeing them as somehow passé or perhaps too complex and ambiguous for us to handle. The issue is not just that we no longer allow ourselves and our imaginations to be shaped by these stories (although clearly that is a problem). The deeper issue is that story is crucial to understanding the OT and its message, as we have already seen. Narrative is a key to understanding the OT, but it creates terrible problems for us in Christian ethics. What do we do with a deceitful Jacob or with a Joseph who, wise as he seems to be, initiates a program that enslaves the population of Egypt and sets up the conditions for his own people's future bondage? These issues, along with others, have led many scholars to argue that narrative cannot be used as the source of theological or ethical teaching; rather, it illustrates more "didactic" material. That is, the stories give way to more explicitly educational texts, such as law or the prophets. Such a view (expressed in, for instance, Gordon Fee and Douglas Stuart's otherwise helpful book *How to Read the Bible for All Its Worth*) seems inadequate to me for a number of reasons. But rather than spend time on arguments against that viewpoint, let's look at a particular story and seek to grasp its ethical significance.

A first step in understanding OT stories is to examine the ways that OT narrative works, because OT narrative works differently from the stories that we are used to reading. For instance, OT narrative rarely describes a character physically, and when it does, it has some point. Esau's hairiness (Gen 25:25; 27:1-40), Ehud's left-handedness (Judg 3:15-30), Saul's height (1 Sam 9:2; 10:23-24), Absalom's hair (2 Sam 14:25-26; 18:9)–all are details crucial to the way the stories unfold. We are rarely told what people are thinking or what kind of people they are. We are expected to work that out from what they do and say. Hebrew narrative is also terse. It is short, even abrupt, and to the point. That is not to say, however, that it is carelessly written, that it has no literary artistry—far from it. Much ot narrative, for example 2 Samuel, shows great subtlety, literary artistry, and depth of insight into the human condition. Of course, this does not mean that a story has to be well told and subtle in order to qualify as Scripture. Many of the accounts early in the book of Judges are little more than stereotypical vignettes (short pieces that stick closely to a clear and simple pattern [see Judg 3:7-11, 31; 10:1-5; 12:8-15]). What it does mean is that we need to grasp how ot narratives are put together, what kinds of literary devices are used, how character is portrayed, narrative framed, and so on in order to appreciate their artistry and so grasp their meanings.

There is, of course, a wealth of stories in the ot from which we could choose. Here we'll look at 2 Sam 11-12, in part because it is frequently misunderstood, in part because it raises important ethical questions, but mainly because it nicely illustrates key features of ot narrative and how we should engage with it. I expect that we're all familiar with the story, but I will outline it nonetheless so that we have its basic shape before us. David, staying home while the army is in the field, is captivated by the beauty of Bathsheba, the wife of one of his close companions, Uriah. He sees her bathing on her roof, purifying herself after her period. He calls Bathsheba to his chamber and has sex with her. She becomes pregnant (not surprising, given reproductive physiology: a week or so after menstruation is generally a fertile time in a woman's cycle), and David instigates a cover-up. Uriah refuses to play along (perhaps unwittingly, perhaps not). Since Uriah hasn't cooperated with David's plan to pass off his own child as Uriah's, he has to go. David puts in place a solution with the same kind of political skill that he displayed in his earlier career. And it works. He's in the clear; the personal and political crisis is averted.

But, of course, there is one who stands behind the king, the one who gives the king legitimacy, one who is meant to be represented by the king—God, who is not pleased. So God sends a messenger, Nathan, who, in an act of costly faithfulness, brings God's message of judgment to this king. Nathan's act is truly costly and brave (recall how this king deals with men who get in his way). Surprisingly, David repents and is forgiven (in contrast to the evasions, half-truths, and outright lies that most public figures use to escape blame), but things are never the same again. David's actions send out ripples in the moral universe and come to mold his dark future in the image of his own actions. That's the story: dark, dangerous, depressing, with the glimmer of God's surprising, complicated grace at the end. So, how does this story speak to us?

Let's begin, as we should with any story, by setting the scene. Israel, having been rescued from Egypt, entered the land under Joshua's leadership and enjoyed initial success in the task of occupying and settling it. This first generation is presented as being, by and large, faithful to God and God's call to live as the covenant people. Things, however, rapidly deteriorated to the point of moral, social, and spiritual chaos, as is exemplified in the horrible stories at the end of the book of Judges.

At the same time, there were significant social and technological developments, primarily associated with the Philistines. They were relative newcomers to Canaan, arriving in the twelfth century B.C., and controlled the coastal plains from their power bases in Gaza, Ashkelon, Ashdod, Ekron, and Gath. They became the major threat facing the newly settled Israelites, for a number of reasons. First, in terms of territory, Israel was largely confined at this stage to the central hill district, whereas Philistia controlled the plains. This meant that the Philistines were a rich and unified people, while the Israelites were scattered in small, poor, rural communities. Second, Israel was politically, at best, a loose confederation of tribes, each settled in its own area, largely governing its own affairs; at worst it was a self-destructive fratricidal mess (see Judg 17–21). In contrast the Philistines had a more centralized system of government and more open lines of communication. Third, the Philistines were economically and technologically dominant as they had a monopoly on new iron technology and a stranglehold on major trade routes (the ports on Canaan's Mediterranean coast as well as the coastal plains). This gave them a technological advantage over their rivals (see 1 Sam 13:19–22); it also gave them much greater regional wealth and power. Fourth, with their local monopoly on iron, the Philistines enjoyed a significant military advantage. Israel possessed limited bronze technology, and its older technology was superseded by the Philistines' iron weaponry (iron, which, when made into steel, is harder and more versatile than bronze). An Israelite facing a Philistine opponent would be akin to a soldier using an M1 rifle facing one equipped with an Uzi–not hopeless, but at a serious disadvantage. This, when added to the organizational advantages of the Philistines, meant that Israel was "under the pump"–an oppressed and marginalized minority group on the fringes of Philistine territory.

Enter the kings. Kingship in Israel was initially an unwanted innovation, at least from the point of view of Yahweh (and the prophet Samuel). It was, indeed, presented as a faithless step by which Israel sought a political and military solution to the Philistine threat, whereas Yahweh wanted them to trust him to deliver them as in the (recent) past (see 1 Sam 7-8). Nonetheless, Yahweh intended to incorporate kingship into Israel, as long as it operated under Yahweh's guidelines (see Deut 17:14-20; 1 Sam 9-16). After the failure of Saul, Israel's first king, God integrated kingship into Israel's life as a covenantal community by way of David, even tying God's own divine rule to that of the human king (see 1 Sam 15:10-35; 2 Sam 7; also, e.g., Pss 2; 72; 110; 132). David is, as is well known, presented as the "man after God's own heart," God's own choice as a fitting king for the people (1 Sam 13:14; 16:1-13). Having been established as king over a united kingdom by a combination of shrewd politics and godliness, David established a new capital for the kingdom in Jerusalem, a city previously controlled by its original Jebusite inhabitants (2 Sam 1-5). Despite initial disaster, David brought the ark of the covenant to Jerusalem, thereby uniting Israel as a religious as well as political entity (2 Sam 6).

In my view, David's early career as king is not, as some suggest, a tale of universal faithfulness. For instance, after his conquest of Jerusalem in 2 Sam 5, David takes more wives and concubines, which, though often seen as a sign of his being blessed by God, strikes me as an example of the acquisitiveness of kings against which Israel had been warned in Deuteronomy (compare 2 Sam 5:13-16 with Deut 17:17; 1 Sam 8). Here David seems to be acting as kings tend to act, accumulating wealth, privilege, and power rather than acting as servant, representative, and ideal Israelite, as a king in Israel was supposed to do (see Deut 17; Ps 72). Nonetheless, in this first period David is presented as, though not perfect, a good and godly king on the whole and one who enjoys Yahweh's favor (2 Sam 5:10). From 2 Sam 11 onwards, however, things change. David, his family, and his kingdom all suffer grievously as a result of his actions with Bathsheba and Uriah, when, for the first time, David acts unambiguously as kings are wont to do.

That, in fact, is what 2 Sam 11–12 is primarily about: kingly power, its abuse, and the consequences it brings about for David and Israel. Perhaps because of our cultural obsession with sex (and perhaps our theological traditions?) we tend to see this as a story of sexual sin: it is usually entitled "David and Bathsheba" or "David Commits Adultery with Bathsheba" (NIV and NRSV headings, respectively). That, as I hope to show, is not the focus of the story. It is, rather, about an act of abusive, violent power by a privileged individual. This is hinted at in 2 Sam 11:1 and becomes progressively clearer in both the story's detail and its construction.

The text opens "in the spring of the year, when kings go off to war." Two things are worth noting here. First, there is the historical and cultural question of the conduct of war in the ancient world. Why the spring? Simple pragmatics: in spring the worst of the rains are over, and so the ground is dry and easier to march (and fight) on. Moreover, in spring the men have finished the big job of preparing their fields and sowing their crops, and so they are available to be called up for military service (there's not much value in winning the war but losing the economy). This is when you would expect a king to play the old game of war. Second, and more importantly, in giving us this particular time reference the narrator hints at David's future action: he is about to act like any other king. Interestingly, however, he does so in such a way as to assume all the so-called privileges of kingship but to ignore its responsibilities. For David sends, but he stays. He sends out the army, with Joab acting in the kingly role of military leader—a role David himself had previously filled (2 Sam 5:2). David, meanwhile, stays home. This immediately invites us to read this text as one that speaks of kingly privilege and power; and we need to take up this invitation rather than seeing it primarily as an episode of sexual sin. Although it does speak of such sin, a careful analysis of the text as a narrative shows that this is not its focus.

As we turn to the text, we need to examine how it works as a story. Various devices are used in Hebrew narrative; here the two most important are the use of key words and irony. The text opens with David sending out the army. The word "send" governs the whole of 2 Sam 11 and the turning point at the start of 2 Sam 12.

In 2 Sam 11:3, 4, 6, 14, and 27 David sends (twice in v. 6 [the NIV, unfortunately, doesn't translate "sent" in 11:27; it is present in the Hebrew text and is translated in the NRSV]); in 11:5 Bathsheba sends to David; in 11:6, 18, and 22 Joab sends to David; and the idea, if not the word, of David sending recurs in 11:25. Interestingly, each of these uses of "send" tracks the main action in the piece. In all of these instances David acts as we would expect an ancient despot to act: he sends (or is sent to) at the dictate of his own will. He has authority and control. It is his will that prevails, no matter what covenant or convention might say. This is a story of a man exercising power and running things his own way. He sends the army to do his job. He sends to find out about and then take another man's wife, and, when she sends to tell him the inconvenient news of her pregnancy, he sends for her husband as a cover up. When Uriah fails to do his bidding, David sends him to his death. Expedient Joab stands in stark contrast to faithful Uriah. Joab is the perfect "hatchet man," the one who will always be found "just obeying orders." He sends and is sent to as the unquestioning, unscrupulous agent of David's unconscionable will. So, in 2 Sam 11–12 sending is all about David and his will and the accomplishing of his desires, no matter what they are. There are, of course, two exceptions to this: Bathsheba (11:5) and Yahweh (12:1), who send words that disrupt David's plans and undermine his control.

Let's look at these two senders who do not fit into David's plans. The first is Bathsheba. It is interesting and important that apart from the messenger in 2 Sam 11:3, she is never named in the text; indeed, the narrator never names her, always calling her "the wife of Uriah," as does Yahweh in the message sent to David by Nathan. There are three main reasons for this. First, Israel was a patriarchal society, one in which power was in the hands of men, and so the texts that come to us from Israel reflect a patriarchal ethos in which women tend to be identified rather than named. (This was true, by the way, in Australia during my parents' generation: my mother was introduced on formal occasions not as "[Mrs.] Avril Sloane" but rather as "Mrs. David Sloane"; she was identified, not named—a practice that now, thankfully, is a thing of the past.) Second, the text deals with David's sin. There has been speculation as to what Bathsheba was doing bathing where David could see her. I think that this is beside the point. Topographically, the king's house was one of the highest structures in Jerusalem and so commanded a view of the roofs of others' houses–the natural, most private place, to wash. Furthermore, her bathing was not for the purposes of beauty or hygiene but rather for ritual cleansing (see 11:4; cf. Lev 15). It seems to me that assigning blame to Bathsheba, when she is simply the passive object of the king's lustful whim, is more reflective of the patriarchal biases of some (generally male) interpreters than it is of the text. Bathsheba's not being named means that the text reflects the way she was treated–as a nonperson, an object of desire–and allows the blame to rest where it belongs, on David (this is clear in, e.g., 11:4). But the chief reason for her not being named is to highlight the nature of David's sin. This woman is another man's wife. David is committing adultery. And he is doing so not with just anyone, but with one of his own chosen band (2 Sam 23:39); this is more than an ordinary act of betrayal. This woman, probably intended by David as no more than an evening's casual dalliance–one of the "perks" of the job–sends David two disruptive words (in Hebrew as in English), "I'm pregnant" (11:5). Bathsheba's brief speech both unravels and reveals David's sordid abuse of power and his betrayal of his less powerful friend.

But it is, of course, Yahweh's word, sent by Nathan the prophet, that pulls apart David's universe and initiates another chain of events. Until now, it is David who sends, who is active, who holds the reins of power, who reigns over the destiny of others. But now, all that changes, for Yahweh sends. From here on, David does nothing; except in his humiliating penitence and petition, he is entirely passive. The one who sent is now sent to; the doer is now done unto. Power is restored to its rightful place–Yahweh's hands–and is restored to its rightful role–the (re)establishing of Yahweh's ordering of relations. And there's nothing David can do about it. Indeed, from this point until the end of the main narrative sequence in 2 Samuel, David is puzzlingly passive; even when he should use his power, he does nothing. Was he paralyzed by his memory of abusing power? Who knows? David's passivity certainly is one of the ways Yahweh brings about David's judgment. In this, as in so many ways, the punishment (ironically) fits the crime.

This focus on power (not just sex) is also seen in the use of the threatening word "take." In 2 Sam 11:4 David sends and takes

Uriah's wife. Once again, the text's use of this key word is obscured, unfortunately, in many English translations, including the NIV and the NRSV (the AV, RSV, ESV, and NASB are exceptions). The threat that lies in that word may not be immediately apparent. This word, however, is used in 1 Sam 8 to warn Israel of the consequences of their request for "a king like the nations have." Such a king will take and take and take, exercising the arbitrary power that typifies despots in the ANE. And now David is described as just such a king. He is one who exercises power in his own interests; one who, as the text unfolds, uses the machinery of the military to get rid of an inconvenient truth.

What can stand in the way of such power, of the brutal force of taking? Only Yahweh. Yahweh, through Nathan, identifies the crux of David's sin in 2 Sam 12:4: arbitrary power that takes from a weaker, less powerful man, for the sake of his own pleasure. Notice how Nathan's parable, which exposes David's sin and causes him to indict himself, focuses on power and not on sex. It is about a stronger, wealthier man taking something precious, something of which he had an abundance, from a weaker, poorer man. In the face of all that Yahweh had given him (12:8) David responds by taking from Uriah both his wife and his life (12:9). Even here Yahweh is turning the tables on David. David sees himself as a man of power, an active man in control, a man who sends and takes at his whim. Yahweh undercuts all of this, for David's very power, the wealth and position that he has relied upon and abused, is a gift from Yahweh, not his own attainment. What Yahweh has given, Yahweh can, and now will, take away. And that is the burden of the judgment (12:10–11). David took, and now from him it will be taken; David cynically used the sword (of the enemy!) to achieve his selfish purpose, and now it will not leave him until it leaves him destitute.

Yahweh taking from David in judgment is seen even in the difficult and puzzling fact that the child born to Bathsheba—the "problem" that prompted David's brutal action—will die as part of God's judgment against David. Now, let me be clear: I don't like this part of the story; in fact, I particularly dislike the fact that the child (and, for that matter, his mother) suffers as a consequence of David's sin. I don't like it, but I think I understand it. First, we need to realize that our actions have consequences; we cannot and must not imagine that we act in glorious isolation, affecting only ourselves. Our sins have consequences, even on the people we love, even when they are forgiven. But why should the child die? This brings us to my second point: this is an act of judgment on David. This is not the child paying for David's crime, but David paying for David's crime. How is that the case? Well, in a culture such as ancient Israel's, children (especially sons) are a sign of the potency of the father, a mark of the blessing of God (again, see 2 Sam 5:13-14 or Ps 127). This particular child, who would have been seen as another sign of God's blessing, is one of the ways David might "gain" from this abuse of his kingly power. And that must not be, not in this, not in any area of his life. This child is taken from David, and even his mourning and repentance cannot undo the horrible consequences of his horrendous act. I still don't like it, but even this awful detail is important: from him who takes much, much will be taken.

This is a cleverly constructed narrative that uses words with delightful skill to tell a deplorable tale. It is also a brutally ironic tale. Irony, like the use of key words, appears right from the start of the story. It opens by noting that David sent Joab (remember Joab, the hatchet man?) with David's own band and the army. At the time when kings do their military thing, David is slacking off at home. This is particularly ironic, given that Israel's request for a king was, in part, driven by a desire to have a reliable warlord (1 Sam 8:20); even more so because David's own credentials as king of the united kingdom were headed by his role as an effective warlord (2 Sam 5:2). But there are deeper and darker ironies in this story. The first is, of course, that the man whom David cuckolds (to use a delightfully nasty old-fashioned term) and eventually has murdered is one of his own inner circle, one to whom he owes particular loyalty but treats in this despicable way. In light of this, David's opening words to Uriah in 2 Sam 11:7 are freighted with dark significance. His questions regarding Joab, the people (or army), and the war are literally inquiries regarding their *shalom*. Now, it's true that *shalom* functions as a common greeting and inquiry, similar to Arabic *salaam* ("How are you?"). Surely, however, it is more than a little ironic that David should use this greeting in the midst of such actions. Little could be less in line with *shalom*—Yahweh's vision of well-being, of life in community—than adultery, murder, and the abuse of power.

The second irony arises out of the contrasts the narrator draws between David and Uriah. Uriah is a Hittite, one of the tribes of Canaan that were to be expelled from the land (Deut 7:1). During David's time in the wilderness fleeing Saul, a number of non-Israelites, men on the margins of Israelite and Philistine society, joined David's band (1 Sam 19-27). Uriah is one of them (2 Sam 23:39). And he shows that he was not driven merely by personal loyalty to David but rather by a deeper commitment to his comrades and to Yahweh's purposes (2 Sam 11:11). David, of course, is trying to cover up his sin by getting Uriah to have sex with Bathsheba. Uriah refuses the "comforts of home" in a time of war. Was he aware of David's offense? Was he contrasting his own actions with those of David? Perhaps. Clearly, however, the narrator, with a fine eye for detail, points up David's sins by way of Uriah's godliness. This man, a foreigner, is more faithful to Yahweh and his purposes than is David, who, as king, is meant to be a paragon of Israelite virtue—and in such circumstances! Uriah drunk is more pious than David sober.

Of course, things get worse, and more brutally ironic, in David's actions. When I read of David writing Uriah's death warrant and sending (!) it to his hatchet man by the victim's hand, I feel like screaming. What callous brutality! Indeed, David uses the very trustworthiness that Uriah has always demonstrated as a weapon against him, for the plot will work only if Uriah is a good and faithful messenger, bearing the message safely to Joab without violating the official seal. There are no words for such cynical manipulative violence, which probably is why the narrator records it without comment, allowing the bare account to strike us with full force. That brutal, self-serving cynicism reaches perhaps its deepest, almost irredeemable, point in 2 Sam 11:25. There David tells Joab, who doubtless was concerned that he might be the next fall guy (after all, no one likes to leave damaging witnesses around), not to worry about Uriah's death and the other deaths occasioned by the "strategic withdrawal" (see 11:17). Such cynicism: "Don't let this upset you; the sword is indiscriminate in its appetite." Perhaps—David certainly is!

But again, the irony goes deeper, for the perspective David warns Joab against is precisely Yahweh's point of view. Here, again, something is lost in translation (except in the old AV), for in Hebrew

David tells Joab not to let this thing "displease" him (2 Sam 11:25); but the thing does "displease" Yahweh (11:27). On both occasions the same Hebrew words are used. David says, "Do not let this thing be evil in your eyes," but we are told that indeed, "The thing that David had done was evil in the eyes of Yahweh." David had been acting as moral arbiter of his own actions and of others' fate; Yahweh reclaims that right. Yahweh alone can truly determine what is right or wrong, what should or should not "displease" us, what is truly "evil in the eyes" of those who see the world aright. David's "truth" is a lie, a destructive, manipulative, abusive, oppressive lie. All that follows in condemnation and judgment is Yahweh's way of putting the world to rights, as far as this is possible, and of showing that this thing is truly evil, that it destroys David and Israel's world. Violence such as David's is never a good but rather always begets violence, and even Yahweh's forgiveness cannot undo the dreadful repercussions of such abuse of power.

This is indeed a dark and powerful story, and one that has much to teach us. None of its instruction is by way of "do or do not do this"; it is all done by way of the masterful telling of a story of power and its abuse. Fee and Stuart are wrong, for this story does have moral force beyond its illustration of commands issued elsewhere. In fact, looking at the story itself shows us that this is not primarily an illustration of the eighth commandment against adultery. Of course, one of David's wrongs is committing adultery, but that is not the focus of the story. As we have seen, it is ultimately about his abuse of royal power and privilege. In this story we see David, an ambiguous but generally positive figure until now, becoming a "king like all the nations have," with all its devastating consequences for Uriah, the army, Bathsheba, David, and the nation. We see, in fact, this become the pattern for Israel's future. The kings who follow in David's line follow his example: they become those who abandon Yahweh's call to uniqueness, refusing to rule Yahweh's people Yahweh's way in favor of a kingship like that of all the nations. They too face the inevitable judgment of God, who is meant to be represented in the kingly project, with the resulting loss of their throne and their land in exile. God's concern for the proper exercise of power extends throughout this history (1 Kgs 21; Jer 22) and beyond it into the anticipated restoration of monarchy and land after the exile (Isa 11; 61; Jer 23:1–8). It is seen also in Jesus, who shows us how power ought to be exercised: not in pursuit of selfish goals at the expense of all others but rather in costly service (Matt 20:20-28); in him, truly, one greater than David is here.

In 2 Sam 11-12 we are reminded of the dangers and responsibilities of power. As we know all too well, those in power tend to abuse their positions of privilege: "Power corrupts and absolute power corrupts absolutely." Furthermore, those in positions of abusive power rewrite the legal and moral universe in an attempt to justify their behavior and escape the consequences of their actions. This story reminds us that in Israel (as in the church) power does not make one immune to critique, that no one is "above the law"; even the most powerful must someday face the moral consequences of their crimes. It also tells us that power must be monitored, and if we won't do it for ourselves, there is a judge of all the earth who will do right. And this, surely, is a message that leaders in both the church and the world desperately need to hear. It is easy for us to look at the "world" and see the corruption and abuse of power so evident in multinational corporations, foreign governments, our own government and its agencies, or international organizations such as the United Nations and the World Bank. But we are not innocent; we have no grounds for the self-righteous accusation of the "world."

We in the church buy into the patterns of power and privilege that David demonstrates in 2 Sam 11-12, and that are so clearly contrary to the character of Jesus and the nature of Christian community. Moreover, these patterns are always destructive of our reputation and ministry and, more importantly, of persons and community. This is tragically evident in the sex scandals (including, tragically and horribly, child sexual abuse) that are currently rocking the church worldwide, lead people to doubt the God whom we claim to serve, and, more to the point, have destroyed the lives of so many people. And as was the case with David, so also in these instances, it is generally more about the abuse of power and position than mere sex (as bad as sexual sin is, especially child sexual abuse). It is also evident in the damage caused by financial mismanagement and embezzlement perpetrated by Christian leaders. This is not limited to televangelists in the United States, for all their self-serving prosperity theology and manipulative rhetoric; it afflicts the church worldwide, damaging the reputation and ministry of churches and Christian organizations from Indianapolis to India and harming the lives of countless people defrauded of their money or deprived of their needs. Power is dangerous, and it needs to be handled with care. We are warned here of the danger of power and shown the need for what we would call accountability structures, systems that carefully monitor power and those who wield it so as to ensure, to the best of our ability, that things don't get to this stage.

Second Samuel 11–12 also speaks of the destructive force of "moral autonomy," the arrogant claim that we can determine for ourselves what is right and wrong, that we can best determine on our own how to run our lives. People of power and significance are perhaps more prone to this temptation, though none of us is immune. We all attempt to wriggle out from under the commands of God, to see that they don't really apply to us, not in this situation; or we consciously or unconsciously reject what we know of God's will and do things our way. This story about David stands as a stark warning: if you run your life the way he did here, this is the kind of thing that is liable to happen. God may or may not act as directly as was the case with David, but sin will always end up destroying us, our lives, and our relationships. David's story shows us that no matter how well we think that we've covered it up, sin sets up ripples that will spread and disrupt our futures. And note: it is the story that does this. It is the story itself that exposes the dangers of moral autonomy; it is the story that shows us what happens to unfettered power. Stories such as this, with their power to draw us in, delight and horrify us, and they are crucial moral resources that do more than merely illustrate more abstract commands. They shape a moral vision, engage our moral sensitivities, empower our consciences, and shape our lives. Such is the power of stories.

POETRY: PSALM 24

If people live by stories, they celebrate—and mourn and protest—with poetry and songs. Poems have the ability to evoke and express our deepest feelings, to connect with others, even to reshape our world. But writing good poetry is hard work, and reading it can be as well. This skill is not one I grasped at school. I suspect that most of my failure is to be placed at my feet rather than with the education system. I was, in this respect at least, a typical adolescent boy, deaf to poetry, except when it had been put to music. Although they may not have been subtle, I can still recall the way albums such as *The Wall* or *Animals* (both by Pink Floyd) expressed and evoked my anger and distaste at the injustice and constraints of the social world I was discovering. They did it with their imagery, with the way their poetry revealed things about the world and helped me to know how I felt about them. *Animals,* in my view, did this better than *The Wall,* largely because it draws on the imagery of George Orwell's *Animal Farm* to portray human and social characteristics. "Getting it" meant grasping the extended metaphors, the shifts between metaphor and reality, and the way that the music matches the message. I may not have really got hold of poetry at school; I did get hold of Pink Floyd. I grasped how that kind of poetry worked. To really grasp what's going on in a song or poem, we need to know something about the kind of poetry being used and how it works. That is as true of Hebrew poetry as it is of Pink Floyd.

Hebrew poetry doesn't use some of the devices that we expect to see in English poetry. Instead it tends to use key words, word plays, and particular ways of putting lines together known as chiasm and parallelism. These may sound puzzling, but they are simply ways of putting phrases and ideas together to make an impact. Let me explain. The term *chiasm* is related to the name of a Greek (not Hebrew) letter, *chi,* shaped like an English "X." Like an English "X," the Greek *chi* is in the shape of a cross, which is where the term *chiasm* comes from, for a chiasm is a crossover pattern in a text. They occur fairly frequently in Hebrew poetry but are not often reproduced in English translation, largely because of the different way sentences are put together in Hebrew and English. For instance, the first verse and most of the second verse of Ps 2 have a chiastic structure in Hebrew, which is not reproduced in English translation. This means that some of the subtlety of the poetry is lost in translation, which inevitably, if unfortunately, happens whenever we move from one language to another. Similarly, word plays are hard to translate, as they often depend on the sound of the words in the original language— something hard to take across to another language. One instance that does come across in English occurs in Ps 127:1, where "build" and "watch" (or "guard") are used to describe divine and human action: without God's building and guarding, human building and guarding is futile. However, these subtleties of language generally require some understanding of Hebrew, and so generally we will need to leave them to one side and focus on other features that can be picked up in a good English translation.

The chief of these is parallelism. Parallelism is fairly self-explanatory. It occurs when one phrase, line, or idea is paralleled by the what immediately follows it in the poem. It is perhaps the most distinctive feature of Hebrew poetry; indeed, it is characteristic of ANE poetry in general. It is found throughout the book of Psalms and is a prominent feature of the poem that we will examine, Ps 24. This psalm uses the most common kind of parallelism, one in which an idea is picked up and repeated or developed in the next line or phrase. You can see it in v. 1, where "earth" is paired with "world," and "its fullness" with "those who dwell in it." Indeed, if you look closely, you will see that every verse in this psalm displays this poetic device, with the exception of the last, which is an example of another poetic device, a refrain. A refrain is a little like the chorus in a pop song: it repeats key ideas in the poem, sometimes with minor variation. Here v. 10 repeats the key idea of v. 8: Yahweh, the mighty warrior, is the glorious king. We will look at this in more detail as we turn to the psalm.

First, however, we need to realize that we find different kinds of poems in the book of Psalms, as elsewhere in the OT. We are perhaps most familiar with hymns, those songs of praise that are reflected in much popular Christian worship music (see, e.g., Pss 145–150). There are many other kinds of songs, however, ranging from prayers for forgiveness (such as Ps 51) to complaints of abandonment by Yahweh (such as Pss 22; 88). Indeed, complaint songs are the most common kind of poetry in the book of Psalms—a fact that much of the music we use in our worship today unfortunately fails to reflect. It is important to remember this when reading Psalms, as different songs work differently and were written and used for different contexts and purposes. With that in mind, let's turn to Ps 24.

Psalm 24 is one of a (very) small group of psalms called "entrance liturgies" (see also Ps 15), and it falls into three clear parts.

Entrance liturgies are poems used to frame the public worship of Israel and shape how worshippers approached the formal worship of Yahweh in the temple. Verses 1-2 are a hymn celebrating the universal lordship of Yahweh, the creator God. Verses 3-6 speak of the qualifications of those who would worship this God, while vv. 7-10 celebrate the presence of the majestic God of history in the temple. The last two sections consist of a series of questions and responses and may have been said/sung by different groups of worshippers or temple servants. To grasp this, we need to imagine two processions: one of worshippers coming to seek the presence of God in the temple, the other of temple servants symbolically representing the coming of God to dwell in and rule from the temple on Mount Zion in their midst.

To get a feel for this psalm and its function, we need to have some idea of the worship life of Israel as it focused on the temple. The temple, built by Solomon in the tenth century B.C., was a larger and permanent version of the wilderness tabernacle, where the glory of Yahweh was visibly manifest among the people of God (see Exod 25-31; 35-40; 1 Kgs 8). After a tumultuous period of "exile" at the end of the period of the judges and the beginning of the monarchy, David installed the ark of the covenant (and presumably the tabernacle that housed it) in Jerusalem, thereby making it the center of Israel's religious as well as political life (2 Sam 6:1-23). Jerusalem (also called Zion), an old Jebusite hill fortress, became the location for the symbolic presence of God. It was the place where God's people went to worship, hear God's instructions through the priests, pray and give thanks for God's mercy, receive God's forgiveness through the sacrificial system, and celebrate together God's glory and grace that they had experienced in their history and their lives. This was a serious business, in both practical and theological terms. Practically, it meant that worshippers had to come on pilgrimage from their towns and villages, leaving their homes and fields to travel to Jerusalem—not an insignificant feat in an era when walking was the only way most people could get around. And this they were called to do at least three times a year (see Deut 16). It was also theologically significant in that those who came to worship were meant to be faithful covenant partners of Yahweh as evident in their lives and in their ritual preparations for worship. We'll look at the issue of cleanness and uncleanness a little later, but for now it suffices to remember that careful ceremonial preparation was essential for an Israelite coming to worship, lest the temple be defiled and God's judgment fall.

Imagine, then, how Ps 24 might have been used in Israel's worship at the temple. A group of pilgrims, having traveled, say, twenty miles on foot from southern Judah, is coming to the end of the journey. They have trekked through the hill country of Judah, probably carrying their offerings, with animals for sacrifice in tow, and now are coming out of the last valley and heading up to the citadel of Jerusalem. As they come up through the city and approach the temple, they are met by a group of priests and temple singers and musicians: "The earth is Yahweh's!" the singers exclaim, reciting the opening lines of the psalm. The worshippers respond, knowing that Yahweh is the sovereign Lord, asking whether they will be permitted into Yahweh's presence: "Who may ascend the hill of Yahweh?" The priests respond with the qualifications of those who may rightly worship Yahweh: those who meet the religious (clean hands) and ethical (pure heart) standards of God's covenant. The people say, "That's us. We are those who seek to know the presence of God." Perhaps the company of pilgrims is already in the temple, or perhaps they are still on the way. In any case, now comes the climax, the great announcement: here comes the king, Yahweh, the God of glory, the God who acts in history. The one whom they seek in worship is there to be found. Yahweh is not there to do their bidding; God is not subject to their control—after all, this is the king of glory, the God of all the earth. Yahweh is there as sovereign Lord, willing to receive the people of God and their worship and grant them divine favor.

The question-and-answer pattern, especially in the middle section, makes this psalm participatory; that is, in using these words, we are interrogated as to our fitness for worship and asked to make the claim that we are indeed those who are entitled to be in the presence of *this* God. That, as we will see, means that worship understood in this light is as ethically challenging as we can imagine. The idea that "religion" and "ethics" are separate spheres makes no sense in the world of this text. True worship of this God requires lives that reflect God's own character and show an appreciation for God's holiness. Anything less is a sham. Let's look, then, at some of the details of Ps 24.

The song opens with an extraordinary, even revolutionary, claim. The whole world is the Lord's; all that exists belongs to Yahweh. To us, that sounds commonplace; the Nicene Creed opens, "We believe in one God, the Father, the Almighty, maker of heaven and earth, of all that is, seen and unseen." Nonetheless, this is an extraordinary claim in light of how it fits (or doesn't fit) in with ANE understandings of the gods and their rule: it claims that this particular god, the god of this particular people, is lord over all the earth, not just this particular territory or this particular people. That is a big claim, especially given the tribal and regional nature of gods in the ANE. The standard view of ANE religions was that particular gods were tied to particular territories and peoples (e.g., "Their gods are gods of the hills" [1 Kgs 20:23]). That was partly due to the idea that particular acts of provision or power on behalf of a particular regime established the gods' authority and control over them, and these political entities were limited to a particular locale. In one sense this psalm shares that viewpoint, or at least it doesn't dispute it. What it does, however, is show that Yahweh (and Yahweh's rule), unlike the gods of the nations, is not restricted to a particular regime or territory. Yahweh's actions are as extensive as the world itself; this God's sovereignty is universal. That is why, of course, the first two parallel statements in v. 1 are followed by the two parallel justifying claims in v. 2.

How can Yahweh claim ownership and authority over the world and all its inhabitants? As v. 2 says, Yahweh is sovereign creator. Now this too may not be particularly clear at first glance. Once again, we need to understand the cultural context and the world of ideas that this psalm reflects. There are a number of stories and songs from other cultures around Israel that speak of the world and its creation. Many of them speak of the act of creation as a series of conflicts between rival gods, with the victor demonstrating lordship in creating the world. One of the most prevalent of these pictures the chief rival god as a chaos beast, symbolized as a cosmic sea that, once defeated, formed the substance out of which the world was made. Similarly, in the Bible the world is often pictured as a kind of disk sitting on the cosmic ocean, stabilized by the great mountains that reach down into the waters (see Ps 46). I don't think for a moment that the psalmist is endorsing the polytheistic view of the world and its creation present in other

ANE creation accounts. Rather, the psalmist uses imagery like that in ANE accounts to express this chief claim: Yahweh is sovereign creator. Note how this claim is made. There is no hint of conflict; there are no other gods here whom Yahweh must defeat, no sense of struggle. This is a sovereign act of power. Yahweh founded the earth upon the seas. Whether that founding is pictured as overcoming chaos or is simply an expression of a common view of the shape of the world at the time, the claim is clear. Yahweh, and Yahweh alone, is sovereign ruler and owner of everything. Yahweh made it; it is Yahweh's possession.

We must bear this in mind as we come to the rest of the psalm, for it reminds us that this song deals with the worship of Yahweh, the one to whom all things and all people, including those who claim to worship *this* God, belong. As we worship, we recall that we are God's handiwork, that all that we know, all that we do or say, takes place on the stage of God's creation, in the theater of God's glory. We are Yahweh's possession; true worship simply acknowledges this. So the opening of the psalm, while it deals with big theological claims, also has important ethical implications. We'll look at how the theology of God as creator relates to environmental stewardship in a later chapter in relation to Gen 1-3; here I want to focus on the implications drawn in the psalm itself. Our lives as well as our worship ought to honor the one who made us and who owns us. God's territory is not restricted to the temple, Jerusalem, or even Israel, nor should our response be. And that is precisely what is reflected in the requirements for true worship that we find in Ps 24:3-6. Indeed, with this claim in mind, the question of the worshippers in v. 3 is all the more powerful and significant. The god whom they are coming to worship, after all, is the one, true, living God, who made all things, including them, and rules over all things, including them. The hill that they are climbing is the hill *of Yahweh;* it is the place where Yahweh is to be found, the holy place, that one place on earth set apart from all others for God's special use. Interestingly, in one sense Jerusalem is a place like any other—*all* the earth is Yahweh's, not just this hill— Yahweh cannot and must not be seen as confined to a particular locale (as Isaiah and, later, Stephen clearly show [Isa 66:1-2; Acts 7]). Nonetheless, the temple is on that hill; it does not confine God, but God does choose it as the place for divine self-revelation, the place where the worshipping people have special access to their God. If Yahweh, Lord of all the earth, is symbolically present there, then it really matters who can come to Yahweh in worship and on what basis they can come.

So, who can come there to worship? One who is faithful to the covenant in all its dimensions. This is important, for some people seem to think that OT worship was ritualistic and formal, and that only with the coming of Jesus did people come to recognize that true worship was "spiritual," that it involved the whole person as an individual. Quite wrong. Notice what Ps 24:4 says. True worshippers, as individuals, need clean hands, sure; they need to be ritually prepared to meet with the holy one of Israel. However, they also need pure hearts. The word "pure" generally is used in the context of ritual and worship, but here it clearly is extended beyond a narrowly ritualistic sense, for it refers to the heart. The "heart" here, as generally in the OT, refers not to feelings or emotions but rather to fundamental commitment and identity, what's at the "heart of things," who we really are and what really counts for us. It speaks of our moral character. Indeed, although the earlier phrase "clean hands" relates to ritual purity, I suggest that it has a much broader meaning. It speaks of how the worshippers' actions would be judged by God. Here, then, we have two fundamental elements of morality—what we do and who we are—both subject to the scrutiny of Yahweh, the cosmic lord, both needing to be right in order for us to come to God in worship.

The second half of Ps 24:4 gives us two key examples of what right action and character entail: right relationship with God and right relationships with others in community. To have clean hands and a pure heart means, in the first instance, not lifting one's soul (or self) to what is false (an idol). Clearly, this speaks of being in right relationship with God; indeed, it references the first and second commandments. If true worship means being a person of covenantal faithfulness, then at the very heart of that is worshipping the one true and living God, Yahweh, and Yahweh alone. Covenantal faithfulness, the prerequisite of true worship, requires that we "love the LORD our God with all our heart and soul and strength" (Deut 6:5; Luke 10:27). But it also means loving our neighbor as ourselves (Lev 19:18; Luke 10:27) and thus, as the psalm goes on to say, not swearing deceitfully. Here again we see the concern of the OT for justice, for such swearing, or oath taking, occurs in the context of legal deliberation. To swear deceitfully is to undermine the foundations of justice and thus good order in community, for all such deliberations require getting at the truth of the matter, and for that to happen, the truth must be told. But it also shows a concern for right relationships in community, for such decisions aim at correcting relationships when they go wrong and seeking to make sure they go right.

Yahweh, then, requires that those who come in worship be people of character, people who are committed to right action, people who live out the purposes of God in their life in community. Not only are such people permitted to come to worship God, but they are also free to receive the benefits of God's presence: blessing and vindication. The favor that they receive embraces God's sovereign work as creator and God's powerful acts as savior, both tied to the covenant. Blessing is, in the first instance, God's favor shown through the created order working well. It is seen in productivity, fruitfulness in harvest, and family life. The God of all the earth and its creator brings that creational power to bear to bless those who truly worship God; they come to express relationship with God and leave with its benefits. It is worth remembering in this regard that two of the major Israelite religious festivals (Weeks and Tabernacles) were associated with the land and its produce. In worship God's people express their dependence on God's sovereignty over nature; the creator God, sovereign over nature, responds with blessing.

However, Yahweh is also the God of salvation, as the final verses make plain and as was celebrated at Passover. It is, then, no accident that the psalm says that one of the key benefits for those who rightly worship Yahweh is receiving "vindication [literally, 'righteousness'] from the God of their salvation." This God is the one who has acted in history rescuing the people of God from slavery and creating a new community in which people are called to live in right relationship with God and each other. This God continues that saving work in temple worship; central to Israel's worship was the sacrificial system, much of which was directed toward receiving the grace of God in forgiveness of sins. Sinful as they are, those who come in covenant faith, seeking to be God's people and to express that in their relationship with God and each other, will receive the great blessing of forgiveness and restored relationship–truly, a gift of God. No wonder, then, that the worshippers in Ps 24 are so keen to claim that they are such people, those who seek God's face.

The reference to God's saving action partly explains the shift at the end of the psalm to God's kingly rule as seen in history; it is also prompted by the acknowledgment of God's presence and the nature of that presence as the sovereign Lord, symbolized in the temple and the ark of the covenant. The ark is seen in Psalms as either the footstool of Yahweh (Pss 99:5; 132:7-8) or Yahweh's throne (Pss 80:1; 99:1). Its construction is described in Exod 25:10-22; 37:1-9; it was the central piece of cultic furniture in the tabernacle, which in turn was at the symbolic center of Israel (Num 2). It served as both meeting place and receptacle: God met with the people of God through their priestly representative there; the Decalogue, the key reminder of the covenant, was lodged there (Exod 25:16, 22; 40). The ark was closely associated with Yahweh's saving and guiding presence with Israel in the early narratives of wandering and settlement (Num 2; 10; Josh 3-4; 6). In Josh 3-4 it is used to part the waters of the Jordan, enabling Israel's entrance into the land, symbolically repeating the crossing of the Reed (Red) Sea and demonstrating that Israel's journey was now over (cf. Exod 14-15). In Josh 6, as in Num 10:35, it is associated with Yahweh the warrior, the one who defeats Israel's enemies and acts for their sake. This connection between the ark and Yahweh the victorious warrior was so clear that Israel presumed it in 1 Sam 3-4, with disastrous consequences. Yahweh may choose to act on behalf of Israel, but they cannot manipulate God. All of this is associated with the ark, to which Ps 24 now turns.

What most likely lies behind the call and response in Ps 24:7-10 is either the memory or ritual reenactment of the ark's coming to Jerusalem and (eventually) being installed in the temple (see Ps 132). Given the associations of the ark with Yahweh's wars on behalf of (and at times against) the people, the coming of the ark to the temple is the arrival of the great, conquering king, the lord of history, which demands a fitting response from everyone and everything present. Hence, the call "Lift up your heads," most likely coming from those reenacting the ark's arrival, demands an honored entrance for the king of glory. It is similar to what happens in naval tradition when an admiral is piped onto the deck of another's ship. The admiral has every right to enter; the piping is both a courtesy to the junior officer (which doesn't pertain here!) and a demonstration and acknowledgment of an existing right and the authority that goes along with it. Here that authority is openly acknowledged: the one who claims right of entrance deserves it, for this one is the king of glory, Yahweh the victorious warrior, Yahweh of hosts. This last term clearly relates to the ark and its use in battle in Num 10:35 and elsewhere. The term can refer to Yahweh as lord of the heavenly host (stars or angels, depending on the context), but here it refers more directly to Yahweh as the lord of armies, the one who fights on behalf of Israel. Yahweh is king; Yahweh deserves entry to the temple; Yahweh deserves worship because Yahweh is lord of creation and of history. Yahweh is the one who defeated chaos in creation (if that was needed) and who defeated Israel's enemies, gave Israel their land, and enabled them to live securely as the people of God.

So here we see a call to covenant faithfulness bounded by the worship of Yahweh, lord of creation, lord of history. We see that enjoying the presence of the cosmic lord who has chosen Jerusalem as the place of divine self-revelation, where the people of God have special access to the God whom they worship, requires true covenant commitment, a commitment characterized by faithfully loving Yahweh, and Yahweh alone, and faithfully loving one's neighbor and engaging justly in community. But we also see that true worship of the one true God fosters obedience and faithfulness. For here we see that it was as Israel came to worship that they were called to the obedience of faith; as they sought to enter the presence of God, they were reminded not only that this is the holy place but also that in order to worship this God they needed to truly be the people *of God*. They needed to be those who, yes, were properly prepared to enter this place, different from all others, but also those who lived in a way that showed exclusive allegiance to Yahweh and its outworking in their lives and relationships. Worship and obedience are inseparably connected; just as faithful obedience enables true worship, so true worship empowers obedient faithfulness. And we see that the sphere of obedience and worship is as broad as the sphere of God's sovereignty; it encompasses all things and all places, not just what we might count as the "religious."

However, we also need to remember that we do not live in ancient Israel. We do not come to the temple to worship and this, of course, changes how we read the psalm. Interestingly, that is also true for those who put the book of Psalms together, for, as we can see from psalms such as Pss 74; 89; and 137, the book as we have it must have been finally put together after the fall of Jerusalem, the destruction of the temple, and the exile of Judah (ca. 586 B.C.). And yet the book still includes songs like this one, so tightly tied to the specifics of the temple and its worship. This means, I suggest, that the kind of rereading that we need to do as Christians is already beginning in the psalms themselves, even if we have to take it further than they did.

The first clues to this rereading are found in the psalm itself: the whole earth is Yahweh's. So, whatever the significance of the temple and Jerusalem, it is relative rather than absolute, for Yahweh is present in all the earth as lord and king. We also need to remember that history is the sphere of Yahweh's sovereign glory. The very existence of Jerusalem as the city of David, the city of God, and the presence there of ark and temple prove that. In the psalm itself, then, the "holy place" is the focus, not the limitation, of Yahweh's presence and rule. For Israel in exile and beyond, this is crucial; even without the temple, Yahweh is still lord of creation and history. The exile itself proves it, for it is Yahweh's action in judgment against a people who did lift up their souls to idols and who failed to live as a just community (see, e.g., Jer 7). So for Israel in exile, this psalm reinforces Yahweh's kingship in creation and history, and its implications, even when there is no visible symbol of it in the temple and its worship.

This relativizing of the temple is taken much further in light of Jesus. Jesus demonstrates that, important as the temple was for Israel, it has served its purpose. It has, in fact, been replaced: Jesus has torn it down and rebuilt it in his death and resurrection (John 2:13–22). If we want to know where we can find Yahweh, the lord of creation and of history, we need look no further than Jesus. Indeed, if we want to connect with him, we must look nowhere else, for Jesus is the presence of God, the one in whom the living God has "tabernacled" with us (John 1:14). He is the priest, he is the new temple, he is the one who manifests God's grace and God's rule (John 1–2; 4). And by his Spirit Jesus is the one who is present with his people, God's people, making us a new temple built up by God, an acceptable "place" of God's presence, of acceptable worship (1 Pet 2:1-10).

This has enormous implications for our theology of worship and the songs we sing, calling into question the uncritical transfer of temple imagery into Christian worship. After all, the holy place that we enter is not found in a church or a worship gathering: it is a different kind of holy place, and those words do not and cannot directly apply. Our focus, however, is on ethics, and so we must move on. Jesus is not only the "locus" of the presence of God; he also is the one through whom we have "clean hands," through whom we are made acceptable to God (Heb 8-10). He is the one who enables our obedience, our loving God and our neighbor, our coming to the (new kind of) holy place by means of his death, and our living in God's world as people who reflect the rule of the lord of creation and history. In Jesus, then, covenant worship and covenant faithfulness most truly come together, enabling us to live as the people of God.

This inevitably leads us to consider the connection between worship and obedience for us as members of Christian communities; that is the primary ethical implication of a text such as Ps 24. Irrespective of the particular songs or kind of songs that we sing, does our worship challenge us with the presence, in Jesus and his community, of the holy and sovereign Lord? Does it call us to acknowledge the great privilege that we have of free and confident access to the holy God? Does it remind us of the requirements of true worship and foster our lives of faith and love? Is our worship an essential tool of discipleship and faith, or is it a privatized, pietistic, or self-indulgent exercise in consumer spirituality? Not only the Christian community, but also its gathered worship, ought to be a crucial ethical resource for the people of God. We ought to be reminded of the character of our God, God's glorious work in creation and rescue, the nature of the new community that God has created us in Christ to be, the inevitability of our failure and the inescapable grace of God. We ought to leave knowing our identity and our calling; having been confronted again with the knowledge of the one true and living God, the holy lord of the world and its history; and empowered by our worship to love God with all our hearts, souls, and strength and to love our neighbors as ourselves.

Psalm 24 doesn't just remind us of the power of creation theology, or the importance of individual ethics in OT piety, or the holiness of Yahweh and what that means for us, or the connections between worship and faith. It challenges us to recognize the truly revolutionary power of our gathered worship. Worship is meant in the first instance to honor the Lord our God; but also it calls us to meet with God, to know God's gracious, forgiving scrutiny, and be called to fresh faithfulness and deeper obedience because of our time together with God and God's people. This psalm is a call to revolutionize our worship, to have nothing to do with the empty sentimentality of a privatized spirituality but instead to recognize the presence of the living God, the holy one of Israel, to know the demands made on those who come to worship the living God and to embrace afresh the call to live as the people of God. It is time, once again, for worship to serve discipleship, for praise to empower ethics, for our lives to come into church and for church to feed our lives. It is time for us to transform our worship and be transformed by it. The strange land of Israel's worship demands it, and it is there, in Christ, that we find our home.

PROPHETS: MICAH 6:6-8

In September 2006 some three hundred evangelical Christians from around the world gathered for a consultation on integral mission—mission that includes evangelism, mercy, and addressing issues of justice—in a world of conflict. Among the seminars were a number addressing how the evangelical church can be mobilized to speak on behalf of the poor, who so often are voiceless, seeking to help them articulate their concerns and develop their communities. The meetings were organized by the Micah Network and included representatives of the associated Micah Challenge. The conference and the very names of the organizations involved remind us of what the prophet Micah had to say over 2,500 years ago. The call to do justice, love mercy, and walk humbly with God gives a synopsis of the church's mission: this is what God wants of God's people; this is what we ought to be about in God's world.

Micah 6:8 (the signature text of Micah Challenge) is rightly seen as a key text in the understanding of God's perspective on poverty and injustice and how God seeks to address them, which makes it a good candidate for our sample prophetic text. Of course, one thing is immediately obvious: this is not prophecy as it is popularly portrayed. There is no prediction of the future here, nor is there a critique of social systems, but only a call to action. True, other passages from the prophets predict or critique (or both [see Jer 7]); that is not, however, essential to the nature of prophecy. Predictions, critiques, calls to action, and so on are particular kinds of prophetic activity that help us to grasp the nature and purpose of OT prophecy. It is important, then, that we get some idea of this nature and purpose before we move on to the text itself.

There is much of interest and value in examining the historical and cultural background of OT prophecy. The prophet is a familiar figure in both the Bible and surrounding cultures. There are numerous ANE prophetic texts from the second millennium B.C. onward that provide important background on biblical prophets, especially some of their "symbolic actions." Additionally, prophets in the ANE, as in the OT, are closely connected to kings; prophecy is largely a phenomenon of the monarchy in Israel. While it has its roots at the beginning of Israel's history—Moses is both the original and the model prophet in Israel (Deut 18)—prophecy as we know it flourished during the monarchy and didn't outlast it by much.

There are, however, a number of distinctive features of OT prophecy, largely the result of the radical differences between ANE and Israelite political and religious systems. For example, an important concern of both the prophetic narratives and what we call the prophetic books is the relationship between kingship and covenant, as we've already seen in 2 Sam 11-12. The risk is that Israel would get what they asked for: a king like that of the nations around them (1 Sam 8:5, 19-20), one who would come to see himself as having absolute power, even over the covenant and the covenant community. One of the roles of the prophets was to bring them back under the authority of the God of the covenant. Examining these differences between Israel and other ANE cultures and the role of prophecy in Israel's history would take us too far afield; the key thing to note is the function of prophecy in Israel, both with respect to the king and to the people, and its crucial connection to the covenant.

The key to understanding biblical prophecy is covenant. The prophets are, in fact, best understood as covenant spokesmen (and occasionally spokeswomen [2 Kgs 22:14–20]). They spoke to the people on behalf of the God of the covenant; analyzing their lives and society in light of the covenant, reminding them of Yahweh's requirements, calling them to account for failure, and promising them hope. Their social critique had no independent existence; it arose out of their speaking on behalf of the covenant God. Their words about the future had no independent rationale (they were not there to predict the future). Rather they arose out of the covenant, speaking of the future consequences of God's warnings and promises. They also spoke to kings on behalf of the God of the covenant, reminding them that they, like everyone else, were subject to a higher authority, whose will has been made known in the covenant instructions. As we have seen already in 2 Sam 11–12, the kings were not "above the law," not in Israel. The prophets were there to remind them of that and to tell them of the consequences of failing to submit to their overlord.

The prophets, then, were particular people called by God to communicate God's covenant will to God's covenant people in particular circumstances. That particularity and context-driven nature of prophecy is important for us to remember. At times we think of prophets (and the Bible in general) as somehow hanging outside of history, speaking a timeless word to a rootless people. The prophets (and the Bible as a whole, for that matter) bring not a timeless word but rather a particularly timely one (pun intended, I'm afraid). That is, prophetic messages are timely in the sense that they are rooted in particular moments in time, in particular circumstances, and speak to those times and circumstances. They are also timely in the sense that they are words brought to bear at just the right time, telling the people how they need to respond now to their covenant Lord. That is not to say that these words were either ad hoc (made up on the spot) or have no relevance to God's people now. These words are, as I've said, expressions of God's covenant will. Indeed, many are an application to their circumstances of things that they already know from their ancient covenant traditions. As expressions of the covenant will of God they are also ever timely, for God's will is still relevant to us, and, given an appropriate understanding of differences in theological and cultural contexts, are applicable to our circumstances. But, as always, we first must understand their message in their context in order to understand what God might be saying to us through them.

In that respect, one important skill that we need to develop is that of recognizing and understanding the different means used by the prophets to communicate their message. As people of their times and cultures, the prophets used culturally relevant forms—such as oracles (brief spoken messages), visions, and symbolic acts—in order to effectively communicate God's covenant will to God's people (and, for that matter, speak to the nations). Two of these devices appear to modern readers as particularly foreign: visions and symbolic actions. In fact, these are well known from ANE prophetic texts and thus were, so to speak, tools at hand for the prophets that they used frequently, especially Jeremiah and Ezekiel (although, interestingly, not Micah). Perhaps the most famous of the prophetic visions is that of Isa 6, a vision that both commissions and shapes the message of Isaiah and his book. Most readers, unfortunately (if comfortably!), stop a bit too early and fail to go on to the end of the vision and its consequences, for the great interplay between Yahweh and prophet in Isa 6 does not end in v. 8 with the prophet's accepting his call. Rather, it goes on to speak of the content of the prophet's message, one of unrelenting judgment until God's new beginning. Nonetheless, it nicely shows us how these visions work: they give a picture of God, God's will, God's purposes, which then is articulated in the prophet's message. Although they may seem odd to us, they are a powerful means by which God addressed the prophets and, through them and their communication of the visions to their contemporaries, God's people.

Perhaps even stranger are the prophets' symbolic actions. Probably most familiar are Jeremiah's visits to the potter's house (Jer 18-19); the weirdest and most confrontational are found in Jer 13; Ezek 4-5; and 12 (and, for that matter, Isa 20). Our (until recently) word-dominated culture has tended to see the actions primarily as illustrations of the message. So, for instance, we see Isa 20 as an illustration of God's word against Egypt, speaking of their humiliation and defeat. It seems to me, however, that there is more to them than that. They are embodiments of the word, not just illustrations. They show the prophets' involvement in their message: they are not dispassionate onlookers, speaking a word from the sidelines; they are on the field, intimately involved in the play, bearing in their bodies both God's passion and the people's need. That element of the embodied message is not limited to the prophets' symbolic actions; it is seen in the way their own stories are intimately connected with the message that they are sent to proclaim. That is perhaps most powerfully and poignantly seen in the prophets Hosea (Hos 1-3), Jeremiah (e.g., his "confessions" in Jer 11:18-23; 12:1-6; 15:15-21; 17:14-18; 20:7-18; his confrontation with Hananiah in Jer 28), and Ezekiel (the symbolic acts in Ezek 4; 5; 12 and his personal grief in Ezek 24:15-27). To wax theological for a moment, even in the "many and various ways" in which God spoke by the prophets, the word was already being made flesh.

There is much I could say about visions and the connection between the prophets and their message, but there are limits to what we can cover, and they are not a prominent feature of Micah. So let us turn now to their words per se and the devices that they used. First, let me introduce this word "oracle": as it is used of prophets it simply refers to a (generally brief) prophetic utterance, a message from God spoken by the prophet. Most prophetic books are collections of oracles. In general, rather than writing a text, the prophets speak their messages to their audience, be it king or people. As such, they put their words together as spoken and heard discourse, generally using Hebrew poetic techniques similar to those found in Psalms. Perhaps the most common and familiar forms are the oracles of judgment and the oracles of hope, in which God utters the verdict against a sinful people or offers them hope beyond judgment.

The prophets also drew on forms of speech found in their social worlds that suited their purposes. For instance, Amos uses the world of a funeral to lament the fall of the northern kingdom in Amos 5:1-2; echoes of that language can also be found in the "woe" speeches in Amos 5:18-20; 6:1-7; and Mic 2:1-5. They also frequently draw on the language of local community legal proceedings, particularly disputes and lawsuit forms. A dispute is an attempt to mount an argument before the judges, normally envisaged as the elders of the community, to persuade them of the plaintiff's case. We will look at one such case in Mic 6:6-8. A lawsuit is, so to speak, a prosecution brief aiming at conviction or the demonstration of guilt, and often it is used by the prophets in the context of the "covenant lawsuit" that Yahweh brings against Yahweh's rebellious people (see Isa 1:2-4; Amos 1-2). Hymns and other echoes of temple worship are employed as well (see Amos 9:5-6; Isa 12) and could be used with devastating force to attack Israel's false claims to righteousness (for Amos's powerful reversal of a priestly call to worship, see Amos 4:4-5). The prophets use these forms with great flexibility and freedom, often combining a number of forms of speech, building up a rich array of images and techniques to make their point. Amos 5:4-17 is a case in point, using a sequence of dispute, hymn, lawsuit, and dispute, and culminating in an oracle of judgment or woe.

These individual messages were then recorded, collected, and edited together in their final form. The rationale for their arrangement varies: books may be arranged more or less chronologically (like Ezekiel or Jer 1-24) or more thematically (like Amos) or theologically (like Isaiah); sometimes it is hard to figure out (like Jer 25-51). In general, however, even when the rationale for the arrangement of a particular sequence of sayings is hard to pin down, there is an underlying theological coherence to the books, giving each of them a unique character. So, then, when we come to a particular passage in the prophets, there are a number of things we need to think about. First, what is the unit of speech here, and what is the context of this passage in the book of which it is a part? Is there an overarching argument or structure in this (section of) the book? How does this fit into it and advance the argument? What are the circumstances being addressed by the prophet? What are the issues, and how does the prophet speak of them here and elsewhere? What kind of text is it, how is the unit put together? What ideas and existing traditions are used? Are they endorsed, rejected, or used ironically? Let's turn to Mic 6:6-8 with these questions in mind.

In order to understand Micah and his message, we need to grasp some of the historical context of Judah in the eighth century B.C. The eighth century B.C. saw a period of prosperity unmatched in the history of the divided kingdoms of Israel and Judah, in part resulting from a relative power vacuum in the ANE. The result was a large and growing gap between the rich and the poor, accompanied by a complacent belief that the nations' prosperity was a sign of God's approval of Israel. There was no transfer from faith to practice: people believed that they could do as they wished and still worship Yahweh. As long as they performed the right religious actions, the rest of their actions didn't count. They could, to put it in our terms, spend Monday through Friday exploiting the poor, setting up unfair and monopolistic trade practices, perverting the law courts for their own ends, and enslaving the innocent with their "sharp" business practices and still come to worship on Sunday and expect that God would accept them and their offerings. These issues are addressed in the book of Micah and elsewhere in the eighth-century prophets.

Let's turn to our text, Mic 6:6-8. The passage is one of a number of disputations in the book of Micah. A disputation is an argument calling for acknowledgement and response, often using rhetorical questions. (These are questions posed to produce an effect or make an assertion, not to actually elicit a reply, except perhaps by the one doing the asking. For example, a parent or teacher asks a kid, "How do you expect to get anywhere if you never do any work?" The answer "By a series of fortunate coincidences and the influence of friends" is probably not going to cut it.) Micah 6 is a chapter of disputations, using a number of rhetorical questions. The first, in vv. 1-5, is in fact a particular kind of disputation known as a lawsuit. Our text is not so specific; it is a general disputation, and one that stands in relative isolation from the passages before and after it. It is located here for reasons of genre rather than a logical or thematic connection; that is, it is here because ch. 6 is a collection of disputations rather than it being (as the NIV implies) the conclusion to the previous argument.

The structure of these few verses is fairly clear. Verses 6-7 are a series of rhetorical questions, with v. 8 being the prophet's response. The questions of vv. 6-7 are asked by Micah in the guise of someone coming before Yahweh and use the language and imagery of worship, similar to what we found in Ps 24 but with very different intent. These questions come in four sets–the third and fourth escalating to deliberately ridiculous and shocking heights of extravagance–before the prophet gives his famous answer in v. 8. Each of the questions consists of two parallel lines; Micah's response– the point of this short speech–breaks that mold, thereby giving it added impact. The introduction to the answer ("He has shown you . . .") consists of a pair of parallel lines; the climax, however, breaks that pattern, ending with a series of three succinct statements. It is worth noting here that the use of patterns, and their being broken, generates force in the "argument" of a text. The use of patterns ties things together, and at times (almost) precise repetition is a way of making a key point (see Ps 8:1, 9; Amos 1:2–2:5); at other times the breaking of a pattern serves to make the point, highlighting that this is the key moment (see Amos 2:6–16). That is what happens here: the pattern is broken, the point is driven home. Now, let's look at some of the details of this brief oracle.

The opening recalls what we have just seen in Ps 24: it deals with God's people coming before God in the temple in worship. Although the words used for "coming before Yahweh" and "bowing down" in v. 6 are unusual ones to find in this context, they clearly speak of approaching the God who is symbolically present in the temple. Normally, worshippers would be expected to bring something to sacrifice to God, be it a thank offering or one that has atoning significance. The burnt offering, described briefly in Lev 1 and 6, was the only regular offering that was to be completely burned on the altar; other offerings generally were shared among the priests or the people (see Lev 2–7). This, then, along with the reference to a year-old calf, suggests a costly offering, one that was meant to indicate the worshipper's dedication to Yahweh. The problem, as we know from the rest of the book, was that worshippers had come to believe that this was the only form their dedication needed to take. If they made the right sacrifices, God would be pleased with them, regardless of their conduct. In order to point out the faithless foolishness of these ideas, Micah piles up the sacrifices to ridiculous and even offensive extremes. A burnt offering should be good enough; if not, then make it a yearling calf, one that you've had to expend time and energy to raise but have had no benefit from as yet. But that may not be enough, so let's pile on (literally!) the sacrifices: thousands of rams, ten thousand rivers of oil. The temple would have been awash with blood and oil. That kind of sacrifice, while perhaps fitting for the dedication of the temple (see 1 Kgs 8), is ludicrously excessive for an individual. It is laughable, and certainly unrepeatable.

Micah, however, is not satisfied with that. He takes legitimate sacrifice to its illogical extreme, but then he turns to the deliberately offensive: human sacrifice. This is the ultimate expression of religious abomination and was never tolerated in the OT. In many ANE cultures, however, it was the ultimate expression of religious dedication, the ultimate way of winning (divine) friends and influencing (divine) people (i.e., gaining a hearing with the gods and getting them to act [see, e.g., 2 Kgs 3:27]). Why does Micah refer to it? To shock his audience into realizing that this is fundamentally the wrong route to take, that no possible multiplication of mere sacrifice—whether familiar but costly calves and rams or vilely despicable human sacrifice—will please Yahweh, the God of the covenant. The way to please this God is not by way of religious obligations, good as they are when used properly; something different is required, not something more.

So, what is this something different? Micah makes it plain: what God requires is already clear. This is not news, or at least it shouldn't be, but rather something that they've known all along. Here, in this familiar refrain, we see that Yahweh's requirements are not strange, that they are not an innovation; they (should) come as no surprise. To reinforce this, Micah uses key terms and ideas related to Israel's covenant response to God. As we have seen already and will see again, "justice" (*mishpat*) is a central requirement of the covenant. The people of Israel have experienced the liberating benefits of God's gracious justice and are called to reflect it in their own lives; elsewhere Micah and the other eighth-century prophets demonstrate Israel and Judah's striking failure to do justice. If they really want to please God, Micah tells them, they should remember the covenant instructions and do justice.

They should also love "mercy" (or "kindness" [NRSV]). The Hebrew word here, *khesed*, is a rich and loaded one, difficult to capture in translation. This mercy is inextricably tied to the covenant and its terms and requirements. It is often used in the sense of "steadfast love," of a commitment that demonstrates the reality of relationship and its requirements. It is, for instance, what the book of Ruth is about: the *khesed* of Ruth to Naomi, of Boaz to Ruth (and so Naomi), and of Yahweh to all concerned. It may entail mercy, as we understand the term (think, for instance, of Boaz's concern for Ruth, and of course of Yahweh's actions for Israel), but given that it is used so frequently of Israel's call to be faithful to Yahweh, that cannot be the sum of it. Micah uses this rich term to remind his hearers of the covenant and its requirements: they are called to express faithful commitment and steadfast love toward God and each other; indeed, they are called to *love khesed*. This is meant to characterize them at the deepest level.

If justice relates to society, and mercy to relationships with God and others, the last requirement is clearly God-directed. Walking with God, or walking in the ways of Yahweh, is characteristic language of the covenant, especially in the book of Deuteronomy. It calls Israel back to their primary relationship, the one on which the covenant and their existence as the people of God depends. And it reminds them that this relationship operates on God's terms, not theirs. They are not free to determine how they are to worship, nor are they free to run their lives their own way and expect God to approve. They are to walk with God, and they are to do so according to the terms of relationship that God has laid down in the covenant.

This also shows us the rationale behind Micah's scathing, sarcastic rejection of his hearers' understanding and practice of worship. This is language reminiscent of Deuteronomy (and, for that matter, Leviticus); it is covenant language. Sacrifice had a clear and important role to play in the covenant: it provided a means by which sinful humans could relate to God, experience God's forgiveness, express their commitment and gratitude, and enjoy fellowship with God and other members of the covenant community. But all of that was within the confines of the covenant (see Deut 16). Sin could be forgiven, commitment could be expressed, thanks could be offered, restitution could be made, but only in the context of covenant commitment (see especially Lev 16). Micah here demonstrates that without that commitment the sacrificial system is worthless, of no more value than a pagan abomination. And he also makes plain what is at the heart of covenant commitment: justice, mercy, and walking in the ways of the Lord—in short, living as the people of God. This brings us back to familiar territory as we are once again confronted with the OT's commitment to justice and to properly expressed relationship with God. It also shows us God's values, what Yahweh sees as important (seen also in Jesus' reference to Mic 6:8 in Matt 23:23). Yahweh's concern, ultimately, is with a particular pattern of relationships: these relational terms illustrate Yahweh's values and tell us the shape of a faithful human life. True "spirituality," truly living as the people of God, requires an integrated life involving the social (justice), the personal (mercy), and the spiritual (walking with God).

This view of being in right relationship with God challenges the contemporary church's morality and mission. In public ethical discourse evangelical Christians have been strong on personal morality. Indeed, in Australia and the United States talking about "moral issues" in the public sphere is often reduced to matters of personal, especially sexual, morality (abortion and gay marriage come to mind). These are matters of legitimate concern, and Christians ought to be engaged in conversations on these matters as they affect public policy, but they do not exhaust God's moral will. Similarly, in the practice of mission evangelical Christians have been strong on personal evangelism and helping people. These are areas of mission in which Christians ought to be engaged, and evangelical mission has much to be proud of (mission history, after all, is more than a litany of cultural imperialism), but they do not exhaust God's missional heart. Micah reminds us that if our morality is to reflect God's will, and if our mission is to express God's heart, we must be passionate about justice, mercy, and faithfulness.

This has practical implications for our mission as God's people. We must seek to create churches that are true communities of justice, love, and faithfulness, communities that model God's purposes and God's new future. But there is an unbreakable link between the life and the mission of the church; central to our mission must be speaking and acting for justice in God's world, for such is God's desire and purpose. In light of the reality of poverty in the world in which we live, and the fact that so much of it is the result of injustice in human politics and society, we must speak and act on behalf of the poor and disenfranchised. The church has a reasonable track record of caring for the poor; if we are to reflect God's own passion for justice, we also need to engage in advocacy and action that address the structures and social systems that generate and perpetuate poverty and injustice. The scale of the issues faced by our now global economy demands it. Statistics are cold and impersonal, but they nonetheless tell a sorry story: 1.2 billion people worldwide live on less than one dollar per day; over 9 million children die every year, largely from preventable causes; 1 billion people do not have safe drinking water, and over one-third of the world's population lacks decent sanitation; 115 million children have no access to primary school education; AIDS and malaria have devastated communities in Africa and are spreading rapidly in Asia. We need to do something about this story, for these statistics represent people and communities who suffer as a result of the inequalities and injustice of our global economic systems. When the profits of coffee manufacturers have increased but the proportion that coffee growers receive from their labors has fallen in the last decade (from 30 percent to 10 percent), so that they are no longer able to support themselves and their families, something is seriously wrong. When the net repayments of foreign debt paid by developing nations greatly outstrip the amount of development aid that they receive (by more than ten to one), something is seriously wrong. This is a system that must be changed. This is not something that we can safely leave to the UN or some other organization; justice is central to our existence and purpose as the people of God and so to our role as leaders and the life of God's church.

The UN Millennium Development Goals

1. Eradicate extreme poverty and hunger

Reduce by one-half the proportion of people living on less than a dollar a day; reduce by one-half the proportion of people who suffer from hunger.

2. Achieve universal primary education

Ensure that all boys and girls complete a full course of primary schooling.

3. Promote gender equality and empower women

Eliminate gender disparity in primary and secondary education preferably by 2005, and at all levels by 2015.

4. Reduce child mortality

Reduce by two-thirds the mortality rate among children under five.

5. Improve maternal health

Reduce by three-fourths the maternal mortality ratio.

6. Combat HIV/AIDS, malaria, and other diseases

Halt and begin to reverse the spread of HIV/AIDS; halt and begin to reverse the incidence of malaria and other major diseases.

7. Ensure environmental sustainability

Integrate the principles of sustainable development into country policies and programs; reverse loss of environmental resources; reduce by one-half the proportion of people without sustainable access to safe drinking water; achieve significant improvement in lives of at least one hundred million slum dwellers by 2020.

8. Develop a global partnership for development

Develop further an open trading and financial system that is rule-based, predictable, and nondiscriminatory; address the special needs of the least-developed countries and land-locked and small-island developing states; deal comprehensively with debt problems of developing countries through national and international measures to make debt sustainable in the long term; develop decent and productive work for youth; provide access to affordable essential pharmaceutical drugs in developing countries; make available the benefits of new technologies, especially information and communication technologies.[3]

There are many things that we can do in response to the reality of our world and in response to Micah's call. Here's one of them: today we have a great opportunity to be involved in a global movement calling for justice and the eradication of poverty. On October 15–16, 2006, over twenty-three million people around the world joined in the Stand Up against Poverty campaign. The organization Make Poverty History is becoming a major force calling on governments around the world to keep their promises and achieve the UN Millennium Development Goals (see p. 85), thus halving world poverty by 2015. In some ways the church has been a leader in the worldwide fight against poverty. The Micah Challenge, for example, is one movement of God's people that is part of this broader global movement for justice in its seeking justice

---

[3] See http://www.un.org/millenniumgoals (accessed June 9, 2008).

and the eradication of poverty. The Jubilee 2000 campaign also comes to mind, in which the church, driven by an understanding of the implications of the Year of Jubilee in Lev 25, called for the cancellation of foreign debt for the world's poorest economies, thus stimulating a worldwide campaign that was, if only partially, successful.

In other ways the church has been a follower. Tragically, and somewhat justifiably, in the twentieth century the church has been seen in both the "developed" and the "developing" worlds as a follower in, even an impediment to, action on the environment and women's issues (I will say more about both issues in a later chapter). I am thankful to God that through organizations and movements such as TEAR, World Vision, Baptist World Aid, and the Micah Challenge, the church in the United Kingdom, Latin America, parts of Africa, Australia, and other parts of the world has become a leader in the call to "make poverty history," or at least to halve absolute poverty by 2015. The prophet Micah, whose great message calls for such action, challenges us to join with these movements to make the most of the opportunity to add doing justice to our love of mercy and our desire to see people walk humbly with God.

WISDOM: ECCLESIASTES 11

Wisdom literature, an important resource for Christian spirituality and moral formation, as is evident in the popularity of editions of the Bible consisting of the NT with Psalms and Proverbs, was for a long time something of an orphan in OT studies. This is largely because it is so different from the rest of the OT in its emphases and methods; indeed, one of the characteristics of Wisdom literature is that it does not deal with many of the great themes of the OT, such as God's saving acts in history or covenant and law. Other sections of Wisdom literature have been similarly orphaned in popular Christian usage, largely because we don't quite know what to do with them (Song of Songs and Ecclesiastes in particular). What are we to do with Song of Songs' reflections on the wondrous and dangerous power of human sexuality? How should we respond to Ecclesiastes's explorations of the fleeting, puzzling, frustrating, and even depressing nature of human existence? Before we look at Ecclesiastes, however (Song of Songs must await another occasion), it is important that we come to grips with some of the key characteristics and features of Wisdom literature. I believe that such an introduction will also help us to be wiser in our use of a book such as Proverbs, which is, in my view, often misunderstood and abused by Christians. This is partly because it is seen as giving timeless moral instruction applicable to all circumstances rather than, as we will see, being a series of nuanced, often deceptively complex, reflections on particular circumstances of life and how we should respond to them.

In our Bibles Wisdom literature is found, most obviously, in the books of Job, Proverbs, Ecclesiastes, and Song of Songs, but it is not confined to those books. Wisdom influences are found in, for instance, the prophets (see Isa 1:2-4), a number of significant poems in Psalms (e.g., Pss 1; 19; 119), the Joseph narratives in Genesis (Gen 37-50), the court tales in Dan 1-6 and the dream sequence in Dan 7, and probably the book of Esther. Due to limitations of space, our focus here will be on wisdom as we find it in Job, Proverbs, Ecclesiastes, and Song of Songs.

Let me note in passing that there are other books, such as the Wisdom of Jesus Son of Sira (known also as Ben Sirach or Ecclesiasticus [not to be confused with Ecclesiastes]) and the Wisdom of Solomon, which appear (along with other books) in a section of Roman Catholic and Orthodox Bibles that Protestants call the Apocrypha (found in, e.g., the NRSV). Protestants do not treat them as canonical Scripture, though many see them as useful for understanding developments in Jewish thinking between the Testaments. The reasons for this decision are complex but are, in my view, based primarily on the fact that these books were never accepted as Scripture by the Jewish community; they are not part of the Hebrew Bible, which is the Bible of Jesus and the apostles and, so, our OT. Here, I'll confine the discussion to Wisdom literature apart from the Apocrypha.

One of the first things to strike us in these books is the absence of key features of other parts of the OT: they don't deal with the law, recount saving history, or bring God's word to bear on specific circumstances. Indeed, there is a certain "rootlessness" in Wisdom literature compared with other parts of the OT; wisdom books are not anchored in particular times and places but rather generalize about human life. That general quality is reflected in the fact that there are a number of texts from the ANE that bear startling similarities to OT wisdom texts; indeed, the connections between OT wisdom texts and these nonbiblical texts seem closer than those between the biblical Wisdom literature and the rest of the OT. The clearest of these are the parallels between Prov 22:17–24:22 and the Wisdom of Amenemope, written around 1100 B.C. in Egypt. There has been much recent discussion of these parallels, along with speculation as to the date and social context of the production of Proverbs. Wisdom has been seen as the product of a "secular," privileged group that flourished during the monarchy after the so-called Solomonic Enlightenment. I find these arguments, and the evidence used to justify them, dubious. Given the way Wisdom literature deliberately avoids tying itself to particular times and places, it seems better to me to describe the literature and its emphases and seek to understand it theologically rather than tie it to particular historical periods and political interests.

The first ten chapters of the book of Proverbs give us a fairly good sampling of the kind of texts that we find in the Wisdom literature. Whereas ch. 10 is a series of relatively disconnected short sayings, chs. 1–9 are a series of loosely connected longish poems on the benefits and characteristics of wisdom and exhortations to choose wisdom (and life) over folly (and death). Proverbs 1–9 introduces and sets up the book and how we are to read the variety of instructions that we find in it; all is governed by the recognition that "the fear of Yahweh is the beginning of wisdom" (Prov 1:7). That also gives us crucial insight into the nature of wisdom and folly. They don't deal with being clever or stupid but rather with how we conduct ourselves in the world. Some of that conduct is clearly moral, even "religious"; some of it is not.

Wisdom deals with successfully navigating our way in the world as we know it, the world that is also God's world. It covers such things as what works and what doesn't (Prov 10:5; 27:14), how relationships work and fail (10:12; 11:13; 12:17–20), how society should be governed (11:11, 14; 31:1–8), and what pleases God (1:7; 3:4; 11:1; 14:2, 26–27; 30:7–9). But all of that is situational—it depends on the context—and a key aspect of wisdom is knowing the times, knowing whether this is a time for action or inaction, words or silence (compare, e.g., 26:4 with 26:5). Moreover, much of what Proverbs says about the world is a distillation of observations of the world and how it works, and sometimes how it *ought* to work, and consists of advice on wise conduct rather than categorical commands. Proverbs' advice on prosperity, for instance, tells us that properly conducting ourselves in the world ought to, and generally will, result in things going well (10:3; 11:27–30). But it also reminds us that wealth may be a sign of oppressive wickedness rather than a blessing on righteousness (15:16; 16:8, 19), that human evil can sweep away the fruits of a good person's labor, and that injustice is also a feature of the world (13:23), albeit one that God detests and that the wise will avoid and, where possible, combat (11:16; 17:5; 31:8). We need, then, to be wise in our use of Proverbs and other wisdom teaching, recognizing that it gives us advice that we need to consider rather than necessarily providing commands that must be followed or promises that we can claim, let alone using it as a bludgeon on others. Job (and Ecclesiastes, for that matter) reminds us of that.

Job and Ecclesiastes also remind us that not all Wisdom literature is like Proverbs, with its relatively optimistic view of the world and our ability to grasp its workings. Key themes of both books are the puzzling nature of human experience of the world and the limits of our ability to grasp it and its ordering. If Proverbs can be seen as "creation theology," a series of reflections on the world as it comes to us as the work of God's hands, Job and Ecclesiastes remind us that there is disorder as well as order in the world. Job tells us, among other things, that God's purposes are beyond our grasp. We cannot always discern from the world what God is doing and why we experience the world as we do (something that Job's "friends" are forced to acknowledge, as is Job himself). Ecclesiastes perhaps goes further, calling us to recognize that there is apparent disorder in the world itself, which is not necessarily the result of God's inscrutable purposes (but, then, how could we know that anyway unless, by God's revelation, they become scrutable?). Sometimes the world just goes wrong; and even when it doesn't, we aren't able to fathom it (see, e.g., Eccl 9:1–12). Wisdom is, in short, a product of practical and theological reflection on creation, and, in the case of Job and Ecclesiastes, creation as we now know it, as fallen.

Let's turn, then, to Eccl 11. Ecclesiastes (also known by its Hebrew name, Qohelet) is a neglected and much misunderstood book of the OT, but it is nonetheless one of my favorites. Ecclesiastes is often seen as a bleak and pessimistic book with a jaundiced, even cynical, take on life—the kind of view of the world that a dissipated skeptic might have at the end of life. Some find that pleasing. One commentator, James Crenshaw, states, "For many years I have been fascinated with Qohelet, perhaps because he makes my own skepticism appear solidly biblical. Like him, I observe a discrepancy between the vision of a just world, which I refuse to relinquish, and reality as I perceive it." Others are less pleased and see it as being hardly a work of faith at all, let alone a contribution to it. Indeed, they believe that it functions as a warning against cynical, autonomous human wisdom and as a call back to a more straightforward faith and obedience. Another commentator, Tremper Longman, argues that a literary and theological distinction should be made between the bulk of the book (written by Qohelet, "the teacher") and what he calls the "frame narrative." He argues that Qohelet's theology is not that of the book; the frame narrator has the last word and negates all of Qohelet's skeptical claims. Neither view, it seems to me, does justice to the book: for while Qohelet clearly despairs of human ability to understand and control the world, this is not the sum total of his reflections; nor does the "frame" clearly contradict the body of the work. To understand this, and the place of our text within the book (and so in our ethical reflection), we need to spend some time grappling with the book and its main theme.

The word that dominates the book, and OT scholarly discussion of it, is *hebel*, traditionally translated "vanity" or "meaningless." Ecclesiastes alone contains about half the OT uses of this word. It is particularly prominent in the opening chapters, but it is found throughout the book, with the exception of ch. 10. Clearly, *hebel* is an important word in the book; but what does it mean? Elsewhere in the OT it means "breath" or "vapor" (e.g., Job 7:16; Ps 62:9), although it is also used in the sense of "vain" or "worthless," especially when used in the plural with reference to idols (e.g., 1 Kgs 16:13, 26; Jer 14:22). Its use in Ecclesiastes, however, is both so frequent and characteristic of the book's thought that we need to examine how Ecclesiastes itself uses the word rather than being informed solely by its use elsewhere. On some occasions Ecclesiastes uses the word simply to mean "fleeting" or "transient," like a breath or vapor (6:12; 11:10). At other times the word seems much darker, more puzzling and frustrating, and almost threatening in its implications (6:2, 4). Still other passages seem ambiguous (1:12–2:26), and, I suggest, deliberately so. I suspect that the writer is in general deliberately ambiguous in the use of the word, as he is with so many other things in the book.

Indeed, I think that the book's form matches its message, for the dominant idea running through the book is the transient, enigmatic, and elusive nature of the world and human experience. But, due in part to wisdom's desire to understand the world and navigate successfully through life, this quest for understanding becomes frustrating in its elusive, enigmatic ambiguity. Indeed, given the reality of death that looms so darkly over the book and that erases permanently any gain that humans have in their labor or their pleasure, life becomes ultimately meaningless. If death is the end—and in Ecclesiastes, as in most of the ot, there is no clear hope of life after death—then we gain nothing from life, and the world doesn't seem to make sense (Eccl 1:12–2:26; 3:19; 7:15; 8:14). Despite the darkness of that vision, it seems to me to be faithful, for the ways of the world often seem awry. Godly people who have committed themselves to serving the needy are killed in acts of senseless violence or in random accidents, while the heedless, selfish rich "live long and prosper." If all we have to go on is the world as we see it—the perspective adopted in Wisdom literature—then surely we must agree that some things make no sense. We know that this is a world that is beyond our grasp, and that although sometimes we can figure out how to live well in it, often we cannot. Random and horrible things happen. That's life.

Ecclesiastes tells us, among other things, that such a view of the world, when we have it, does not stand in contradiction to our faith. It is a true perception of the parts of the story that we see, but it is not the whole story (which is one of the reasons we need the whole canon of Scripture). The psalms and the prophets remind us that God is sovereign judge of the earth, Daniel reminds us that death may not be the end (Dan 12:1–4). The nt tells us the great good news that judgment and hope have come in the person of Jesus; that because of his resurrection and the coming transformation of all things, death is not the end; that there will be a final reckoning in which the balances will be put right and the enigmas resolved (as much as they can be); that creation will be set free from its bondage to frustration; and that none of our labor will have been in vain (Rom 8:20; 1 Cor 15:58).

Let's turn to Eccl 11. As we do, I need to introduce an aspect of literary analysis that so far we have been able to ignore: identifying the unit, or section of the text, that we'll be examining. In our earlier passages the unit was fairly straightforward; here it's a little more complicated, in part because of the characteristic ambiguity of Ecclesiastes. I mentioned earlier that the form of the book matches its content; that includes the structure of the book and identifying its flow of thought. The quest to understand the clear structure of the book is elusive, hard to grasp, puzzling, and, in the end, frustrating. This is particularly clear in Eccl 9:13-10:20, where the previous thematic ordering breaks down and the sayings seem to be piled on each other with no underlying rationale— in ch. 10 even *hebel* vanishes like the mist. Once we come to chs. 11-12, however, order returns; the book closes with an extended meditation on old age and concluding reflections.

Chapter 11 brings some of Qohelet's reflections to as much of a resolution as he ever achieves, and it seeks to bring them to bear on practical strategies for life. The chapter falls into two sections: 11:1-6 and 11:7-10, each of which contains two connected reflections on life and its ambiguities. Here is where the question of the unit of thought comes in, for 11:7-10 fits naturally with what follows in 12:1-7, as both passages deal with the evanescence of youth and its potency and pleasures. Indeed, the long poem in 12:1-7 (and the final summation in 12:8) can be seen as an extended motivation to grasp the opportunities that youth offers in 11:7-10. Nonetheless, although 11:7-10 is clearly connected with what follows, it is in my view an independent unit that also has connections with what precedes it. So, strictly speaking, we will be examining two passages: 11:1-6 and 11:7-10. Dealing with them together is justified, I believe, because Ecclesiastes returns to more obvious coherence in these final chapters and because both texts deal with how we should respond to the enigma of life.

The first section, Eccl 11:1-6, is a collection of typically pithy wisdom sayings and falls into two main sections: vv. 1-2 and vv. 3-6. The first, as we will see, gives practical advice on investment strategies, the second on agriculture. Both fall into two sections (v. 1 and

v. 2; vv. 3-4 and vv. 5-6), but in vv. 3-6 each of the sections is comprised of paired sayings. The result of this small collection of aphorisms (brief, pithy sayings) is elusive (in Ecclesiastes–what a surprise!) but comprises an argument of sorts, suggesting a practical policy in the face of our inability to understand the world or control or predict the outcomes of our endeavors. Let's now turn, after this brief foray into literary analysis, to exegesis proper.

Verse 1 is often taken as an ethical charge to give alms: even though it seems to be a fruitless enterprise (casting bread on waters), it is a long-term strategy, for the kindness will rebound (after many days you will find it again). In the same way, v. 2 is seen as a call to generosity in the face of the many problems that people encounter. I think that this interpretation, though popular in the tradition, is wrong, mainly because it doesn't fit with the rest of 11:1-6 and the wording of the text. Verses 3-6 clearly deal with how to conduct ourselves in light of the unpredictable and inflexible nature of reality. Verses 1-2 make better sense when read in a similar way: the exhortation to cast bread (or food) on the waters is, I think, a reference to business endeavors. It may, indeed, be an allusion to overseas trade, which was (and was seen to be) a risky business in Israel–hence, casting your food on the waters. The world is an unpredictable place, so you might as well have a go! But–and here is the wise balance–if v. 1 says, "Have a go," v. 2 says, "Don't put all your eggs in one basket." True, after many days you may find your investment and find it a success, but it doesn't always work out well, as we know already from our reading of Ecclesiastes (and from life). And because you don't know which enterprise will fail (for surely in this uncertain world something is bound to fail), make sure to "spread your investments." The alternative is paralysis in the face of the pitfalls and possibilities of life, which is a waste of what God has given us.

That is clearly picked up in vv. 3-6, which turn from business (where we can have some say over events that matter, I suppose) to agriculture (where we have none). Verse 3 speaks of our inability to control the world: clouds rain (or don't), trees fall in the wind, and we can do nothing about it. If we seek understanding and control before we do anything, then we'll do nothing. The wind may blow our seed (and topsoil) away; rain may fall during harvest so that our grain and hay rot in the barns. If you seek certainty and

control, you'll be paralyzed. Verses 5-6 put it (a little) more positively. The ways of the world are beyond our ken; how much more
so are the ways of God. So, get on with it. You never know—it may
even work! So, figure out what makes sense and do it rather than
worrying endlessly about whether it's going to work or not. Success, after all, is beyond our control.

Ecclesiastes's brilliant insight is clearly counter to our culture.
He is at pains to affirm what he has already stated: the world is too
complex or unpredictable for us to be sure that our plans will work.
But his conclusion is radically different to what we would expect,
at least what we in our culture might expect. Rather than advising
a conservative, protective, controlling way of life that seeks to gain
power over all the variables and hedge against all possible disasters, he exhorts us to banish anxiety and the paralysis that it brings
and embrace a liberality of lifestyle that is truly freeing. True, he
is far from optimistic. But then, how could he be, given his observations of the world? Ecclesiastes's advice arises out of resignation
rather than hope. Nonetheless, he calls us away from an anxiously
conservative grasping after control to a (resigned, yes, but) carefree
embrace of life and its possibilities. From an ethical point of view
this challenges the vision of life and values so prevalent in Western culture. It also has clear implications for how we conduct our
lives and our business affairs, as we'll see shortly.

In v. 7 the chapter clearly changes focus, though it still deals
with "So what?" questions in the face of the fleeting and frustrating
nature of life. The opening of this section praises the sweet, pleas-
ant nature of light, of a human's ability to live "under the sun"—an
interesting contrast, it seems, to what Ecclesiastes says about the
bitter pain of human existence (see 2:17; 4:1-3). Here, however,
he is contrasting the joys of life with the inevitability of death and
its erasing of all opportunities to experience the relative goods of
human life (see also 9:3-6). Life and light, he says, are to be enjoyed
while we have them, and that's not for long; darkness and death
will come, and when they do, there is no going back. In light (so
to speak) of 12:1-7, the darkness of 11:8 must be seen as including death but going beyond it. The images from that final poem
suggest that the dark powers of death can intrude on a human
life, robbing it of sweetness and light. Enjoy it, then, while you've
got it. Ecclesiastes has something of an interest in enjoying life as

a good, if fleeting, gift of God (see 2:24-26; 3:12-14; 5:18-20; 9:7-10; 10:19). That is affirmed here and is applied especially to the young.

Ecclesiastes focuses on the young for two reasons: first, the capacity for pleasure that comes with youth; second, the looming depredations of old age and the diminishing the capacity for joy that comes with them. As an aside, I would note that these observations, typical of Wisdom literature, are general, not universal. I have known many older people with a great zest for life; a few years before my mother's death, we took her on a "Sydney Harbor Bridge Climb" for her sixty-fifth birthday, which she did with great delight. And I have known many young people who have no enthusiasm for life, the kind for whom a new X-Box is a peak experience. The generalization nonetheless stands, especially in a society such as ancient Israel's, one without state-of-the-art geriatric services. The call, then, is to avoid anxiety and to embrace pleasure while you can. Interestingly, *hebel* is used in two distinct ways in these verses, nicely encapsulating key elements of how the word is used in Ecclesiastes. In 11:10 it clearly means "fleeting"—like breath, youthful vigor is evanescent, it passes all too soon, as those of us over age forty can attest. In 11:8, however, it has the darker meaning of enigmatic, frustrating, or yielding no lasting value or meaning for life. These paired uses of *hebel* also nicely balance the exhortation: in the first instance (v. 8) because of the dark futility of what is to come, in the second (v. 10) because youth and the ability to enjoy life soon pass.

There is, nonetheless, another "threat" in the passage, as seen in the second half of v. 9: God's judgment. But for what is God judging us? It cannot be because of our enjoyment of life, for that is specifically encouraged: despite what some commentators have thought, the language of "ways of your heart" and "what your eyes see" is neutral. It seems to me that there are two possibilities: we will be called to account either for our abuse of God's good gifts or for our neglect of God's good gifts. It may seem that the first is the obvious answer. Given the OT's clear passion for justice and its hatred of self-indulgent complacency, God's judgment here must be directed toward such abuses. But it is important to remember the context. This is part of a clear exhortation to enjoy life as a good gift from God while we are best able to do so, as is made plain in the following verse. Yes, excess is to be avoided, but so is a miser-able, miserly, minimalist restriction on life. I suggest that both are in view—that the ambiguity is deliberate—encouraging us to con-sider all the ways that God's gifts can be misused or neglected. The latter is somewhat startling, at least in the Australian context, where the church is seen as "a bunch of wowsers" (a wowser is a killjoy, someone out to spoil everyone else's fun). It is surprising that the Bible might encourage us, under God, to embrace life and to enjoy its good gifts. It certainly reverses those images that many of us have of God as the ultimate killjoy, the heavenly schoolmas-ter just itching to see us step out of line so he can whack us with a cosmic cane. The call to liberality in enjoyment might be unex-pected, but it's indisputable.

That, in fact, is what ties the two parts of ch. 11 together: the call to liberality in life, both in how we conduct our lives, and how we receive the good things of life. In both respects it is a clear counter to our culture's anxious desire for control and its obsessive quest for systems that will allow us to avoid, contain, or command the hap-penstances of life. Nor does it share our culture's anxious search for more and more stimulation; it receives these good things as gifts for which God will hold us accountable. It is a call to "be not anxious," because God is in control and we're not, nor can we fully grasp the ways that God or the world works. It points out the fruitlessness of anxiety—something that Jesus states in the Sermon on the Mount (Matt 6:27). It also sets us up for the other, more positive rationale to the same liberality of life that we find in Jesus' famous sermon. Our heavenly Father loves us and cares for us (and he runs the world and we don't), so be generous, not anxious (Matt 6:19-34). Jesus reminds us not only that we are not in control, but also that God is, and by showing us the depths of God's love we know that we can trust God in this puzzling and frustrating world.

So, we see here, in sum, a call to surrender anxiety and the desire for mastery that drives it, and to embrace responsible lib-erality in life. That is very clear in relation to the call to enjoy the benefits of youth while you have them; it is also, as we have seen, behind the advice in Eccl 11:1-6. God, I suggest, is interested in our investment strategies and the view of the world that drives them. Given that we do not run the universe (and that God does), God calls us, I believe, to a responsible mix of defensiveness and risk in our use of the resources that God has entrusted to our care. Some opportunities will come our way that seem attractive, that are good investments, holding out the prospect of enriching people's lives and enabling human communities to flourish. But they may be risky. Well, as we say in Australia, have a go. The whole thing might fall in a heap, but at least you had a shot at doing something good and significant. (I think that a similar strategy lies behind Jesus' parable of the Talents in Matt 25:14-30.) Of course, both in our service of God and in our use of God's other gifts we need to balance our risks, ensuring that we have spread ourselves widely enough so that if one endeavor fails, we have something to fall back on. But that is driven not by a miserly managerial mindset but rather by the recognition that, in the end, nothing is subject to our ultimate control.

Ecclesiastes reminds us, then, that we're not in control, and therefore we shouldn't live as if we were. But it also reminds us that life is fleeting, and so we should enjoy the good gifts that God has given us, and enjoy them *as gifts* and in honor of the giver. This is something that Paul also picks up on, negating the false asceticism that comes from our false view of God as one who wants to limit and constrain our existence. He reminds us that all things can be received (and enjoyed) as God's (1 Tim 4:1-5). We must use them in a way that honors God and fits God's purposes for us and creation; but the very fact of doing so also honors God. All things, including the pleasure of good food and drink and the delight of sex (the latter always understood to belong in the context of marriage alone) can be accepted and used in honor of God, the gracious giver of all good gifts (1 Cor 6:12-7:7; cf. Eccl 9:9; 11:9). Sure, we need to use what God has given us in responsible ways that reflect God's own generosity and justice and the purposes for which God has given them (a particularly pertinent consideration in relation to sex). However, part of that responsibility is to delight in these gifts. Love, justice, and faithfulness are all essential to *shalom*, but so is delight. Ecclesiastes reminds us to round out our images of *shalom*, to enjoy what God has given us and so demonstrate our trusting gratitude for God's good gifts. That too is integral to Christian ethics, to our call to live as God's people in God's good and beautiful world. That too is one of the ways we can reflect God's character and represent God in God's world.

CHAPTER 3

AVOIDING PITFALLS, HACKING THROUGH THE JUNGLE

NOT ALL TERRAIN IS SAFE and easy going. Sometimes we have to work hard—very hard—to get over the ground. We face tangled undergrowth, tightly packed trees, and paths that are obscure at best. To get over that ground we need to get out the machete and do some hard work hacking through the jungle (presuming, of course, that we are not damaging a protected national park!). And we have to watch our step because the undergrowth may hide pitfalls, places where the ground has subsided and the vines grown over. All serious bushwalkers and hikers know that. Some journeys, or stages on the journey, can be dangerous and taxing tasks. We are now at that stage of our journey into the strange land of the OT where we turn aside to some of the difficult terrain and try to figure out how to make our way through it. Let's turn, then, to those issues that I raised back in the introduction: slavery, ritual purity, and holy war.

SLAVERY

Slavery is a significant problem for evangelical Christians, who take the Bible as the authoritative word of God. This is only accentuated if we believe, as I do, that it speaks of a God of liberty and justice and shapes a vision of life in community that reflects God's own character. How can that be the case when slavery is both an obvious reality in the Bible, particularly the OT, and an offense to our basic ideas of justice and freedom? Furthermore, it is an oppressive reality that distorts and destroys the lives of millions in our world today, whether it takes the form of debt slavery in India, sweatshops in Asia, conscripted child soldiers in North Africa, bonded domestic workers in the Middle East, or children sold into prostitution worldwide. Anyone who knows about slavery in the (post)modern world, now or in our recent past, also knows that such slavery is an intolerable offense against God and human dignity. Yet we find slavery in the Bible, and it is not condemned. That problem, as I mentioned earlier, was brought forcefully home to me in early 2006 when the question was raised by someone who was both a Christian and passionate about justice: "How can we say that God has a passion for justice, that the Old Testament shapes our vision of justice and integral mission, when slavery is never challenged in the Old Testament?" That is the question to which we now turn.

As we do so, let's not pretend that we don't have a problem. We do. Slavery is present in the OT, where it goes unchallenged; it is taken as a given in Israelite society, not presented as a problem to be solved. Does this mean, then, that far from being a resource in our fight against slavery, the OT endorses it? Certainly, that is what many eighteenth- and nineteenth-century evangelical Christians believed. They believed that their fellow Christians who campaigned against slavery, such as William Wilberforce, were fighting against the clear teaching of Scripture. Is that right? Have the long years of struggle against slavery gone against the Bible? In answering these questions, I won't look at every text in the OT that refers to slavery; that is too big a task and would be fairly repetitive. I will, however, look at some representative, problematic instances of slavery in the OT, before moving on to other texts that moderate slavery as a social institution or limit its effects. I will then briefly discuss slavery in redemptive history and the question of the divine accommodation of God to the realities of fallen human society, before looking at what this means for us as Christians. We begin by tackling some of the problem texts.

The OT assumes the existence of slavery as an institution and also that the people of God can own slaves and count them as part of their property, even as marks of prosperity (see Gen 12:16; Eccl 2:7). Lest we dodge the issue by claiming that these are merely descriptive texts with no prescriptive force, we must recognize that male and female slaves are specifically included in the property that is protected by the last of the Ten Commandments in Exod 20:17 and Deut 5:21. We are not to covet any of the possessions of our neighbor, including his male and female slaves. By the way, we should also note that Deuteronomy, while making it clear that our neighbor's wife is not to be counted as a possession, does not so distinguish slaves: they are counted as property that we should not covet. Slavery is an assumed institution, and slaves are property to be protected.

This idea of slaves being property is graphically clear in Exod 21:20-21. It is worth quoting these verses: "If a man strikes his slave or his female slave with a staff and he dies under his hand, he is surely to be punished [or, "avenged"]. However, if he stands [after] a day or two days, he shall not be punished, for he is his money" (my translation). I should note that the NRSV and the NIV differ significantly on v. 21. The NIV has "if the slave gets up after a day or two," while the NRSV has "if the slave survives for a day or two" (and then, presumably, dies). This is not the place to get bogged down in translation issues, other than to say that although either one is a possible translation of the Hebrew of v. 21, the NIV translation is a better fit with the normal use of the key word, "stand." That, however, is an aside. The key point for our purposes is that the slave is clearly identified as the master's possession, his property—literally, his silver or money. That is why the loss of the slave's labor is the only punishment the master receives for inflicting a nonfatal, nonpermanent injury. Indeed, this law assumes that masters have the right to strike their slaves, presumably in punishment for disobedience or laziness. Whatever protections existed in Israel for slaves, they were treated as property, as a possession, and they could be beaten if their master thought fit. Their status as property is seen, in the case of foreign slaves, in the fact that they and their descendants born in the master's house could be bequeathed from one generation to the next (Lev 25:44-46). So far so bad for the OT: slavery is assumed as a practice in the OT, the law legislates it as such, and it is nowhere rejected. But that's not the whole story, as Exod 21 itself makes plain; for there, slaves are treated as persons, not just property.

I will return to this notion in a moment; for now, we turn to an issue that may not initially strike us as particularly pertinent: the way that provisions regarding a dangerous animal in Exod 21 apply to slaves. Exodus 21:18-36 deals with cases of what we would call "culpable negligence" and the proper exercise of "the duty of care." The cases in Exod 21 cover the kind of dangers for which a person in a rural community might have responsibility–things such as dangerous animals, like a bull that gores people or other animals (vv. 28-32, 35-36), and holes in the ground (vv. 33-34). In the case of an animal with a "history," one known to be dangerous, the owner of the animal is held responsible if it causes anyone's death (vv. 28-32). Not only is the bull to be stoned, but also the owner must either be executed (a very serious penalty for culpable negligence) or, if the family of the dead person so chooses, pay a fine. The family has suffered a loss, and although they are entitled to demand the death of the one responsible, they are not required to do so; nonetheless, compensation must be paid to cover their loss (including but not restricted to the economic loss suffered with the death of a productive member of the family). If, however, the animal kills a slave, then the owner of the animal is fined–fairly heavily, but merely fined–since the loss is seen as being incurred by the master of the slave, not the family of the slave. So far, this is consistent with the slave being seen as property, as an economic commodity for which the owner must be compensated. But the slave is not merely property, for the bull is still to be stoned. The bull's action has cost a human life, and, whether that life was slave or free, Gen 9:5-6 applies. True, slaves are slaves; however, they are also human beings and are to be counted as such. This, as we will see, is not an isolated instance of limits being placed on slavery; it is, in fact, typical of how the OT treats the institution. It is assumed and tolerated, but it is also moderated.

As we come to look at the way slavery is qualified and moderated in the OT, it becomes clear that it bears little resemblance to slavery as seen in the world today (see Anna's story below) or on plantations in the Caribbean or North America in the nineteenth century. To see that, let's look at some key texts. First, we go back to creation. In Gen 1-2 all humans are made in the image of God and are granted the rights and responsibilities of productive labor in the world. There is no hint that some humans are created inferior, that some are created to toil for a separate, leisured class; the OT knows nothing of slave races. Slavery is a social institution, not an ontological (or a nature of being) category. Let me explain what I mean by that. Slavery and the subjugation of one "race" by another have at times been justified on the grounds of the natural, inherent inferiority of the "slave race," or of the existence of an innate "slave class." It is consequent on their being a particular kind of person rather than their playing a particular role in society and the economy. In contrast, slavery in the OT is no more than a social institution that, furthermore, comes into existence only after the advent of human sin; it is not a feature of God's created order. That, it seems to me, is the only way of understanding the law regarding the goring ox in Exod 21:32: the ox is to be stoned because it has killed a human being. In this matter, slave or free, all humans are equal (Gen 9:5-6). Job 31:13-15 presents the same creational perspective: slaves have rights and are to be treated fairly because they too have been made by the sovereign Creator. Slavery, then, is not part of God's creative work; it forms no part of God's creative intentions for humanity.

When we turn to God's work of redemption, we find that fundamental to Israel's story and the identity of Yahweh is the understanding that Yahweh is a God who sets captives free. God is commonly identified as "Yahweh your God, who brought you out of Egypt, out of the land of slavery" (e.g., Exod 20:2; Deut 5:6). This is not a "dead" creedal identity, a mere name doing no work in Israel's understanding of God and their responsibilities. As we've already seen, it shapes their understanding of the character of God, the nature of God's purposes, as well as an understanding of their responsibilities as God's people living in God's world. That is evident in the frequent call for Israel to "remember that you were slaves in Egypt and Yahweh your God brought you out of there with a mighty hand and an outstretched arm" (Deut 5:15). This repeated call in Deuteronomy is often used as the motivation for them to act in justice and mercy (e.g., Deut 10:12-22; 15:12-15; 16:11-12; 24:17-22). Not only is Yahweh the God who sets the captives free, giving justice to the oppressed and being kind to the poor, but the beneficiaries of Yahweh's mercy and justice, the people of Israel, are to do likewise. As we will see, they are to do so with respect to the Sabbath, ensuring that even slaves can enjoy rest that, in Deuteronomy's version of the Sabbath command, is specifically motivated by Yahweh's deliverance of Israel from slavery

(Exod 20:10; Deut 5:12-15). Slaves are even to be included in the celebration of festivals at the central sanctuary (Deut 12:12, 18; 16:11). God's character and the character of their story are to shape their treatment of slaves.

Indeed, slaves in Israel have rights. As we have seen, although slaves are treated as property in OT law (and in Exod 21 no distinction is drawn between Hebrew and non-Hebrew slaves), they still are regarded as persons. That lies behind the interesting example of compensation for a permanent injury found in Exod 21:26-27. The injuries range from the serious and debilitating (the loss of an eye) to the trivial but disfiguring (the loss of a tooth). Rather than inflict a similar injury on the offender, the slave (male or female) is to go free in exchange for the loss of eye or tooth. Two things are at work here. First, there is a cost to the offender: in this case, valuable property—with significant economic worth in terms of the slave's future labor—is lost. Second, there is a compensatory benefit to the injured party: in this case going free, meaning, for an Israelite slave, the cancellation of whatever debt led to his or her period of bonded labor (see below for this), and for a foreigner, freedom from perpetual servitude. Slaves have rights, and these rights, and the slave's well-being, cannot be casually disregarded.

We just noted the distinction between Israelite and non-Israelite slaves. That is important to remember because, with the exception of prisoners of war, most slaves in Israel would have been Israelites. As we can see in Exod 21:1-11; Deut 15; and Lev 25, for Israelites slavery was generally a temporary condition, not a permanent state, and was a way of dealing with crushing debt. It was a period of bonded labor that was used to clear a debt and was terminated in the seventh year. In this regard, it is interesting to note that in Jer 34:8-22 one of Zedekiah's many crimes is his reversal of the Sabbatical freedom that he earlier granted his people (see also Neh 5:1-13). Furthermore, debts were to be canceled in the Sabbatical year, meaning that the slave went away debt free; indeed, if Deut 15:14 were followed, the slave went away with the provisions needed to become economically stable. In the case of severe economic hardship requiring the sale of their prime resource, their land, this too would be reversed in the year of Jubilee, when all people were restored to their original inheritance, without debt. For Israelites, then, slavery was voluntarily entered into (at least by the head of the household) and was, in effect, a form of social security, and one that ensured that debts could not be passed on from one generation to another. It is fundamentally inappropriate that those liberated by Yahweh could be subjected again to permanent slavery, either literally, by becoming perpetual slaves (except by their own free decision [Exod 21:5-6]), or metaphorically, by way of perpetual debt; hence this provision. This, by the way, is in stark contrast to the intergenerational debt slavery so prevalent today on the Indian subcontinent in which three or four generations can be effectively enslaved for a debt of a few dollars that rapidly compounds at the 300 percent annual interest charged to the original borrower.

There is, however, an exception to this law regarding the free release of slaves. In Exod 21:7-11 maidservants are not to be released in the seventh year but rather stay in the master's house indefinitely (as is also the case for a servant who loves his master or his slave-born wife [21:5-6]). This, at first glance, seems to be an example of the patriarchal values of the OT, in which men are granted greater freedom and value than are women. But this, I suggest, is a case where appearance is deceiving. It is important to look at the instruction in its entirety because, as v. 8 implies and vv. 9-10 make plain, the female slave in question is bought as a wife (or perhaps concubine, or subordinate wife) for the master or his son. What is most probably in view here is a case in which a woman is "sold" in light of her family's debt with the intention of her becoming the wife of the "purchaser" or, more likely, his son. For the "selling" family, this is a way of honorably dealing with a debt; for the "purchaser" it is a way of ensuring that he or his son has a wife.

Though limited, the woman's rights in this transaction are clear. First, she was not to be treated as property: if for some reason she was not acceptable to her master and he chose not to marry her or have her marry his son, she was not to be "sold on" to foreigners but rather must be redeemed by her original family. On the other hand, if she was found to be acceptable, although she had no say in whom she married, she was nonetheless an Israelite woman and could not be casually treated as sexual object; whatever other domestic arrangements the man might make, she was still his wife and must receive her due. Failure to treat her in this way is equivalent to a personal injury (most likely related to the role of honor and shame in social relationships in Israel; cf. Deut 21:10–14, where a similar provision is extended to a woman captured as a slave in war). Clearly, whatever limitations of rights women had in Israel (especially women prisoners of war), they nonetheless had rights that, if seriously infringed, meant they could go free. Once again, this is in stark contrast to the callous and dehumanizing way women often were treated on the plantations of the eighteenth and nineteenth centuries, let alone in contemporary sexual slavery (see Anna's story below). Clearly, there were moderating influences on the practice of slavery in the OT, influences that sharply differentiate it from the more familiar and brutal patterns of modern slavery.

The most striking instances of that moderating influence are seen in Deut 23:15–16; 24:7 (cf. Exod 21:16). Let me deal with the latter first. William Wilberforce famously recognized that 1 Tim 1:10 condemns the practice of slave trading; in Deut 24:7 the OT definitively outlaws it. An Israelite could own a foreign slave or could have a fellow Israelite under his control for a period of bonded servitude; kidnapping someone (anyone in Exodus; a "brother Israelite" in Deuteronomy) in order to sell them into slavery is not only forbidden but even punishable by death. Foreigners, presumably, would become slaves if captured as prisoners of war; otherwise, no Israelite could be sold into slavery unwillingly (in contrast to Joseph's treatment at the hands of his brothers in Gen 37). Indeed, Exod 21:16 suggests that any such act by a private person, be it directed at an Israelite or not, was a capital offense. Once again, this is in stark contrast to the brutality of the slave trade in the eighteenth and nineteenth centuries or today, where, in effect, every slave was taken in breach of this law.

The most revolutionary instruction, however, and one that effectively undermines slavery in the OT as a potentially oppressive institution, is Deut 23:15–16: "You shall not capture for their master a slave who has escaped to you from their master. They may live in your midst in the place which they choose in any of your towns [literally, "gates"] as seems good to them. You shall not oppress them" (my translation). There is debate among OT scholars as to whether this law applies only to (Israelite) slaves escaping from masters in foreign lands or whether it applies equally to all slaves

(Israelite and non-Israelite), including those in Israel. Given the absence of the kind of qualification or distinction that we find elsewhere in Deuteronomy in relation to slaves, the latter makes the best sense: it applies to all slaves everywhere. Any slave who found conditions under a brutal master intolerable and fled was to be offered a home (wherever the slave freely chose) as a free person in Israel. This effectively undermines slavery as an oppressive institution. For any master who brutalizes his slaves risks their flight and freedom: whatever rights the master may have under law, his rendering their lot unendurable negates them.

This is, as we noted in chapter 2, a unique law in the ANE. The Code of Hammurabi, for instance, specifically requires that an escaped slave be returned to the master; failure to do so undermines a central social and economic structure and was to be severely punished (by death, in many instances). Deuteronomy explicitly reverses such laws, in so doing, demonstrating a radically different social vision. Whatever role slavery may have played in ancient Israel, it was not such a pivotal institution as to require that it be hedged with draconian legislation and onerous penalties. On the contrary: Israel's social vision, shaped as it was by their story of liberation and a God who sets captives free, valued freedom so highly that it superseded a slave owner's property rights. This applies not only when slaves are injured but also when they are so mistreated that they flee their bondage. A nation of escaped slaves is called upon to welcome all their fellow fugitives and to allow them to settle where they wished. Deuteronomy, far from giving comfort to (post)modern slave owners, would have heartily endorsed both the nineteenth-century Underground Railroad from the Confederate states to Canada and current campaigns to end human trafficking.

So, what do we find when we piece this all together? We must begin, not with slavery as a tolerated institution, but rather with the creation of humanity, which affirms that all people have worth and dignity no matter their ethnicity or social standing. Slavery is a tolerated but fallen institution, which is not part of God's creational purposes. God, furthermore, is identified as Yahweh, the one who sets the captives free. As the OT story progresses, we see the liberating action of God at work not just in the exodus but also in the restoration of exiled Israel, indeed, the restoration of a fallen creation.

This last is seen in Isa 40–66 as well as in Neh 9:36 and Joel 2:29; indeed, Joel speaks of slaves as recipients of the great gift of God's spirit. The great theme of God liberating the oppressed, setting the captives free, is central to Jesus' own ministry (Luke 4:16–21). True, slavery is an assumed institution in Israel, and the OT nowhere bans it (nor, for that matter, does the NT), but as we have seen, slavery in the OT is remarkably different from slavery as we know it. Israelite slaves were not, in fact, seen as a permanent possession; rather, they were subject to a period of indentured labor as a way of dealing with debt. No slave, Israelite or foreigner, was to be mistreated; if such did occur, the slave was to go free. Indeed, a slave who fled the condition of slavery was not to be returned to it but rather was to be granted freedom. Far from endorsing those oppressive sets of practices that we know of as slavery, the OT condemns the forcible enslavement of people and their oppressive treatment as disposable goods. Indeed, paradoxically, those very texts that cause us most concern most clearly condemn slavery as we know it.

Although I don't think so, perhaps the eighteenth- and nineteenth-century defenders of slavery were entitled to use the Bible in support of their claims; but if so, they should have looked more carefully and seen that what they were defending bore no resemblance to what the Bible presents. Indeed, had they implemented the OT, slavery would have been revolutionized and, for all intents and purposes, undermined as an oppressive social institution. I don't think that the plantation owners would have been quite so pleased with that (not when they are called themselves to join the Underground Railroad), but at least it would have been a defensible use of the OT. Surely, nineteenth-century slave owners could appeal to the Bible in support of slavery only if they did so consistently and sought to re-create Israel and its particular social shape, including its passion for the dignity and ultimate freedom even of slaves. But, unsurprisingly, that is not what they wanted, for then any runaway slave would be granted freedom, and all slave owners would need to respect their rights and grant them freedom if their bodies or honor were irreversibly damaged.

As I've said, however, I do not believe that we can appeal to the Bible in support of slavery; rather, we are called to enable all people to live free from slavery in all its forms, including the crushing burden of intergenerational debt. One reason for that is that we are not called to re-create Israelite social institutions. Nor can we pick and choose those social institutions that we want and ignore the rest; for, as we have seen, slavery in Israel operated within a broader social and theological vision that established clear limitations and moderations of the institution. Where that vision doesn't operate or where it is flouted (as, for instance, by Zedekiah in Jer 34), slavery is untethered from its social context and sundered from its purposes under God and becomes just another oppressive human social institution. Furthermore, however paradoxical it may appear, it seems to me that both what the OT actually says about slavery and the way the OT moderates it and undermines its oppressive practices fit well with the call to end slavery in all its modern forms.

Even so, the OT tolerates slavery. Given all that the OT does to undermine it as an oppressive institution, why not simply abolish it? I have no simple (or entirely satisfactory) answer to that. I cannot offer a set of reasons and arguments demonstrating that God could have done it this way and no other. In fact, I'm deeply suspicious of all such claims to second-guess God. However, I do have some thoughts relating to slavery, redemptive history, and the notion of divine accommodation that may help. The notion of divine accommodation is not a new one; it goes back at least as far as the reformers of the church in sixteenth-century Europe. John Calvin, in particular, was fond of the idea. He argued that God accommodates the nature of God's communication and action to us and our abilities, and necessarily so. God, the infinite, personal, sovereign lord of the universe is beyond our grasp; in order for us to understand anything of God and God's purposes, God has to "package" that knowledge in a way we can understand. Furthermore, if God is to act in human history and at the same time allow that history to have its own integrity, God's speech and actions must be accommodated to the limitations of particular human cultures.

This has a number of implications, the most important for us being that societies and their institutions are not commanded by God and do not perfectly express God's character and purposes. Although Israelite society was shaped by God and God's redemptive purposes, it was not created from scratch as the perfect embodiment of human community. It was a paradigm of God's creative and redemptive purposes, but it was not a perfect society.

I would add this: if, as I believe is the case, God's intention was that all people be invited into relationship with the one true God, it makes sense for God to work with fallen human societies. Otherwise only those who live in a perfect society that fully reflects God's kingly purposes will be able to live as God's people; but how can they do that when all human culture, though reflecting God's good creational purposes, is also fallen?

This means that God doesn't overturn all flawed social institutions (and what in human affairs isn't flawed?), replacing them with perfect expressions of God and God's purposes for humanity. On the other hand, God doesn't simply let things be and call people to lives of individualistic piety with no reference to society and its goods and evils. God's intention is that God's redeemed people, in the midst of fallen human society, might express God's sovereign purposes in their lives, including their life as a community. Some institutions and social forms reflect (more or less) God's purposes for humanity, such as family and other kinship systems or various forms of government, which enable humans to live together in community—these God endorses (and molds). Some institutions and social practices fundamentally conflict with and undermine God's intentions for human community, such as idolatry and flagrant injustice—these God condemns and replaces with alternative systems. Still other institutions and social practices, though far from perfect, can be tolerated as vehicles partially expressing God's intentions for human community; they are, at the same time, clearly fallen and in need of significant reshaping. In such cases the institution remains but is evacuated of its fallen, oppressive content and filled with new content that more adequately (if only partially) reflects God's creative and redemptive purposes. An existing institution gains new, redemptive content. That pattern is seen not just in the OT but also in the NT (see, e.g., Eph 5:21-6:9; Col 3:18-4:1). God's concern is not to overturn the existing human social order—that radical transformation awaits the return of Jesus—but, rather, to ensure that whatever institutions exist, God's people use them, where possible, as opportunities to reflect God's character and purposes for society. And even slavery can do that, at least in the forms in which it appears in the OT.

We can see that when we think again of the social function of slavery in its OT theological and relational context. First, it acts as an effective means of "social security" for those facing a temporary financial crisis. This, in an agrarian culture such as Israel's, would most likely be the result of crop failure. In such a case an Israelite could choose a period of bonded labor, limited to six years at worst, to pay off his (or her) debt and at the end of that time leave (if Deuteronomy were obeyed) and be set up for a new life. In more serious cases a family might need to sell its land; but even then, after forty-nine years and a year of celebration, the land would return to them, enabling them to start afresh with their assets intact. Of course, for non-Israelites and those Israelites who chose to stay with a master indefinitely, slavery was a permanent condition. However, there were clear protections for such permanent slaves, which also applied to the period of temporary bonded labor for an indebted Israelite. Slavery was a social condition, not a created state, and slaves, for all that they could be counted as property, were nonetheless to be treated as human beings. If a slave died as a result of negligence or brutality, the death was a serious crime and was to be punished accordingly. In less serious cases in which their bodies (and for women, also their honor) were irreparably damaged, slaves were to be compensated with freedom. And should some master forget his place and act like a pharaoh oppressing his slaves, they were free to flee and find shelter and freedom wherever they wished—reenacting a "little exodus," recapitulating God's liberating action for Israel.

Anna: A Story of Slavery Today

Antislavery advocates estimate that there are twenty-seven million slaves in the world today, more than at any time in human history. One of the most prevalent and horrifying instances of contemporary slavery involves children being sold into prostitution. Here is one such story.

Anna (not her real name, of course) was born into a poor rural family in Thailand. She was sold at the age of thirteen to a woman who claimed that Anna would be employed in Bangkok as a domestic laborer. She was taken to Bangkok and "sold on" to the owner of a brothel, where she was forced to have sex with six to ten men a day. She doesn't know whether her parents realized this would be her fate. People in Thailand know that this often happens, but perhaps her parents hoped for better in her case. Perhaps they didn't care—after all, she was "just a girl."

The brothel owners charged more for unprotected sex, especially with a girl who was so obviously a minor, so condoms were rarely used. Life was harsh. The girls were fed enough—if a girl is too skinny, she won't get any customers—but their accommodation was appalling, and they were never allowed to go out (certainly, not alone). Anna never saw any of the money that she earned. All of it went to the brothel owner. She was there for four years before she escaped. It wasn't the first time she tried to run away. On each previous attempt she had been caught and beaten, sometimes until she lost consciousness. They tried not to break any bones, as that would put her out of commission for a while, which would be bad for business.

Anna is now dying of AIDS in a hostel for rescued "sex workers" run by a Christian aid organization. She doesn't know when she contracted HIV, or who gave it to her. She does know that she can't go home. People in rural Thailand have little understanding of and less sympathy for those suffering from AIDS. She doesn't want to bring the shame of being an infected "prostitute" onto her family. Despite the fact that she is dying, she feels safer and more cared for in the hostel than at any time in the last four years.

That's one glimpse of the modern slave trade.

The implications for us are clear. Yes, the OT allows for the institution of slavery (as does the NT), but this does not mean that we are forced to stand mute in the face of the evils of modern slavery, silenced by our own Scriptures. Rather, these texts call us to recognize the rights and value of all people and to oppose the violence and oppression inherent in slavery in all its current forms. When people are forcibly abducted and compelled into slavery—soldiers in the Sudan, servants in Saudi Arabia, sex workers in Saigon—the OT compels us to protest. When generations are deprived of their rights and their land, forced to work to pay off a crippling debt first imposed on their great-grandparents, the OT compels us to protest. When people in sweatshops are required to work incessantly for a pittance, the OT compels us to protest. When immigrants (legal or otherwise) are manipulated into working off their so-called visa and travel costs in intolerable conditions for ludicrously small wages, the OT compels us to protest. They are human beings made in God's image; they are the special objects of concern for our loving, liberating God; they are those whom we are called to love and liberate. The God of the exodus, the God and Father of our Lord Jesus Christ, demands it.

CLEAN AND UNCLEAN

If slavery is a moral problem for us, Israel's system of ritual cleanliness is simply puzzling. What are we supposed to make of this seemingly obsessive system of prohibitions and practices? Surely it is now of interest only to antiquarians and OT scholars, having no relevance for contemporary Christians. After all, hasn't the ritual code, with its particular picture of holiness and difference, been done away with in Christ? Isn't the moral code the only thing that matters? The problem with this view, apart from its cavalier treatment of the OT and its misunderstanding of the NT, is that it fails to do justice to the way that the OT itself deals with these matters. Every OT law code deals with moral, ceremonial, civil, and criminal matters and, to our eye, does so somewhat indiscriminately (see, e.g., Exod 22–23). On what basis, then, can we discard such an important part of our Scripture? Nonetheless, ritual purity is a problem for us, particularly given that the rules do not apply. As Christians, we are simply not required to maintain the distinctions between clean and unclean food, exclusions from community on the basis of bodily emissions or skin diseases; indeed, regarding the latter, Jesus' example suggests we are required *not* to do so. Are we back, then, to dismissing this as irrelevant material? I want to suggest an alternative: rather than being caught in the dilemma of ignoring or obeying the purity system in all its details, we are called to understand its function in OT theology and seek to be shaped by it. But before we get there, we need to look at the code of ritual purity and seek to understand the underlying reasons behind it and its function in Israel's life as the people of God and then consider what role that might play in Christian ethics.

There is a surprising amount of material in the Torah dealing with ritual purity and worship ceremonies, where it is found in every major collection of legal material (see Exod 20:22-26; 22:28-31; 23:14-19; Lev 19; Deut 14; 16; see also Num 18-19). It is surprising, at least, to most Gentile Christians, though not so much to Jews or Jewish Christians. We will focus on Lev 11-15, the largest block of material specifically dealing with distinctions between clean and unclean, found, not surprisingly, in the book that deals with worship and ritual in the most detail. The first thing for us to do is to briefly go through the instructions themselves to see what they cover. When we think of clean and unclean, our thoughts generally turn first to the question of food, partly because that seems to be the focus of Jesus' and Paul's concern in the NT. That too is where Leviticus begins. Leviticus 11 deals with the distinction between clean and unclean animals, specifying which quadrupeds, fish, birds, and insects (oh, great!) may or may not be eaten, as well as how to deal with their corpses.

The first thing to note is that we are not specifically given a rationale for why some animals may be eaten and others not; it is simply a matter of them being clean or unclean (or detestable). We are given, however, some general descriptions and particular instances. For example, only those quadrupeds that both chew cud and have cloven hooves may be eaten (11:1-8); only water creatures with both fins and scales are clean (11:9-12). For quadrupeds, we are given both general characteristics and particular instances of both clean and unclean; for fish, only general characteristics are given. In the case of birds, we are given only particular instances of detestable flying creatures (including bats [11:13-19]); all insects, with a few exceptions, are unclean (11:20-23). The instructions on quadrupeds, the dominant domestic animals for an agrarian culture, are the most detailed and explicit and give us a guide to understanding the reason for the distinctions; it seems concerned with two things: locomotion and diet. We are also told what to do in regard to the corpses of these animals, both clean and unclean, whether encountered accidentally or deliberately. Both people and objects, including containers and their contents, that come into contact with a dead, unclean animal are rendered unclean. People and some objects can be restored; others are to be destroyed (11:24–38). It is interesting to note that even the corpses of clean animals render those who touch them unclean. The concern seems to be with death and the way it intrudes on life. We will return to this matter, along with the question of the diet and movement of clean and unclean animals, when we look at the possible rationale for these distinctions.

Leviticus 12 covers the cleansing of a woman after the birth of a child. Three things are apparent. First, a woman is unclean for a time after childbirth; she then experiences an extended time of cleansing. Second, the period (sorry!) of her uncleanness and her corresponding cleansing is twice as long for a daughter as for a son (14 + 66 rather than 7 + 33). Third, sacrifice needs to be offered before she is fully restored to the (worshipping) community. Let me stress: the uncleanness following childbirth is not a matter of her being ill or dirty or sinful; it is a ritual matter preventing her from being a fully functional member of the worshipping community (12:4). It raises interesting theological questions, which we will address below.

Leviticus 13–14 addresses the issue of "infectious skin diseases" (better: abnormalities of the external surfaces) of persons, clothing, and objects and their cleansing, if possible, or their treatment as being (semi-)permanently unclean if not. The first thing to note about these chapters is that, unlike chs. 11, 12, and 15, which are addressed by Yahweh *through* Moses (and Aaron in 11:1; 15:1) to Israel, these instructions are addressed *to* Moses (and Aaron in 13:1). That suggests that they are given primarily to the priests (of whom Moses and Aaron are the founders and representatives) rather than the people. They are to guide priests in their determination of whether a person or item is afflicted with the kind of "skin" ailment that renders the person or item unclean. The criteria are detailed, including things such as the depth of the lesion, the color of the hair, whether it is an open wound, and whether it spreads or changes. These are, however, "naked eye" criteria that do not relate to whether a disease is contagious or not. Here the NIV is misleading, for it translates the term *tsara'at* as "infectious skin disease." The NRSV's traditional translation, "leprosy" (what we know today as Hansen's disease) is equally unfortunate (even with the NRSV's footnoted caveat). The conditions described with the term *tsara'at* are not necessarily contagious. They are persistent abnormalities of the skin (other than straightforward scars) that are a demonstrable defect, rendering the person unclean.

Such uncleanness is not permanent but rather persistent; if the condition clears up or becomes inactive, the unclean person can be made clean by a series of physical and ceremonial rites of cleansing. For a short-term problem confinement or quarantine is required, and if the condition clears up or is obviously a trivial case, the person is to wash and return to normal life. In more serious cases the person is excluded from the camp and cut off from the community and its life, inhabiting, in a sense, the realm of the dead. Here, a more elaborate cleansing process is required, involving sacrifices for the restoration of the affected person (similar to what we saw in relation to childbirth). It is interesting to note that the culmination of the process is an atoning ritual that bears remarkable similarity to the consecration of priests (Lev 14:12-18, 21-32; cf. 8:22-24). This indicates that the concern is not primarily with physical health but rather with ritual purity and whether the affected person can participate in tabernacle worship. This "reconsecration" enables such as person to be clearly and demonstrably a member of the covenant community, once again entitled to participate in the full life of the (worshipping) community; indeed, it symbolically enables the person's transferal from the realm of death outside the camp to the realm of life within it.

Finally, Lev 15 deals with genital emissions, be they normal or abnormal, for both men and women. The chapter opens and closes with instructions regarding abnormal discharges, first penile then vaginal (vv. 2-15, 25-30), and in the middle section it deals with normal discharges, first ejaculation then menstruation (vv. 16-18, 19-24). Ejaculation, be it during sexual intercourse or not, renders a man and all that touches his semen unclean, including his sexual partner. Menstruation likewise renders a woman and all that she touches unclean. In both cases washing and the passage of time (waiting until evening) render them clean. It is important to note that this does not indicate that sex, reproduction, and menstruation are "dirty," any more than childbirth is. This, once again, is a matter of ritual purity, not a moral or medical matter. Finally, abnormal discharges also render a person unclean, in a manner similar to childbirth or a chronic skin disease. Similarly, dealing with them requires both physical and ritual cleansing, including, once again, sacrifices.

I will make a few preliminary observations before we consider the underlying rationale behind the system of ritual purity. In particular, we need to consider the categories found here and elsewhere in Leviticus and how things can move from one category to another. The key categories are unclean, clean, and holy, and there are temporary and (almost) permanent examples of each. "Clean" is the default state of persons and objects (and animals) and roughly equates with that which is "normal" and has no association with death. "Uncleanness" is the result of some defect—permanent for some animals, temporary for people (if of indefinite duration in the case of, say, a chronic skin abnormality of the relevant kind)—or contact with death. Things that normally are clean can be made unclean: for objects, by way of contact with the unclean or the dead; for people, by way of contact with the unclean or dead or because of sin. Sin is best understood as a violation of Yahweh's (and Israel's) holiness, and it is a serious matter, both morally and ritually. Most temporary abnormalities are relatively easily dealt with, say, by washing; sin, however, requires sacrifice to make the person clean again.

Finally, if clean equates with normal, "holy" means special. It is that which preeminently characterizes Israel's God; other people or things become holy because of their relationship with Yahweh. It is a theological category, not a moral one. With reference to Yahweh, holiness speaks of God's otherness, that is, transcendence. Yahweh is the quintessentially "special" one. Other things are holy because they are set apart from the ordinary and set apart for Yahweh (more on this below). Nothing that is unclean can be holy; some things (including people) that are unclean can be made clean, normally by way of cleansing (with or without sacrifice), and some things (including people) that are clean can be made holy, normally by way of cleansing and sacrifice. Gordon Wenham has produced a helpful diagram of these categories and how things move from one to another.

The Dynamics of Cleanness

← WASHING & SACRIFICE ←

← sanctify   ← cleanse

holy   clean   unclean

profane →   pollute →

→ SIN & INFIRMITY →

Source: Modified and adapted from Gordon Wenham, *The Book of Leviticus* (Grand Rapids: Eerdmans, 1979), 26.

A question remains, however: what is this all about? The theories abound, ranging from the obscure to the puzzling. One of the oldest Christian attempts to wrestle with this issue is found in the *Epistle of Barnabus* (written in the late first or early second century A.D.), which allegorizes the biblical text, finding within it a moral or spiritual meaning. For instance, the prohibition of pork was understood to mean that Christians should avoid those who forget the Lord in prosperity and only turn to God in need (*Barnabus* 10:3). The call to eat animals that have a cloven hoof and chew cud really means that we should seek out the godly, those who meditate on the word of God (chewing "spiritual cud," you might say) and who live in this world but also look for the world to come (having part of each foot in both worlds, or, we might say, having a foot in both camps). Intriguing and entertaining as such readings may be (readings that regrettably pop up with dismaying regularity in evangelical preaching), these allegorical approaches separate the true meaning of the text from its communicative intent and rely upon fanciful flights of insight that can (and often do) lead anywhere. Such meanings are not what the author intended, nor is this how God now speaks to us through these texts.

A more popular view in recent times is that these laws are primarily directed toward public health and hygiene. Animals such as pigs and shellfish are common bearers of disease, and, unless their flesh is prepared carefully, they can make us seriously ill; thus, banning them is a health measure. Similarly, the separation of "lepers" is a form of quarantine, ensuring that their disease doesn't infect the whole community. The instructions on penile and vaginal discharges are aimed at preventing the spread of sexually transmitted diseases, as intercourse with a man or woman with a discharge renders his or her partner unclean. Now, it is true that some of the legislation has public health benefits, but it seems unlikely that this is the underlying rationale, first because it doesn't explain all the inclusions, and second because there are too many puzzling omissions.

The most obvious inclusion that has no public health benefit is the uncleanness that arises from normal sexual intercourse and from menstruation. The latter seems to be associated with blood, but what about the former? Moreover, I fail to see the public health benefits of a woman being unclean while menstruating or of a couple being unclean for the rest of the day after having sexual intercourse. True, such legislation ensures that sex and procreation are treated with due care and seriousness, but public health and hygiene benefits? I think not. So, too, it is not clear that the instructions on skin abnormalities would identify all and only infectious diseases. Many infectious skin diseases are not particularly contagious (for instance, folliculitis or acne), while others are (such as impetigo or tinea [there is no evidence that Hansen's disease—what we call leprosy—was present in ancient Israel]). Furthermore, many skin diseases that would fit the criteria in Lev 13 are not at all contagious, no matter how gruesome they might appear (for instance, acute eczema or lupus would fit the criteria, as would diabetic or ischemic ulcers, none of which are contagious). In addition, if the concern were primarily with public health and hygiene, then it is puzzling that respiratory and gastrointestinal illnesses, many of which are highly contagious, are omitted. True, elsewhere the Israelites are instructed to build pit latrines outside the camp, and that is specifically motivated by Yahweh's holy presence among them (Deut 23:12-14). That practice has clear sanitary benefits; nonetheless, clearly infectious diseases with obvious public health consequences (such as infectious diarrhea or viral illnesses such as the common cold) are not identified as rendering persons unclean in Leviticus or elsewhere in the ritual purity laws. If the aim is public health and hygiene, then the law doesn't do a very good job, which suggests to me that the law had other aims.

A more recent suggestion draws on the sociology of communities and their practices and looks for an underlying "worldview" expressed in the various restrictions. Gordon Wenham has been one of the ablest exponents of this view, and I will draw heavily on his work in what follows. The basic idea is that the legislation for ritual purity presents us with a picture of an ordered world in which things are embraced or avoided depending on how they fit in the symbolic universe. The key issue is how they relate to the normal and "safe" (that which is connected with life) or the abnormal and "dangerous" (that which is connected with death). Clean animals are seen as "normal," as exemplars of what a food animal ought to be, and those that have the least association with death. For land animals, chewing cud and having cloven hoofs are seen to be the way things ought to be, presumably because such animals are definitively (perhaps paradigmatically?) herbivorous and so have no natural connection with death, which is the ultimate disruption in the symbolic universe. Camels have feet that resemble, in some respects, nonherbivores; pigs (like humans) are definitive omnivores; hence, either in what they actually eat or how they get around, unclean animals are connected, directly or by association, with death. Similarly, many shellfish are scavengers, clearly deriving their life from death, as is also the case with the birds of prey and the scavengers listed among the unclean birds; their diet precludes them. Fish with scales and fins, it would seem, like animals with cloven hooves, have the right appearance and "get around" the right way (i.e., they are not reminiscent of shellfish); hence they are clean. Clean animals, then, are seen as normal, or properly ordered; unclean animals are not. So far so good.

What about the other causes of uncleanness? Here we need to consider the question of danger and death. There are things other than food that are associated with the normal and abnormal, and these have important ramifications for both the symbolic and social worlds of Israel. Only the normal can be clean (and hence associated with that which is holy); that which is clearly abnormal, such as persons suffering from skin diseases, cannot be counted clean—that is, as potential worshippers of the holy God. Thus, they are unclean. Indeed, that which is abnormal, that which does not fit into the categories of the symbolic universe, is associated with danger and with death (the ultimate danger or disruption). Those who have enduring abnormalities and thus are seriously unclean are excluded from the place of life, where God is, and are symbolically consigned to the realm of danger and death, outside the camp (the place where the goat bearing Israel's death-dealing sin and uncleanness is sent [Lev 16]). To return to the community, and so to rejoin the company of those who worship the holy God, requires their symbolic transfer from death to life by way of washing and sacrifice.

What, then, of childbirth and penile and vaginal discharges? Abnormal discharges are clear enough: they are not normal and thus are associated with disruption, danger, and death. A person with such a condition cannot be considered normal—that is, clean, a potential member of the worshipping community. Thus, they are unclean. A different reason lies behind the uncleanness of ejaculation and menstruation, related to the (fairly obvious) connection between genitals and procreation. Childbirth is a clear instance of serious uncleanness; a period of forty or eighty days of exclusion, requiring washing and sacrifice, makes that plain. Sex is clearly associated with the begetting and birth of children, and so it attracts some of the danger; hence, ejaculation renders a man unclean. Menstruation is also clearly associated with begetting and birth, as also with blood, and so attracts some danger; hence, it renders a woman unclean.

The issue, however, is why childbirth should be seen in this light. In my view, there are two reasons. First, childbirth is a bloody affair. Blood is associated not only with life (both literally and symbolically, as in connection with the sacrificial system [see Lev 17:10–14]) but also death: bleeding is dangerous and, unless treated, will lead to death. The bloody business of childbirth is doubly dangerous: each time she gives birth a woman who does not have access to good health care has a one-in-ten chance of dying during or shortly after labor. Second, childbirth is what is known as a "liminal event," one involving a key transition—here, into life and the human community. Such transitions are also dangerous, physically in the case of childbirth (as I mentioned earlier), but also symbolically, for where life is, death can soon follow. But why does giving birth to a girl generate double the uncleanness that follows the birth of a boy? Once again we are speculating, for the text doesn't say. I suggest, however, that the popular idea that it's a sign that boys were valued more highly than girls is wrong, mainly because we have other, more convincing explanations. The first of these suggests that the longer period is a response to the fact that a baby girl may experience a small amount of vaginal bleeding within a few days of birth. What happens is that *in utero* a female fetus is exposed to her mother's hormones, resulting in slight growth of hormone-dependent tissue in her uterus. At birth, the hormone levels drop and the tissue sloughs away, resulting in a small amount of vaginal bleeding resembling a period. Some commentators argue that this occasional phenomenon accounts for the longer period of uncleanness: the woman and her daughter have to deal with that extra potential uncleanness.

The second explanation picks up on something that the text itself mentions: circumcision (Lev 12:3). Circumcision ends the period of uncleanness for a boy and his mother and begins the time of purification; that transition point is not available for a girl. Circumcision is that ritual which "marks out" (both literally and theologically) this new boy: it marks his separation to God and entrance into the covenant community. Boys, then, have a clearer transition into God's special people (life) by way of the "sanctifying" rite of circumcision. The longer period of uncleanness and cleansing following the birth of a girl is an alternative way of marking that transition, a way of ensuring that girls and their mothers are recognized as full members of covenant community even though the girl cannot undergo the sanctifying rite of circumcision. Although this explanation seems to me to be the most plausible, we should note that the text does not tell us, and so we are guessing.

Nonetheless, we now have a clearer picture of cleanness and uncleanness. Cleanness is about avoiding danger and death and embracing life and normality. The system of ritual purity, then, is a pointer to the OT's recognition that this is an ordered universe, and that this order has symbolic/theological and moral dimensions. Now, let me stress: this is a speculative reconstruction of the thought world of the Levitical purity system; it is possible that the underlying conceptual rationale is unrecoverable, that we just don't have enough to go on. I think that explaining the thought world of Leviticus in terms of purity and danger makes sense, but that is not the primary purpose of the system of ritual purity.

We are, in fact, given clear statements of the purpose of the purity system in Lev 11:44–45; 12:4; 13:45–46; and 15:31. Leviticus 11:44–45 says that Israel must avoid being made unclean by food because they are holy to the holy God. Leviticus 12:4 warns that a woman who is unclean after childbirth must not have any contact with the holy place or holy things. Leviticus 13:45–46 excludes someone having a serious skin abnormality from the camp and requires that such a person perform symbolic actions associated with death (mourning rituals) and its danger. Leviticus 15:31 ensures that the Israelites are separated from that which would make them unclean, which would desecrate God's dwelling place (after all, nothing unclean can be holy), turning God's life-giving presence into a source of death. I think that there is enough there to support Wenham's reconstruction, but let me put that to one side. There is a clear common thread here: the maintenance of God's holiness and Israel's. These distinctions are one key way that Israel both shows and guards its holiness, a holiness that derives from Yahweh and is directed to him.

Holiness is an important concept, though it is much misunderstood. For various reasons we tend to see it as a moral category: that which is holy is preeminently good; it is God's goodness (holiness) that means God cannot tolerate sin. Now that may be true, but only by association. Holiness is primarily a quality of God; it speaks of God's transcendence, of otherness. Things and people can become holy—that is, set apart for God and his use. Holiness, then, is primarily "set-apartness." Something is holy to Yahweh if it is separated from the common and set apart for Yahweh's use. A colleague of mine, Anthony Petterson, uses the helpful (if mundane) analogy of a toothbrush. My toothbrush is holy to me. It is set apart from common use for my use only. I share a house with my wife and three daughters, but none of them share my toothbrush. If they brushed their teeth with my toothbrush, it would no longer be holy: in fact, after remonstrating with them, I would throw it away and get a new one. It is holy; it is mine. This helps explain what it means for Israel to be holy: they are set apart for Yahweh and come to share (to some extent) Yahweh's holiness.

That latter point is important. When I used the toothbrush analogy at a church camp recently (with due thanks to Anthony), the pastor's wife confessed that she had, in fact, lost her toothbrush when they packed for camp and had been using her husband's. I was, I confess, rendered speechless. Such a thing certainly wouldn't happen in my house, but it didn't seem to overly bother her husband; they share their lives, so why not a toothbrush? I'm not convinced: my toothbrush is still mine, and mine alone. However, her sharing her husband's toothbrush does illustrate something: because of her relationship with her husband, he counted her as holy (set apart) and so allowed her to use his toothbrush (I hope with clear conditions!). Yahweh does likewise with Israel. By entering into relationship with Israel Yahweh makes them holy and allows them to use Yahweh's holy things. The sanctuary and sacred objects are, in fact, one of the ways in which Israel expressed and maintained their special (holy) relationship with Yahweh. However, for them to use these things, which have been set apart from the common and reserved for Yahweh's use, they too must be holy—that is, different, distinct, demonstrably set apart. That is what the legislation for ritual purity is primarily about; it is how Israel shows and maintains their "set-apartness" from the common and for God.

This primary purpose becomes clear when we place these chapters in the context of the whole book of Leviticus. Chapters 1–7 open the book with instructions on what to do in the newly consecrated tabernacle, instructions for the people on the sacrificial system and its purposes. Then, in chs. 8–9, the text moves on to the ordination of the priests, those who are to serve God and the people in the tabernacle, before recounting in ch. 10 the almost immediate failure of the priests to maintain their distinctive function. The consequences for Nadab and Abihu are devastating: offering "strange fire" leads to their fiery destruction. Clearly, the holiness of this place and its proper treatment are crucial. Immediately after the instructions on distinguishing between the clean and the unclean, ending as it does with a concern for the holiness of the tabernacle (15:31), comes the Day of Atonement (Yom Kippur) in ch. 16.

There we see a complicated set of procedures aimed at cleansing the priests and the tabernacle of residual uncleanness caused by Israel's moral and ritual failures, before the newly cleansed high priest atones for the sins of the people. Chapter 17 immediately addresses a key ritual issue, the prohibition of eating blood, that which has been set aside for Yahweh as the means of cleansing the people of their sin and uncleanness. Chapters 18-19 provide a set of sexual, ritual, civil, criminal, and moral instructions, followed in ch. 20 with instructions on the treatment of those who disobey them. Chapters 21-22 deal with maintaining the purity of priests and the offerings that they make, while ch. 23 addresses the major sacred days of the OT calendar. Chapter 24 discusses the lamps and bread of the presence of Yahweh in the tabernacle and then deals with blasphemy as one representative case of a capital offense. Chapter 25 (since the modern Jubilee 2000 campaign, one of the better known sections of an unfamiliar book) covers the ideal of Jubilee, the provision given to ensure the freedom of Israelites and their land in the face of severe economic need. The book ends with a record of the blessings and curses of the covenant in ch. 26 and detailed instructions on offerings both mandatory (firstborn and tithes of produce) and voluntary (various vows) and their redemption in ch. 27. Leviticus thus closes as it opened, dealing with offerings made by Israel in the newly dedicated tabernacle, that crucial piece of "covenant apparatus" in Israel. Clearly, the worship life of Israel and how it is to be conducted and guarded against "contamination" are of vital concern. That is what the rules about ritual purity are designed to do: guard Israel against contamination so that they might be able to express their special covenant relationship with God in worship.

Now, what are we to do with all this? Clearly, ritual purity plays an important role in the OT. It ensures that Israel is and remains a special people, set apart from the nations for God and God's purposes. These social practices are a way of establishing the boundary between Israel and the nations; the distinction between clean and unclean (especially clean and unclean animals) is the way Israel expresses its distinction from the nations. But that, in turn, serves a "missional" aim: Israel's purpose, the reason they are set apart, is to demonstrate to the nations the nature of true community and so further God's saving purposes for all humanity. For Israel, the failure to be distinct means that they have failed to live as the people of God and thus have failed to be God's agents in the world. However, the nature and basis of our being the people of God are radically different in Christ. The people of God are not a national-political entity whose boundaries are determined by adherence to circumcision, Sabbath, and the food laws. We are a scattered people formed by the Spirit around the person of Jesus, the Messiah, and the boundaries of our community are determined by adherence to Jesus in faith and the commitment to living as his disciples (1 Pet 1:1-2). We are, nonetheless, a holy (set apart) people: the people of God (1 Pet 2:9-10), called to be holy even as God is holy (1:13-16). The expression of that holiness is, however, radically different since the advent of Jesus.

We see the revolutionary nature of holiness in the person of Jesus. Not only does he remind his hearers that God's special people are not defined by purely social practices, such as eating kosher foods, but he also calls them to recognize that they are distinct in the overall conduct of their lives. It is what comes out of the heart, not what goes into the stomach, that can render someone no longer fit to be counted among God's holy people (Mark 7:14-23). In making all foods clean, however (Mark 7:19), Jesus demolished the demarcation between Jew and Gentile, demonstrating that faithfulness, not ethnicity, is the primary criterion for being the people of God, as Peter recognized in his vision in Acts 10. Ethnic holiness and the sociological boundary markers of a separated community are no longer our concern.

However, Jesus' relation to holiness and cleanness was not principally negative. In the OT uncleanness was contagious: anyone, no matter how clean, who touched an unclean person or object was thereby rendered unclean. In Jesus, however, holiness is contagious. This is so in a familiar sense: as Jesus shows in John 13, by his cleansing work, especially his then imminent death, we who were unclean have been made clean (John 13:6-10). It is also seen in an unfamiliar sense, directly related to the paradigmatic cases of uncleanness in Leviticus. Jesus healed the lepers (e.g., Luke 5:12-14). Touching those who were ritually unclean should make Jesus unclean; however, things happen in reverse. Rather than the clean (even holy) being made unclean by contact with the unclean, the unclean is made clean by contact with Jesus; he then calls them to perform those actions that will demonstrate to everyone that they have been restored to health and so to the (worshipping) community. His holiness is contagious; it is, if you like, a saving contagion. Exactly the same thing happens in the interesting story of Jesus healing the woman with prolonged bleeding

(Luke 8:42b-48). There is too much in this story for us to look at it in detail, but we should note here that by touching Jesus, who is holy, the unclean woman is made clean. Her faith (no matter how flawed and faltering) saves her, connecting her with Jesus, who rescues her from her physical, social, and theological brokenness, restoring her to relationship with those around her (and, indeed, in the end with God). In Jesus, holiness is no longer something to be guarded to ensure that it is not negated by uncleanness; instead, it has become a dynamic, life-giving force that negates uncleanness and makes people whole.

Our "cleanness," even our holiness, is assured. We are cleansed and made holy by Jesus. We do not need to guard our holiness, and certainly not by a set of social practices designed to mark us off and keep us safe from "outsiders." We *are* "outsiders" who have been brought into the people of God by Jesus' sacrifice for us (Eph 2). Holiness, of course, still matters. God has called us to "be holy as I am holy"; however, the holiness of the new people of God corresponds to the nature of the new people of God. It is not a sociological holiness but rather a personal and relational holiness, expressed in the total conduct of our lives, lives meant to imitate the God who has saved us (1 Pet 1:2, 13-22). The system of ritual purity is alien to us. It operates in a different symbolic—and theological—world to the one we now live in. It does not bind us and shape a set of social practices that are to distinguish us from all others. It does, however, remind us of the reality of God's holiness and the seriousness of our calling to be a holy people of God. It also, somewhat paradoxically, reminds us of our freedom, a freedom to express our identity as the people of God in other ways. But this is a freedom for obedience. Indeed, it is a freedom that finds its nature and goal in the imitation of God, being holy as God is holy. We are, once again, called to model God's character in our life and community. The chief mark of that holiness, as John and 1 Peter remind us, is love (John 13:34-35; 1 Pet 1:22-23). It is love that is the sign of our covenant relationship with God, and love that demonstrates our imitation of the one who loved us and gave himself for us (1 John 4:7-21). Once again, we are reminded of our moral vision, of our call to live as a community of character, even in this strangest of territory in the strange land of the ot.

HOLY WAR

If the instructions on holiness are strange and puzzling to us, the instructions on so-called holy war are brutal and offensive. Here we encounter perhaps the most acute problem in the OT. When we read texts such as Joshua, with its account of the wholesale slaughter of the Canaanite inhabitants of the land, or Deut 7, which clearly commands Israel's actions, not only do words such as "genocide" spring to mind, but also we recoil in horror and distaste and question how this can be sacred Scripture. In attempting to address this, I will focus on Deut 7, which commands the "Canaanite genocide," the program of holy war. Let me say at the outset that I would rather that this was not in the Bible; I would rather not have to deal with it, and I am not fully satisfied with my own explanation of it. It prompts images of violence, religious intolerance, and hatred—the kind of evils that the rock band Rage Against the Machine decries in their song "Killing in the Name"— and quite frankly, I wish that I could ignore or reject it. The problem is, I can't. I'm an evangelical Christian, and I believe that the Bible is the word of God and thus, in the words of Ps 119, is a delight (v. 16) and a light to my path (v. 105). Or as 2 Tim 3:16 says, it is "useful for teaching, for reproof, for correction, and for training in righteousness." But that leaves me with a huge problem, for it seems, at first glance, that this text is more about training in xenophobic violence than in righteousness. It seems, in fact, to give comfort to the Ku Klux Klan and its hateful racism, or Serbian "Christians" and their "ethnic cleansing" program involving the slaughter of their Muslim neighbors, or the Hutus in Rwanda who used religion to justify their interracial violence against their Tutsi neighbors. Does a text such as this really count as "training in *righteousness*"?

It comes as no surprise that in light of these difficulties some Christians, including evangelical scholars, question or even reject such texts as authoritative Scripture because they contain such horribly violent teaching. That is the position adopted by C. S. Cowles. He writes one of the main essays in *Show Them No Mercy*, a book in which four evangelical scholars wrestle with the issue of the Canaanite genocide. In his piece he argues for radical discontinuity between the OT and the NT. He believes that Jesus invalidates Joshua, that we serve a God of love and not of violence. Jesus, he states, renounced the power of violence for the power of love and shows us the true nature of God. In fact, although Israel may have thought that Yahweh commanded the violent destruction of the Canaanites, they were wrong. These texts show us something of the history of the people of God, but Deut 7, for instance, does not actually reflect the will and the command of God. We can safely renounce it and texts like it, and the violence that they endorse.

As much as I might like to, that is not a course I can easily adopt, in part because it conflicts with what I believe about the nature and function of Scripture, but also because it comes at a high hermeneutical and theological price, as we will see. But before we make any judgments on what we are to do with the text, we first must have a careful look at it. We will focus on Deut 7:1-11, both for the sake of space and because that is where the command is put most sharply. This comprises the first two sections of a larger unit dealing with Israel's entrance into the land. Verses 1-5 deal with the promise of God in giving and holding the land; vv. 6-11 speak of the holiness of God's chosen people. Verses 12-16 go on to speak of God's blessing of the land as matching the people's holiness; vv. 17-26 return to the theme of the promise of God in giving and holding the land, providing a larger chiastic (A [vv. 1-5] B [vv. 6-11] B' [vv. 12-16] A' [vv. 17-26]) structure to the chapter.

The section—God's promise in giving and holding the land—opens with a clear but often neglected statement that Yahweh is the one who will bring them into the land and drive out its inhabitants. This accents the priority and primacy of God's grace, surprising as that may seem: God is the one who is at work on behalf of God's people, keeping the promises of the covenant and bringing them into the land. God's grace is, in fact, a sustained emphasis in the text; its primacy here means that we must see all that follows as a response on Israel's part to the grace of God. This is seen in the statement in v. 2 that Israel's defeat of the Canaanites is the result of Yahweh delivering them to Israel; they are to respond to Yahweh's action by destroying the Canaanites totally. It is that language in v. 2 that most disturbs us. But what does the word translated "set apart for destruction," or "destroy totally," or "utterly destroy" (*kherem*, in an emphatic construction) actually mean? The traditional view, reflected in most translations, including both the NIV and the NRSV, is that it means "dedicate to Yahweh to be [or, 'by being'] utterly destroyed." This is the "ban," as it is called. Most scholars believe that this command's rationale lies in the nature of holy war; this is Yahweh's victory, and so the "booty" belongs entirely to God and is set apart for God's exclusive use (that idea of holy again). No one else can use or benefit from that which is so dedicated; thus, to ensure the preservation of Yahweh's holiness and that of the devoted things, they must be destroyed. Such seems to be what drives the treatment of Jericho in Josh 6, and that of Achan in Josh 7, who, having violated *kherem*, is subject to it, along with all that is his. Thus, destruction is seen as inherent in the ban.

Christopher Wright has presented an alternative view in his Deuteronomy commentary. He argues that *kherem* means "utterly repudiate" or "utterly renounce" rather than "utterly destroy." The primary idea is still that Israel is not to gain booty from Yahweh's action; the bountiful land (and its infrastructure [Deut 6:11-12]) should be enough. They are, however, to have nothing to do with the Canaanite inhabitants of the land by way of marriage or treaty arrangements and are to expel them from it, by force if necessary. This view has the advantage of easily accounting for the details at the end of v. 2 and in v. 3. After all, if all the Canaanites are dead, how could Israel enter in to a treaty arrangement with them or intermarry with them?

There is much to say in favor of Wright's suggestion, but it is a suggestion at best and in any case does not erase violence from the text. For instance, it is possible on the traditional view to understand v. 3 as an example of the "realism" of the text that stands in apparent tension with its rhetoric of absolute destruction. That realism is also seen in v. 22, which speaks of Yahweh driving the Canaanites out over a period of time rather than all at once, and is evident also in Joshua (compare Josh 13 with Josh 10-12). The instruction on intermarriage, then, may be an interim measure applicable to the period between Israel's entry into the land and the final eradication of the Canaanites. Furthermore, even on Wright's account, this is still a violent and bloody business, as vv. 16 ("you shall consume them") and 20 ("they will perish") show; it is unlikely that the Canaanite inhabitants will just pack up and leave

quietly! Even if they are not all annihilated, they will still be removed by force, by military defeat and forcible expulsion. It is a
violent and bloody command.

It is important, however, to look at the rationale for the command and to place it in its cultural context. The first thing to note
is that *kherem* was not Israel's invention; it was a standard feature of
certain kinds of war in the ANE. Mesha, king of Moab in the ninth
B.C., directs *kherem* against Israel during his successful revolt against
Israelite control (see the Mesha Stele). Let's be clear: this doesn't
solve the problem, as if we can say, "It's OK, everyone does it" (as
with cheating on your taxes or on your spouse, a "majority rules"
kind of justification doesn't make it right); it does, however, help
us place it in its context. Although it might be an unimaginable
command for us to hear from God, it was not for Israel. The second thing to note, again something not found per se in our text,
is that God has a clear rationale not just for Israel's occupation of
the land but also for the Canaanites' expulsion. Deuteronomy 9
makes that plain (as does Gen 15:16): God expels the Canaanite
inhabitants from the land because of their wickedness. I'll say some
more about that later, for there is a third rationale for the command,
one found in Deut 7 itself, reflected in the call not to intermarry
or make treaties with them.

Verses 2–3 make this third rationale plain. Israel is commanded
not to make treaties with the Canaanites or show them mercy and,
in particular, not to intermarry with the non-Israelite inhabitants
of the land. This last directive probably refers to marriage alliances
rather than (or perhaps in addition to) ordinary intermarriage. Israel's failure to maintain their distinctiveness will lead, v. 4 says, to
idolatry, either in abandoning Yahweh outright or in attempting
to combine worship of the one true God with the gods of Canaan
(syncretism). This is not just a cultural and social phenomenon, although it is that. More is at stake than peer group pressure within
the home, for making covenants or treaties in the ANE involved
each party calling on their gods, and their treaty partner's gods, as
witnesses to the agreement. How could Israel do that when at the
heart of their identity and purpose is serving Yahweh, their covenant God, the one true God, and serving Yahweh alone? That is
the primary concern of the text: Israel must maintain the integrity
of their covenant relationship with Yahweh. Treaties, mercy, and

marriage all threaten that integrity. And that is a deadly danger, as the close of v. 4 shows (as does Solomon's failure [1 Kgs 11]).

So this much is clear: Deuteronomy is not, in the first instance, about the genocidal slaughter of the Canaanites; rather, it is about the danger that future generations of Israelites will turn away from following Yahweh and thus fall under the same sentence as the Canaanites. This is not, then, xenophobia; it is certainly not ethnic cleansing as a political or racial project. It is, in fact, a theological project, directed not just toward Israel but also the gods of Canaan. The alternative to syncretistic interaction with the Canaanites is iconoclasm–the destruction of idols and all that goes with them. The picture in Deut 7:5, as well as in vv. 16 and 20-26, is of the destruction of the Canaanites' gods. The primary concern in what the Israelites are to do to the Canaanites is the removal of idolatry from the land–in part as a defensive measure to ensure that Israel is not corrupted by the idolatrous religion and oppressive political and economic ideology of Canaan, and in part as an act of judgment against Canaanite religion and society. Their action is primarily about the erasing of Canaanite culture (religious and political) rather than the termination of the Canaanites; this is strictly a case of cultural "theocide" or "polydeicide" (the eradication of the Canaanite gods).

We have, then, a clear rationale for the ban. It is driven by Yahweh's desire to eradicate the Canaanites' religion and the culture associated with it, and it is presented as an act of judgment against them and their detestable practices. Now, lest this be seen as an example of violent, narrow-minded religious bigotry, we need to realize that the detestable practices of the Canaanites include socioeconomic abuses as well as religious ones. Sociological analysis of Canaanite culture shows that the stratified pantheon of Canaan served both to justify and to guarantee the stratification of Canaanite culture. Theirs was a social and economic system in which power and prestige were enshrined, almost deified, in which "justice" meant maintaining the current social order and the vested interests of the elite while the poor and marginalized were kept in their "proper place." This connection between economics and politics is clearly reflected in 1 Kgs 21, where, under Ahab and his Sidonian Baalist wife, royal power comes to trump covenant rights, at fatal cost to Naboth. Religion and politics always mix, and though Jezebel's Baalism was of the Sidonian variety, the Canaanites shared the same Baalist ideology that was so viciously at work in 1 Kgs 21. Canaanite Baalist culture was religiously detestable and morally bankrupt. Yahweh's action here is specifically an act of judgment against that religious and social culture and the ideologies that supported it. It also aims to defend Israel against being corrupted by them, seen in their renouncing (and/or destroying–that word *kherem* again) the Canaanites and the "spoils of war," ensuring that they do not profit from the oppressive and violent economic system of the Canaanite city-states. Destroying everything but the infrastructure of the land ensures that they have no part in that idolatrous and unjust culture and are not tainted by it and its proceeds. That is the negative rationale.

There is, however, also a positive motivation given for the command. Deuteronomy 7 opens with reference to the grace of Yahweh, who gives the Israelites victory and enables them to possess the land promised them. This emphasis on Yahweh's gracious initiative is powerfully reinforced by the key positive motivation for Israel to obey, which is given in v. 6: Israel is Yahweh's chosen people and own special possession. This, not the call to expel or eradicate the Canaanites and their gods, is the theological heart of the text, with clear theological implications. First, Israel is holy to Yahweh their God, once again reminding them of their unique relationship with Yahweh: that they are special, set apart from the nations and their idolatry and oppressive ideologies for God and God's purposes. Yahweh chose them, furthermore, to be his own special possession and "personal portion" (*segullah*) out of all the nations of the earth (see also Exod 19:5).

But why did Yahweh choose them? Deuteronomy 7:7–8 make this plain, as does 9:4. It was not because they were more powerful or numerous than other nations and thus a stronger instrument for Yahweh's purposes; it was not because they were more righteous or noble than other nations and thus more deserving recipients of favor. This is a matter of grace, not merit. True, God does keep God's promises, as v. 8 also says. But those promises too are a matter of God's free, sovereign, electing love. What motivates that love, what lies behind Yahweh's grace? Nothing. Yahweh has broader purposes that that motivate the decision to initiate a saving plan (gracious saving purposes, we might note, also motivated by grace alone), but nothing compels Yahweh to select Israel (or Abraham before them) other than Yahweh's free, sovereign, loving choice. Theirs is a uniquely privileged position. They have been chosen by God, set apart and treasured. All that they are to do follows on from that choosing, arises out of that choosing, and expresses gratitude for that choosing by God. Theirs is a life bounded by grace and obedience; their life is a creation of God's grace, but they are called to obedience, which is seen as a necessary response to grace.

That pattern is clearly seen in Deut 7:9-11, which both calls Israel to respond to God and presents them with clear warnings. Verse 9 reminds them of God's identity: Yahweh is God, and Yahweh is faithful, exhibiting that faithfulness (*khesed*, "covenant love," "faithful love," once again) to those who show covenant commitment. That commitment is described in the typical style of Deuteronomy: it is a matter of love and keeping God's commands (see Deut 6:4-9). But God's faithfulness has a dark side, for God's faithfulness means being true to God's word, and that word both promises and warns. Verse 10 reminds us that God, extravagant as God's loving faithfulness is, is also faithful in judgment. Israel is, so to speak, shown both the carrot (God's grace and promises) and the stick (the reality of God's judgment); both are meant to motivate their obedience. The carrot should be enough, but if not, then there's always the stick. It is a stark reminder that with the privilege of election comes the responsibility of holiness expressed in obedience. Election is no grounds for complacency, for this God is the one who judges the nations for their sin, and who will do the same to Israel if they fail to express obedient holiness. This command, then, aims at enabling Israel to express and maintain their holiness, as well as receive God's promises. This is a dark text, but it also clearly demonstrates God's electing love. It also shows the "even-handedness" of Yahweh: this God shows no favorites, and if the Israelites identify themselves with the Canaanites in their religious and social life, they will share that group's terrible fate (Deut 7:10; see also 8:19-20; 11:16-17; 28:15-68; Lev 18:24-30; 26:14-39; Josh 7). Whatever else this text may be, it is not an expression of arrogant xenophobia.

We've looked at the text, but what are Christians supposed to do with the commands of Deut 7? To begin with, it should be clear that the Ku Klux Klan and "racial purity" or "ethnic cleansing" programs get no comfort from this text, for it's not about racial purity but rather absolute holiness and radical commitment to Yahweh and Yahweh's purposes. Indeed, the very things that justify the violence of Deut 7 invalidate it for us. In Deuteronomy this is about God giving Israel the land, and Israel living faithfully as God's people in God's land. This nation, at this point in its history, is given this clear instruction. That instruction, we should note, is not the universal pattern for Israel's wars (see Deut 20). Indeed, with the exception of 1 Sam 15, it is not a command that continues past the initial phase of Israel taking (in part) the land. It belongs to that period of Israel's history when God gives them the land and punishes its current inhabitants. Indeed, this is not primarily a matter of Israel fighting and Yahweh giving victory; it is about Yahweh fighting for Israel and Israel being Yahweh's instrument. This is not holy war, human warfare given divine sanction; it is Yahweh war, God acting as a warrior, bringing victory and achieving God's purposes in the world, albeit through (and manifestly for) God's people. And that simply does not apply to us, for the church, the (re)new(ed) people of God, is not a national-political entity. We have no particular territory that is ours alone; we are not called to that kind of holiness; we are not called upon to be God's instruments in that kind of battle. This text cannot be read as justification of Christians using violence to take land away from others in the service of God's purposes (no matter how our forebears may have used it).

Furthermore, this is about God bringing judgment on a sinful nation. Israel is called by God to be God's instrument of judgment on an idolatrous, unjust, sinful nation. That, once again, is a specific command, applying to this particular occasion and not others. And that command never applies to us. As far as I can tell, the only way we act as God's instrument of judgment against the world is by way of our mission of living and proclaiming the gospel. That gospel aims at bringing freedom and forgiveness; but where it is rejected, it brings God's condemnation (John 3:16-21). So, although the Israelites may be agents of God's judgment on the Canaanites, Christians cannot legitimately see themselves in the same light. Furthermore, while we can rightly see these historical events as God's judgment in history (as, we must remember, we must also see the fall of Jerusalem and the judgment of exile as God's judgment at work in history), we are not in a position to make those claims about events in our day. First, unlike Israel here (or, for that matter, in the exile), we are not told by God that any particular event in our history is a specific act of judgment. God may act in judgment in history—Mark 13 and 1 Cor 11:27-32 suggest that is the case—but we cannot say that any particular event is God acting in judgment. Indeed, Jesus tells us otherwise. Second, we are in no position to pass judgment on others, for we ourselves are sinful (Matt 7:1-5); we are also in no position to self-righteously claim that a particular event is God's judgment on particularly sinful people. The horrors of history should, rather, prompt us to acknowledge our own sinfulness and need for God's grace (Luke 13:1-5). Third, the NT is clear that God has reserved judgment, through Jesus, for another occasion: the end of human history as we know it (more on this shortly). We are neither judges nor God's agents of judgment in history.

The question remains: why did God choose to judge the Canaanites on this occasion, and with such ferocity? Again, we return to Deut 9 (which, we must recall, gives Israel no grounds for the kind of complacent self-righteousness that so often characterizes Christian public statements on "sinful society"). There we are reminded that God is judging the Canaanites on the basis of their detestable practices. On that the evidence is fairly clear. Their culture and society, so deeply imbued with Baalist ideology, was detestable both in religious terms, such as sacred prostitution and child sacrifice, and in political and social terms, such as what we see in 1 Kgs 21. Nonetheless, I wouldn't claim (nor does the text) that Canaanite culture was the most detestable of the time and region; there are lots of contenders for that prize (including Sidon, on the coast to the north of Canaan). So, why were the Canaanites judged and others spared? To put it bluntly, God chose in their case to renounce forbearance. Here we need to reckon with a very unpopular notion: all human beings stand under the just condemnation of God. The fall and the flood demonstrate that (Gen 3; 6:5-7; see also Rom 1:18-32). The puzzle has more to do with the forbearance of God than his severity. The puzzle is not that the nations of Canaan were judged for their sinfulness; rather, it is that all other nations were not (and are not). Furthermore, God's giving up forbearance in this case is not arbitrary but is, as we have seen, connected with God's larger purposes.

Finally, Israel is called, as a nation-state, to live as the people of God and demonstrate their holiness by a distinctive, separate, national life that demands the eradication of all foreign, ungodly elements from their territory and national life. And that simply doesn't apply to us. We have no particular territory; there is no such thing as a Christian state. There may be more-or-less Christianized countries (depending on your view of how church and state interact; I tend toward the traditional Baptist and Anabaptist renunciation of political power as a tool of Christian endeavor, but be that as it may). There is no such thing as a Christian country, as if a particular national body were ever able to say that it represents God and God's purposes in the world (and only God and God's purposes and not its own). Even if there were, it would not be its role to exclude non-Christians from its territory in the interests of national purity. We are called to holiness, but as we have seen, that is not to be expressed in a body of social practices that act as a barrier between us and an unbelieving world. We are called to be distinct, reflecting God's character and purposes in our lives and communities. There is a clear imperative to Christian cultural nonconformity; that is the character of our holiness as the people of God, a matter central to our existence. However, we are called to a hospitable holiness that invites others, by way of the particular practices of the church (practices such as welcoming strangers, working for justice, proclaiming the good news of God's welcome in Christ), to join us in faith. Let me make it plain: the violent, racial, or cultural destruction masquerading as Christian activity that we have seen in the Ku Klux Klan, or Bosnia, or Rwanda (or wherever) must be understood by Christians as an abhorrent aberration.

Let me also be clear about this: I am not entirely happy with my explanation of these troubling texts, nor would I claim that my reading of the texts deals with all the questions that we have about them. This is not because my reading offers a theological rather than an ethical justification of the "Canaanite genocide," however; a theological justification is the only one there is, in my view. The biggest residual problem is the question of why women and children are subject to the violence of destruction or repudiation. The immunity of noncombatants is deeply ingrained in my moral instincts. We are rightly outraged when we hear of the indiscriminate slaughter of civilians by suicide bombers (or, for that matter, misdirected Israeli military strikes or badly or wrongly targeted American "smart bombs"—bombs that turn out to be as ignorant and misguided as the hands that direct them). I am similarly repelled by the thought of ancient Israel slaughtering (or violently expelling) the original Canaanite inhabitants of their new land.

Although it is foreign to our understanding of how warfare ought to be conducted, however, the practice of *kherem* elsewhere in the ANE suggests that it was not foreign to Israel. Still, it is also important to remember that none of these texts serve as an ethical justification of human warfare and its conduct. Not Israel's, and certainly not ours. They are presented as a theological account of Yahweh's action as a warrior in judgment against the Canaanites and in grace on behalf of the Israelites. In relation to that, we need to remember that the aim of the ban was the eradication of Canaanite (religious) culture. Women (and even older children, I guess) are just as much bearers of that culture as are men (the dark side of "equal opportunity," you might say). Nonetheless, it does seem harsh and horrible, especially given that the texts do not seem to exclude very young children, those who would not yet have been shaped by their native culture. Perhaps Christians can claim that this was judgment in history and may not reflect the final state of those children. That's cold comfort, though, and I do not find it an entirely satisfactory explanation.

Some have suggested that a possible way out is to see this as a (later) theological ideal that was not actually enacted in history. Given the terrible consequences of Israel's failure to live as the people of God, partly due to their "buying into" Canaanite religion and culture, this is what they *should* have done: they should have utterly repudiated (or destroyed) them, although that is not what they actually did. Now, it is true (as we have seen) that the actual taking of the land was not as abrupt and violent as a casual reading of the text may suppose, especially if Wright is correct in understanding *kherem* as "utterly repudiate" rather than "destroy." This view goes further, saying that these texts do not reflect Israel's actual history but rather are a rewriting of their theological history in light of a particular ideal of Israel's call. I have some sympathy with that view, but apart from the difficulties that it raises for our understanding of Scripture and OT history, it is, in the end, unsatisfactory theologically. Indeed, it doesn't help solve the problem at all, for according to this view although the story might not be intended as a historical account, it is presented as a theological ideal. In this case, though the problems may not confront us in relation to Israel's actual history in the land, the theological ideal is still subject to them. Israel may not have slaughtered them all—men, women, children—but that is what they *ought* to have done. The problem persists.

There is, however, in the biblical text itself a clear moderating element, one that directly relates to the primary purpose of this Yahweh war. The "campaign" in Joshua, for example, opens with the destruction of Jericho. A handful of inhabitants, however, are saved from annihilation (Josh 2:1-21; 6:17, 22-25). Rahab and her family, Canaanite inhabitants of the land, are spared on the grounds of her faith and faithful action on Israel's behalf. It is worth noting Josh 2:9-11, where Rahab says that the knowledge of Yahweh and his actions for Israel (past and future) are known to the inhabitants of the land. She is not the only one who is aware of what God is doing. Rahab shows the reaction that this knowledge should evoke: fear and faith. And note, in accepting Yahweh as her God she is incorporated into Israel as a full member of the covenant community, so much so that one of her distant descendants comes to sit on Israel's throne (Matt 1:5). The response of the Canaanites is generally otherwise (with the exception of the Gibeonites in Josh 9). Their vested interests—especially those of the ruling elite, the kings of the Canaanites—overwhelm the good news of this saving and liberating God, good news that confronts them and their established systems of power and domination. Their response, as is so often the case when injustice is confronted with the call to freedom, is one of violent rejection. It is not surprising, perhaps, that Rahab responds as she does, as she is (most likely) one of the marginalized rather than the powerful in this Canaanite city-state. It is likely that she stands not as an isolated example but rather as an illustration of those Canaanites who embraced Yahweh's new program; certainly, she is a model of how they could (and should) have responded to the news of Yahweh's liberating presence. Clearly, there is an alternative to the violence of judgment (be that destruction or expulsion): the alternative of faith and the salvation that it brings.

So, we have seen that there are some features of the text that soften the harshness of the account, and, furthermore, that the text does not warrant the Christian use of violence. Nonetheless, I am not entirely satisfied with this explanation of the violence of Israel's entry into Canaan; indeed, there are, as I've said, a number of residual problems. Nonetheless, it has fewer problems than the alternatives, and so, as much as I am tempted by it, I can't embrace the "Jesus, not Joshua" line of interpretation such as is provided by Cowles. It doesn't fit an evangelical commitment to Scripture and its authority, for it forces us to pick and choose which bits of the Bible count as Scripture. But, more to the point, we can't simply reject this text and the *kherem*, for the ultimate purpose of this violence is central to our existence. In Deuteronomy this is grounded in election and holiness. It arises out of God's call to Israel to be God's own, special people. They are called to live as a nation, adhering only to Yahweh and demonstrating in their life together Yahweh's character and purposes. And that, in turn, arises out of God's commitment to the world, for as Gen 12 and Exod 19:5-6 show, Israel is called to be God's own people for the benefit of the world. Maintaining their purity as the people of God, worshipping Yahweh alone, and living according to Yahweh's liberating law are essential to Israel's existence as the people of God and their purpose in God's world. And is that not absolutely true of us? There's a lot riding on this, on the distinctiveness of the people of God: the spread of the knowledge of this gracious, saving God depends on it. For without that distinctiveness, there is no mission.

Further, this violence reflects God's passionate hatred of sin. God takes sin this seriously. And so should we. Sin, after all, both offends God and destroys human community and God's world. And that is something that God will not tolerate, as Deut 7 makes plain. That same violent response to sin is found also in the NT. It takes Jesus to the cross; that, if anything, surely shows us how seriously God takes sin. It is also important to remember that our God doesn't play favorites. The same uncompromising (violent) response to sin is directed against Israel as well as the nations (Deut 7:4b, 10, 25-26), as is seen, tragically, in their future history. Israel is called to share Yahweh's abhorrence of sin. And is that not absolutely true of us? However, that violence is directed not at those outside who are sinners but rather at that within us that offends God's holy purposes: it is our own sinful hand or eye that we are called to destroy, not others (Matt 5:29-30). Deuteronomy reminds us of God's abhorrence of sin, an abhorrence that we should share. But most of all, this text reminds us of God's grace. It reminds us that this God is the one who works on behalf of God's people, calling them, blessing them, using them in God's own purposes. It reminds us that we are God's people, as was Israel before us, because God loved us and chose us to be God's own special possession. And that is a high and holy calling indeed.

In closing, let me make one thing plain (if it is not already): this understanding of the "Canaanite genocide" is theological in nature, not ethical. That is, this is a justification not of human acts of violence but rather of God's action in the giving and keeping of the land for Israel. The nation of Israel then responds to God's actions. There are indeed serious ethical issues relating to Christians and violence—whether Christians can use violence, and if so, when and how that relates to the OT—but dealing with that must await another occasion. We have done enough for now, and in the end, Yahweh's war in the OT is a matter of theology, not ethics. Furthermore, we see that the violence of judgment is the eschatological prerogative of God. God, in the person of Jesus, acts directly in judgment on the last day and no longer calls God's people to be agents of divine judgment in history. God, so to speak, takes the violence of judgment on sin out of our hands and into God's own. What is more, the aim of that judgment is the final eradication of all that destroys and distorts God's world and human existence so that God's final purposes of *shalom* might be fully realized. So this much is clear: no nation can claim to be a "Christian nation"; no one can claim that theirs is a "holy war" commanded by God; no one can claim that their violence against other races or religions is committed in the service of Yahweh our God. This text doesn't allow it, and the very nature and purpose of our existence as the holy people of God forbid it.

Chapter 4

Exploring the Territory

I GREW UP IN THE western suburbs of Sydney, but I was born and spent the first eighteen months of my life in Scotland. My mother was Scottish, my father Australian, and when he decided to train to be a specialist surgeon he chose the Royal College of Surgeons in Edinburgh, then one of the world's best places to do surgical training. I was born in the small town of Kilmarnock, where Dad was surgical registrar, but, being eighteen months old when we left, I had no memories of the place. Mom and Dad took us back there for a holiday when we were in primary school. We had a great time touring through England and Scotland, seeing the sights, sampling the food (fighting in the back seat of the car, but I'll draw a veil over that). Having heard the stories many, many times, my wife, Alison, and my daughters, Elanor, Laura, and Alexandra, had long wanted to go to the United Kingdom. So, since I was doing some research and presenting a paper at a conference in England in 2006, we decided that it would be a good opportunity for the girls to see Scotland, the land of my birth, and something of England on the way. We didn't have long–neither the girls' schooling nor our finances would permit a long trip–but we did have a month or so. But what should we see while we were there?

We could have decided to go on a package tour, seeing the highlights of the United Kingdom, spending each night in one of a dozen new places. That didn't appeal to us. The thought of being stuck on a bus with a bunch of strangers for days on end wasn't attractive; more importantly, it wasn't how we wanted to get a feel for the country. We wanted to spend some time in a few places, seeing what was there, getting to know at least a little bit about them, rather than hurriedly skipping from one place to another, shallowly skimming the surface of them all. So we visited London (Laura demanded it), Bath (Jane Austen's hold on Alison, Elanor, and Alexandra demanded it), Portsmouth (proximity to Alison's sister demanded it), Cambridge (my research demanded it), the Peak district (Alison's love of beautiful countryside demanded it), and Glasgow and the Scottish Highlands (my history demanded it). It was still only a few days, a week at most, in each place, but we did have time to explore, see some key landmarks, and think about their significance. I must confess that Kilmarnock was a bit of a disappointment for us. Glasgow and the Highlands, on the other hand, were all that we could have hoped for. I would have loved more time there, but we had only enough to whet my appetite for further exploration. I'm glad that we decided on that kind of trip.

This is the kind of exploration that we will undertake in this chapter (and in the book as a whole, I suppose). Here we will spend a bit of time on only two texts, Gen 1–3 and Deut 5:6–21. Any more would mean lightly skimming the surface of several texts, finding none of it particularly satisfying. Of course, I can't cover all that Gen 1–3 and Deut 5:6–21 have to say; indeed, there will be much that I will simply have to ignore. The material is too rich and theologically significant to do otherwise. As we look at these two texts, then, we will focus on their importance for understanding the OT and Christian ethics, and also their richness. For instance, my focus as we come to the Ten Commandments will be on how they shape Christian moral vision rather than on the many ways they have shaped theories of personal and social ethics both in Jewish and Christian tradition and in Western culture. With Gen 1–3, the first and foundational section of the Bible, it would be possible to undertake a brief overview of what it says, touching on some of its ethical significance as we go. But that would be too shallow an approach to this deep and complex text. Instead, we will look at how it addresses two key issues facing evangelical Christians: the environment and gender relationships. I trust that with both texts we will do enough to get a feel for what they say and their significance for Christian ethics, and also, perhaps, whet your appetite for further exploration.

THE CREATION STORY: GENESIS 1-3

GENESIS 1-3 AND THE ENVIRONMENT

Surely, we don't need to be reminded of the enormous pressure that our environment is under, whether or not it is rightly called a crisis, and whether or not climate change is a result, irreversible or not, of human industrial enterprise. (As an aside, I think that the evidence is now compelling, and has been for over a decade, that climate change is real and is a consequence of our activities; what is not so clear is whether it is reversible, and if so, what it would take to reverse it and what the long-term consequences will be.) We know of the loss of forests, and thus habitat, and the way it threatens biodiversity and the sustainability of ecosystems. We know the history of multiple species extinctions due to human activity and its acceleration in the last century. We know of the deterioration of air and water quality in industrialized countries and its impact on river and coastal systems and human health. In Australia we are all too familiar with soil degradation, especially as a result of salination from misuse of our scarce water supplies, and its devastating impact on agriculture and rural communities, as well as the effect that unrestrained coastal development has had on key habitats and breeding grounds for fish and water birds. I could go on indefinitely cataloging the damage that we have caused and the issues that we face, but I won't. Other books do that. You are, I expect, familiar enough with the issues, and my purposes are otherwise. My interest is in what Genesis has to say on the matter.

Before we move on to that, however, I need to acknowledge that many environmentalists see the Bible (especially Gen 1:1–2:3) and the "Judeo-Christian tradition" that is shaped by it as largely responsible for the ecological crisis that we now face. One of the earliest and most influential of expressions of this is found in a piece by Lynn White Jr., who identifies himself as a "churchman" (i.e., one who identifies with the Christian tradition in some form) and makes a number of important claims that have been echoed in many subsequent discussions of the issues. Genesis 1 and the Bible as a whole are seen as safe and comfortable texts that justify our exploitation of the world for our own selfish benefit with no regard either for the rights of others or for the benefit of the world, now or in the future.

Historical Roots of Our Ecologic Crisis

[In the Christian view,] God planned all [creation] explicitly for man's benefit and rule: no item in the physical creation had any purpose save to serve man's purposes. . . . Christianity . . . not only established a dualism of man and nature but also insisted that it is God's will that man exploit nature for his proper ends. . . . [A]s we now recognize, somewhat over a century ago science and technology–hitherto quite separate activities–joined to give mankind powers which, to judge by many of the ecologic effects, are out of control. If so, Christianity bears a huge burden of guilt. . . . Our science and technology have grown out of Christian attitudes toward man's relation to nature which are almost universally held not only by Christians and neo-Christians but also by those who fondly regard themselves as post-Christian . . . We are superior to nature, contemptuous of it, willing to use it for our slightest whim. . . . Since the roots of our trouble are so largely religious, the remedy must also be essentially religious, whether we call it that or not. We must rethink and refeel our nature and destiny. . . .[1]

As we will see, although White may be right in his assessment of the dominant Western Christian attitude toward nature (which is open to question) the view that he presents as the dominant Christian one–of unrestrained lordship over inferior creatures–is radically inconsistent with the Genesis account. Indeed, I suggest that an alternative religious vision, the remedy for our ecological crisis, is found in Gen 1:1–2:3 (and Gen 2:4–3:24) and what it tells us about humanity and our role in the world. So, let's turn to the text.

We need to begin by examining the genre and literary structure of the text because that is an important step in the interpretive process and because they are significant in themselves for understanding the ethical implications of Gen 1:1–2:3. The first thing that we notice as we come to this creation account is that its form

---

[1] Lynn White Jr., "The Historical Roots of Our Ecologic Crisis," in *Ecology and Religion in History* (ed. David and Eileen Spring; New York: Harper & Row, 1974), 15-31.

differs from other OT texts; indeed, it is virtually unique in the Bible, with only John 1:1–18 (deliberately) paralleling it. The language is not poetry per se (with the exception of Gen 1:27), but neither is it straightforward prose. It is a carefully organized, tightly structured theological text. The most obvious organizational feature of Gen 1:1–2:3 is the structure of a series of six days plus one, in which there is a clear progression and a correspondence between the first three days and the second three days. The seventh day sits outside the normal pattern of the days: it is, for instance, the only day that doesn't end with "and there was evening and morning, the *x* day." That has significance in itself, but here it is important to note the way that this places the seventh day in a different category from the others because of its clearly different literary form and its content.

The Structure of Genesis 1:1–2:3

Summary statement (1:1)
Initial conditions: chaos (1:2)

Day 1 **Day 4**
light (1:3-5) luminaries (1:14-19)

Day 2 **Day 5**
firmament, separation of flying and swimming
waters (1:6-8) creatures (1:20-23)

Day 3 **Day 6**
dry land and plants (1:9-13) land animals, humans;
plants as food (1:24-31)

Day 7
Final goal: Sabbath rest (2:1-4a)

Genesis 1:1–2:3 uses many other devices, especially key words and phrases, to order the text. For instance, there are eight acts of creation grouped into six creation days (two acts on the third and the sixth days, those "days" that matter most to land-dwelling humans). As an exercise in "close-reading" of the text, read through Gen 1:1–2:3 and note the number and pattern of announcements ("[and] God said"), commands ("let there be," and the like), reports ("and it was so," and the like), and evaluations ("[and] God saw that it was [very] good"). Clearly, it is a carefully organized text. This, I suggest, has broader implications for how we read Gen 1:1–2:3, especially as we look at its implications for our theology and an ethics of the nonhuman environment.

Another thing to notice is that it is a measured, sober text in which there is no conflict, crisis, or problem for God to combat, no enemy for God to defeat, no hint that God's purposes might be even temporarily thwarted. The closest we get to that is the chaos of Gen 1:2 ("formless and empty," or "utter waste"; the deep; the waters), and even that is under God's sovereign superintendence (the spirit of God was hovering, or brooding over it). In Gen 1:1–2:3 God says, God does, it happens, that's it. Now, given the long-standing and well-established church doctrine of *creatio ex nihilo* ("creation out of nothing"), this seems perfectly plain and obvious and of little interest to us. In the ANE, however, it is quite remarkable.

There are many creation accounts in ANE religious texts and most of them share key characteristics. They are clearly polytheistic, envisioning a divine realm inhabited by numerous gods, both greater and lesser. These gods, like their human counterparts, are an unruly lot and are at war among themselves, particularly the younger gods against their older forebears. Moreover, ANE accounts often tell of gods who control the forces of chaos, who must be vanquished in order for an ordered cosmos to be created. Creation is the result of a conflict between rival deities, with the outcome in question until the climax. Indeed, in one ANE account the earth and the sky are made out of the corpse of a defeated goddess, and humans fashioned from dirt and the blood of other slaughtered (lesser) gods. In this account not only is the creation act an uncertain struggle against chaos, but the cosmos is dependent on the nature of defeated chaos gods for its form and substance. This is an uncertain order, depending on the whim of the gods and on which of them is ascendant; there is the ever-present threat that the cosmos will collapse into chaos once again.

The contrast with the orderly, controlled, unconstrained, sovereign creative work of God in Gen 1:1–2:3 is striking; here, creation is an orderly process, the product of an orderly God, reflecting God's own orderly nature. This has enormous significance for our understanding of the world as an orderly, dependable system, and it has had an incalculable effect on the development of science as we now know it. This is seen not only in a desire to control the world but also to understand it. As White notes, early modern science, shaped as it was by the Christian commitments of many of its exponents, saw its task as "thinking God's thoughts after him" or, in Francis Bacon's estimation, understanding the book of nature as well as the book of Scripture. This view has, at times, expressed itself in a desire for domination of nature and its total subjection to human interests. But that is an aberration and does not arise from the Christian roots of modern science, as is witnessed by the fact that some of the worst environmental disasters of the twentieth century were perpetrated in the (hardly Christian!) former USSR. Lest these be seen as a relic of Marxism's Judeo-Christian origins, it is also seen in the fact that Japan is a notoriously poor environmental citizen, especially in its vigorous (and largely illegal) practice of (so-called scientific) whaling in the face of international outrage.

Our concern, however, is with how Gen 1:1–2:3 shapes our moral vision. As we have seen, the OT functions primarily to shape our moral vision rather than to set out a list of rules. It shapes our imagination, forms our character, enlightens our view of the world, transforms our values, portrays how our communities should be, projects our future; it doesn't just "tell us what to do." Genesis 1:1–2:3 is a key to that moral vision, for it tells us who God is, the one who is the ultimate determiner of reality, our existence, and the shape of our lives; it tells us what kind of world this is, the world that is the stage for our lives and moral enterprises and to which we must respond if we are to be faithful to the creator God who has called us; and it tells us, as we'll see shortly, who we are and what our place in the world is.

There is much that I could say about this, but for now I will introduce the idea of the integrity of creation. The orderliness of this God and the world that God has sovereignly made demonstrates that the world as a dependable system that has value in the eyes of God. We need to respect it as God's creation, one in which God delights, one that God blesses. This brings us to two important features of the text: God's affirmation and blessing of creation. Six times in Gen 1:1–2:3 God says that what God has made is good, and finally that all of it is very good (vv. 4, 10, 12, 18, 21, 25, 31).

Three times God blesses creation: God blesses birds and sea creatures, humanity, and the seventh day (1:22, 28; 2:3). It is significant that God see things as "good" long before humans come onto the scene, and that God's blessing is not restricted to humanity. God affirms light, dry ground, vegetation, the heavenly bodies, birds and sea creatures (and blesses them), land animals, and, lastly, all that God had made. The word "good" in Hebrew (*tob*) has as broad a range of meaning, as does our English word "good." We speak of a "good painting" or a "good song," meaning one that is beautiful and well crafted; we speak of a "good bicycle" or a "good dog," meaning one that does what it is supposed to do; we speak of a "good person" or a "good deed," meaning one that deserves our moral approval. The word *tob* can also be used for all of these things, which raises the question of what it means here in Gen 1:1–2:3. It seems to me that the things that God pronounces to be "good," especially creation as a whole, are more like a good painting or bicycle than a good deed; that is, God's approval of creation means not that it is morally perfect but rather that it is well crafted, beautiful, and fully functional. God's affirmation, then, speaks of the goodness, integrity, and value of creation per se, and it does so regardless of human use. Furthermore, creation is intended to flourish for God's purposes and its own, as is seen in God's blessing. Blessing ensures creation's ability to reproduce, flourish, and achieve its purposes, and this extends beyond human beings to the rest of the cosmos.

The goodness and order of creation are important for Christian ethics, most obviously in relation to the environment, but also in other areas, such as work, culture, and sexuality. For now it is important to see that God's interests are not limited to humanity: we are not, as we so often assume or assert, at the center of the universe; that is a place reserved for God, the one in whom we live and move and have our being. What's more, God has given creation inherent value as that which God has made, approved, and blessed. This means that our spirituality and ethics need a "this worldly" dimension. This is a good world, one in which God delights. We should celebrate and delight in the good things that God has made, as Ecclesiastes reminds us, despite its fairly bleak view of the world (see p. 91 on Ecclesiastes's worldview). In Gen 1:1–2:3 we see the creational ground of that delight. Genesis 1:1–2:3 also provides the grounds for our responsibility to care for this world: if God has called creation good and blessed its creatures, we need to reflect that valuing of creation in our treatment of it. Whatever we might say about the responsibility of so-called Judeo-Christian culture for environmental decay, we cannot rightly claim that its genesis lies in this text (please allow the pun). White is simply wrong to say that Genesis claims that other things in the world exist only for human benefit.

So far, we have been focusing on the form and structure of the text and seeking to understand its general features in light of its cultural context, without paying much attention to the details. Now we will shift focus to a key event in Gen 1:1–2:3, one that rightly gets a lot of attention in theology and ethics: the creation of humanity in vv. 26–31. Obviously, we won't be able to deal with all the theological and ethical issues associated with these verses, let alone examine the wide range of views on their interpretation. Nonetheless, there are some key things to notice.

The first is (once again) a matter of form and structure. This particular creative act is different in crucial ways from the others in Gen 1:1–2:3, it being longer and more detailed. It is also differentiated from them by its unique introductory formula. Genesis 1:1–2:3 characteristically has God speaking things into existence and/or making them. For instance, when God announces the new creative act in vv. 24–25, we read, "Let the earth produce living creatures.... And it was so. And God made . . ." Here in v. 26, however, God says, "Let us make," a unique utterance in this chapter. Much has been written about the significance of the plural, "Let *us* make," ranging from the comfortably orthodox (but implausible) claim that it refers to the Trinity of the Godhead to the uncomfortably unorthodox (but impossible) claim that it is a remnant of older polytheistic notions of creation. (By the way, the traditional trinitarian view is implausible because, as far as I can see, the Trinity, while truly describing the eternal relational nature of God, was not made known to God's people until the coming of Jesus, and so it's unlikely that the writer of Genesis is making claims regarding the triune character of God. The idea of a polytheistic remnant persisting in Gen 1:1–2:3 is impossible because the text is so carefully crafted, and so deliberately set against alternative, pagan accounts of creation, cosmos, and the gods, that the idea that a reference to many gods could slip in undetected is preposterous. It is possible that it is a reference to God consulting the "heavenly court"–angels and so on–an idea we find in places such as 1 Kgs 22 and Isa 6. I find the notion of divine deliberation, God, so to speak "thinking out loud," a simpler explanation on this occasion.) These words do something fairly clear in the text: they separate out this creative act from all others; this is the only time that God announces God's intentions rather than God's actions. That, I suspect, is the meaning of the plural: it is a marker of divine deliberation rather than conversation (i.e., the text records God reflecting, not a discussion between Father, Son, and Spirit)–God announces this determination, thus indicating the unique significance of the coming creative act.

The second thing to note is, of course, the content of the deliberation: "Let us make humans in our image, according to our likeness." The idea that humans are created in the image of God is exegetically complex and theologically rich. The ethical implications of this statement are incalculable, especially in its ANE context, and extend far beyond the issue of human dignity and the value of life. There are, as we have seen, connections between the gods and humanity in ANE myth. But the humans created out of blood and clay in an ANE account are created as servants of the gods, put on the earth to lessen the burden on the lower, "peasant class" deities by growing the food that the gods need and offering it to them in sacrifice. Interestingly, in Gen 1:1-2:3 (and Gen 2:4-25) God provides food for human beings, not the other way around (1:29; 2:16), showing a striking contrast between the one true God and the gods of other cultures and the dignity and purpose of humans in their respective creations.

The notion of being created in the image of God (or the gods) existed in other cultures, but only with reference to the kings who were the unique representatives of the god/s on earth (in Egypt even being counted as demigods in their own right). In Gen 1:1-2:3 this royal image is radically democratized: it is not just kings but rather all humanity who are made in the image of God and who represent the one true God and God's rule over the earth. While not identical the statements of being and function, of image and rule, respectively, are integrally connected. Again, ANE context helps us here. Ancient kings were in the habit of erecting statues of themselves in major centers throughout their realm as signs and symbols of their authority over that territory. These images of the kings were expressions of their rule. Much the same thing was done by modern European monarchs. Note, for instance, the ubiquitous statues of (a usually frowning) Queen Victoria erected throughout the old British Empire. The image of this queen and empress over this empire on which the sun never set can still be seen silently brooding over her former dominions from London to Melbourne, Kolkata to Ottawa–signs of a now defunct authority. Humanity has a similar (but more positive) role to play in God's world: as those created in God's image, we are given unique dignity and a unique responsibility as representatives of the divine king and are, consequently, called to express God's rule over God's world.

This is important to remember when we come to the "dominion mandate" of Gen 1:28, the command to be fruitful, multiply, and rule over the earth and its inhabitants. This has been taken by some Christians (and more of Christianity's detractors) to mean unbridled domination of a passive world that has no intrinsic value and exists only for human ends. Despite the fact that the relevant words of that verse can be taken that way–*kabash* and *radah* mean "subdue" and "have dominion" respectively–this idea is wildly mistaken. Not only, as we have seen, does creation have inherent worth and dignity, but also the rule that humans are to exercise over the world is representative of God's rule. Dominion is both entrusted to humanity by God and meant to be shaped by God's own rule over the world. That rule is of a loving, caring provider, not an arrogant, exploitative despot. This God provides food for humanity and other animals, commands the flourishing of all creatures and is delighted by it, and seeks the well-being of all creation. That ought to be the character of human rule over the world.

That quality of human rule may be hinted at in the nature of the provision for humans and the animals. Humanity is given fruit- and seed-bearing plants for food and animals are given green plants. At this stage there is no hint of predation or eating animal flesh. This may be because this is envisaged as an idyll, a golden era of harmony in which death is unheard of. But I suspect that this view would read too much into the text, and that it is simply not mentioned at this stage as it would fit oddly with the notion of God's blessing on humanity and, through humanity, on the rest of creation. What it does mean, however, is that at this point human dominion is not seen as violent, as entailing the subjugation and death of other creatures. That is allowed for in human dominion; it is not required. This suggests that human dominion is meant to be for the mutual benefit of humans and other creatures. This is clearly the case when we turn to Gen 2:4-25.

The account of God creating the garden and humanity establishes both an integral relationship between humanity, particularly the man, and creation and shows the character of care entailed in human dominion. This is first seen in the description of the narrative stage on which God makes the garden and the first humans. Initially this is a barren land, for although there is water, it is useless. There was no rain that would have allowed for the growth of "wild" vegetation, and the groundwater (or perhaps mist [the Hebrew word 'ed is obscure]) is of no benefit, for as the text says, "There was no one to till the ground," no one to put it to good agricultural use in irrigation (Gen 2:5-6). The ground has a need, and human beings are seen as a solution to it, as 2:15 makes plain: once God makes a human, God places the human in the garden "to till it and keep it" (NRSV) or, more likely, "to work it and look after [or even guard] it" (showing, by the way, that work is not a "curse of the fall" but rather a part of God's creational intentions for humanity). The result is that the ground's need is met: God provides a human for the ground. Of course, God also provides for the human from the ground: the human is placed in a garden where God had planted every useful and beautiful tree (2:9).

There is a crucial connection, then, between the human and the ground, as seen in the Hebrew words used in the text: the ground is 'adamah, and the human is 'adam. These similarly sounding (but probably philologically unrelated) words are deliberately used to make this connection (like "earth" and "earthling"). This connection is also seen in the description of the man being created out of the dust of the ground: on this occasion, God does not create by fiat, by just speaking the man into existence; rather, God gets his hands dirty, so to speak, showing not only intimate care in fashioning the human being but also humankind's integral connection to the rest of creation. It is the stuff of which human beings are made. We are in a relationship of interdependence with the rest of creation; we come from it and care for it, and on its bounty we depend. Not only is there this connection, but also the human is created in part for the benefit of the ground: the human is to work (or tend) it and keep (or look after) it. This is a relationship not of domination and exploitation but rather of mutual benefit: the human, caring for the ground, is provided for by it—a very different picture from those exploitative readings that we saw earlier.

Furthermore, this is a garden of delight. The trees that Yahweh God plants for the man are both useful (good for food) and beautiful (desirable to look at). This is a matter not just of utilitarian provision, of base pragmatics, but rather of aesthetic delight, the reveling in beauty. For things don't have to be beautiful in order to work well; beauty is redundant, a useless quality except for the pleasure that it brings those who use them and, for that matter, those who create them. This is a world in which God delights and in which God invites humans to share in God's pleasure. This reinforces, of course, the intrinsic value of the creation in God's eyes. It is not just good *for* us, God's purposes, and so on; it is good, period. This recklessly extravagant beauty and the goods of creation (both for us and in themselves) are accentuated in the little detail (interruption, really) of the rivers of Eden (Gen 2:10–14). Water is life; this garden where God is present is the source of life for the (natural and, I expect, the intended human) world. But this too is not just useful; it is also beautiful, a beauty that itself points us to the presence of God, for in the lands watered by these rivers is (good) gold, gems, and other rich and wonderful substances, many found in connection with the tabernacle and the priests (see, e.g., Exod 35–40). God's desire is that this world work well as well as be beautiful and something in which both God and humanity can delight.

If our rule in the world is meant to reflect God and God's purposes, then we ought to both delight in this world and preserve its "useless beauty." Exploitation that destroys its beauty or results in the loss of creatures in which God delights cannot be a reflection of God's own rule in the world. Ours is meant to be a relationship with the ground, and by extension the whole created order, in which both parties benefit: we receive from the ground the fruit of our labors, that which we need to survive and flourish and develop, but equally we need to ensure that the ground, is enriched not impoverished by our labors, that it is more fruitful because of us and that its inherent beauty is maintained and enhanced. That is the kind of "rule" that God invites us to share in; that is the relationship with the ground that God initiated for us.

Tragically, for the environment as for all aspects of creation, the text doesn't end with Gen 2:25. We are all too aware of the nasty end to the story in Gen 3, the way that humans (then as now) use their God-given freedom to flout the will of God and throw God's good gifts back in God's face. And we are also all too aware of the consequences: the pain, frustration, alienation, destruction, disharmony, and death that flow from the human will to sin. The reality that we know, the world in which we live, is the world that we find at the end of Gen 3–a world that still bears the marks of God's good and bountiful creative work but that also bears the scars of human depredation. What we call "the fall" is best understood as the results of a broken, fractured relationship with God, each other, and the world. There is much that we could look at in this richly symbolic and tragic text, but here we need to focus on what the text shows us regarding human relationship with the ground and the effects of other broken relationships on the created order. For our purposes this is most clearly seen in the so-called curses of Gen 3:14–19, better understood as the judicial sentences of the divine lawmaker on rebellious subjects.

The most obvious point to note is that the man's relationship with the ground is marred by sin. In Gen 2:4–25 the man is put into the garden to work and care for the ground and to enjoy its produce; in Gen 3:17–19 we are told not only that the ground is cursed because of what the man has done, but also that this curse results in alienation between the man and the ground and its produce. There is a certain symmetry here: the man sinned by eating the fruit of the ground (whatever that fruit may have been–almost certainly not an apple); his punishment is that in the future eating the fruit of the ground will come only with toil and trouble. Further, the ground itself, and what it produces, is cursed: it now produces fruitless thorns and thistles rather than the abundant delight of the trees of the garden. The earth itself suffers as a result of human sin. We are not told of the mechanism of the curse, but I suspect that humans are themselves the "vector" by which this curse is transmitted to the ground. In creation we were entrusted with loving rule of the earth; as a result of the fall, that dominion is as distorted as all other human actions, as distorted as human nature itself. Sin is alienation, and it disrupts all relationships, deeply infecting human nature; all that we do is now affected by it. No longer is human dominion characterized by the loving imitation of God and the mediation of God's kingly rule on the earth. Now it is characterized by the same selfish struggle that is evident in the fall itself (note the finger-pointing in 3:12-13).

Moreover, human sin results in the quest for personal power and the struggles that go along with it. This is evident in Gen 3:16, which foreshadows the power struggles between men and women in marriage (and to which we will return in the next section). Although the text doesn't explicitly say so, I think that we can safely infer that similar power struggles will be seen between humans and the world that has been entrusted to our care. Our desire will be to control it, to turn it to our purposes, to use it for our own ends rather than to care for it and seek its flourishing along with the good of all who might and should benefit from its bounty. That oppressive domination is seen not only in how we relate to the earth—raping it rather than loving it—but also in the injustice that typifies what we do with its produce, and even the inequities that exist in the access that different people have to the ground and its produce. The environment suffers as much from the results of our sinful exploitation of one another as it does from our sinful exploitation of the world itself. Deforestation, for instance, is sometimes the result of poor communities' quest for fuel for their fires, which they need to keep themselves warm and cook their food. So too, desertification (the conversion of arable land to desert—happening at an accelerating rate on the southern fringes of the Sahara) is largely the consequence of the overgrazing of marginal land. Goats are the main culprits, being one of the most efficient but destructive of herbivores: killing plants, destroying ground cover, causing the loss of topsoil, and creating a new stretch of desert. Poor communities, those who don't have access to more productive land and adequate social services, rely on goats for their livelihood; this, like many other environmental problems, is the direct result of injustice in the human community. Furthermore, it is the poor who are most vulnerable to environmental decay, as is seen, for instance, in the projected consequences of global climate change. Such are the consequences of sin. If the creation tells us that we have responsibility for the world in which we live, the fall tells us why we face the awful problems that we do.

The connection between sin and environmental destruction is not limited to Gen 3:17–19; indeed, that text sets up (or explains) the conditions for the rest of the scriptural story. It is seen directly in places such as the prelude to the flood narrative in Gen 6:11–12, where the text speaks of the earth being ruined by human violence and sin, and Deut 28 and the prophets, where the curses of covenantal disobedience include agricultural collapse as a result of the effects of human sin on the environment (and, of course, God's judgment on it). That is not the only way, of course, that concern for the cosmos and our relationship with it is reflected throughout Scripture. There is a sense in which the land granted to Israel is portrayed as a new Eden, and their role is to be the kind of faithful and effective stewards of the land that the man and the woman failed to be in the garden (a task in which Israel tragically failed). Further, the prophets have a clear hope for a new creation in which the distortions and disruption of sin, the damaging effects on the world of sin and judgment, are removed in a new golden age (see Isa 11:1–9; 25:6–10a; 55:12–13; 65:17–25). This hope is picked up in Jesus, who not only demonstrates his sovereignty over nature (Matt 8:23–27; 14:22–33) but also is the Lord of the new creation, in which the cosmos is freed from its bondage to decay caused by sin (Rom 8) and all is put right (Rev 20–21).

So, a concern with the world, and with the quality of our relationship with it, is found throughout Scripture, but its roots are here in Gen 1–3. However, although this text grounds us in the importance of valuing creation and its goods, it doesn't mandate a particular set of environmental policies addressing the needs of industrial and postindustrial societies. All these texts were produced in agrarian cultures—the kind of culture in which most human beings have lived throughout history—and address the issues of those cultures. The texts do not give us direct guidance on how to manage urban sprawl or the transport and pollution issues that follow, or how to deal with toxic waste—be it radioactive, biohazard, or industrial effluent—in a sustainable manner. They don't speak to us about how to deal with our ludicrous dependence on (eventually exhausted) fossil fuels, or how to fund the development and implementation of sustainable alternatives in "developed" and "developing" economies, or how (or whether) the patterns of consumption that we enjoy in the West can be enjoyed by our descendants or members of the "emerging economies" in China and India. However, when we see the damage caused by our current relationship with the ground and the way it flagrantly disregards the needs of the future of our planet and our descendants, and the well-being of threatened species, and access to the ground and its produce for poor communities, I cannot imagine how that could be defended as consistent with Genesis's vision of creation. Genesis doesn't tell us what policies we should implement or what lifestyle choices we should make. It does project a vision of the world that calls us to repent of our selfish and destructive relationship with the ground and to embrace a responsible and caring one, and to call upon our political leaders to enact policies that do likewise. It may not prescribe specific policies, but this is a dangerous vision and one that calls for costly action.

GENESIS 1-3 AND GENDER RELATIONSHIPS

Our next topic also calls us to action: gender issues and the pattern of relationships that ought to exist between women and men. It is only in the last half-century that women and girls have enjoyed a measure of equality in the Western world. When my father trained as a doctor, women students were rare and women surgeons almost (but not quite) unknown. That is no longer the case. In the West, women are fairly well represented in the medical profession, for instance, although there is still a long way to go before we see equal and adequate representation of women in some key areas, such as politics and industry, or adequate and fair pay for professions such as nursing and teaching, in which women have tended to predominate. I would not say that the situation my daughters face is ideal—far from it—but it is better than what most women have had to face through most of human history, and what most women in the world face today.

Women and girls in the majority (or third) world not only face serious inequities, they have to bear more than their fair share of the burden of poverty. While women tend to have to run the household economy, shouldering responsibility for providing for their husband and children, men tend to control what money is available and are free to spend it on themselves, leaving their wives to make do on less than a pittance. Whatever the law states, access to education for girls is dramatically lower than for boys, and their access to what social services exist is severely limited. Literacy rates are lower for women than for men and maternal and child health suffers as a result.

There is, correspondingly, a greater "pay-off" in development work that focuses on the needs of women and children, which is one of the reasons why the second and fifth of the UN Millennium Development Goals directly address the needs of women (see p. 85 in chapter 2). Targeting aid to the needs of women, especially when it operates on a small scale in local communities and includes literacy training and education, is one of the most effective ways of delivering development aid. Further, the evidence is overwhelming that where women receive education and basic social services, the birth rate is dramatically reduced, easing the burdens of population growth on both poor communities and the environment. I need say nothing, I suspect, about the difficulties being faced by women in those countries where ultra-conservative Islamic policies are being implemented. Gender issues have been and still are significant ones for the Christian community to address, both here in the Western world and in the majority world. That's one good reason to look at gender relationships in Genesis, given that it is foundational for our understanding of the nature of women and men and the way those relationships ought to be structured.

There are two other reasons to address this issue: first, many people see the OT as a whole as misogynistic and patriarchal and see Gen 2–3 in particular as the source of such views; second, the issue of gender relationships, including in Gen 1–3, has been a source of (often acrimonious) debate among evangelical Christians. My discussion will focus on the specific arguments that have been used to justify a patriarchal reading of the material and how they are not, in my view, supported by the text. I will focus on the debate within evangelicalism between "subordinationist" (also called "complementarian"—a term that I will avoid because I believe that it is not as clear as the alternative and is easily misunderstood) and egalitarian interpretations of Gen 1–3.

Here I will make a couple of preliminary points. First, both subordinationists and egalitarians within evangelicalism presuppose the authoritative status of the Bible as God's word and that the basic goal of interpretation is to understand what the writer intended so as to understand what God says by way of the text. Where they differ (strongly) is on the interpretation of the texts, especially in the case of Gen 2–3. Second, I don't believe that the author of the text is deliberately dealing with the question of relationships between males and females. I believe the focus is on presenting a particular pattern of relationships, a vision of human community as it ought to be in relationship with God, among its members, and with the world, and what it has become as a result of sin. Nonetheless, it seems to me that the picture of community that emerges, and the pattern of relationships that the author presents as God's creational ideal, are profoundly inconsistent with hierarchical orderings of relationships between men and women. Let's turn, then, to examine and critique the arguments that have been used to support the traditional subordinationist point of view.

The first argument is that the woman was created to be the man's helper ('*ezer* [Gen 2:18]) and thus is subordinate to him. This assumes that the one doing the helping is subordinate to the one being helped, since servants help masters and subordinates help their superiors. Generally, the nature of the help provided is also seen as contributing to this picture of one who, though equal in being with the man (ontological equality), is subordinate to him (functionally or relationally). From this point of view, the help that the woman provides is that associated with being a wife and mother: she is created in order that humans might be able to reproduce, and so, in an agrarian society such as Israel's, she might be able to contribute to the domestic economy by providing workers for the ground. There are two problems with this argument. First, the word "helper" in Hebrew does not imply an inferior helping a superior; in fact, its OT usage suggests the contrary. God is frequently spoken of as the helper of Israel or particular persons in Israel; for instance, '*ezer* is specifically used in this sense in Exod 18:4; Pss 70:5; and 121:1–2 and also the Ebenezer (stone of help) narrative in 1 Samuel (7:12); the related word '*ezrah* is used with reference to God in Pss 22:19 and 46:1 and on many other occasions. It is hard to imagine that an OT author would see God as an inferior coming to help a superior! If anything, usage implies the contrary: the helper is the one with superior power coming to the aid of the weaker party. Genesis 2:18 is, of course, not implying the superiority of the woman, for the use of "as his equal" or "as his counterpart" (kenegdo) counters that idea; rather, she is the one whom God creates to provide for the man's need.

But what is that need? What does Eve do to help? Again, the traditional subordinationist interpretation goes astray on this point, for the text identifies the nature of the man's need, and it is not for procreation. Indeed, God tells us, and in the most striking way: "It is not good for the man to be alone." Not good! After Gen 1:1–2:3, this strikes us as a remarkable, even shocking, statement, for there we hear six times "and God saw that is was good," and the seventh time, "it was very good." And now God says, "Not good." In the context of the creation narratives, I suggest, this means that the work of creation is not yet done. This is also apparent when we compare Gen 2:4–25 with Gen 1:1–2:3. In Gen 1:1–2:3 God's creation of humanity is the creation of male and female in the image of God, the creation of a human community. The man alone is not yet a finished creation, not of humanity at least; that requires persons in relationship. And relationship of a particular kind, for, of course, the man in Gen 2:18 is not alone: God is there. But, in this sense, God is not enough. In order for there to be a human community, there must be a human counterpart for the man. That is what is lacking; that is what is "not good." The need that the woman fulfills is the need for relationship, for community, for the finalization of the very creation of humanity. That goes well beyond bearing children, and it is hardly the work of an inferior. What Eve does to help is vital for human existence and God's creational purposes.

The second argument is a more general one and relates to the order of creation events: temporal order (the order of events in the narrative) corresponds to relational order (the order of superordinate to subordinate between men and women). The man was created first and then the woman, and so the man is her superior. This argument is often justified by reference to 1 Tim 2:13, which, it is claimed, shows us that this is how Paul read Genesis. I am not persuaded that that is the best reading of the argument in 1 Tim 2:9–15, a notoriously difficult passage. Paul, I suggest, is not exegeting the text, giving us its original meaning, but rather is using it as a source of a comparison or illustration (as he does also in 2 Tim 3:8 with Exod 7). He uses the woman in the garden as an example of one person's deception leading to others' sin (Eve deceived by the serpent leading to Adam's sin), which is also what is happening in the church at Ephesus (women were the avenue by which false teaching was entering the Christian community, as seen in 1 Tim 5:13-15 and 2 Tim 3:1-9). This explains, I suggest, why Paul forbids women teaching (and claiming inappropriate authority) in that church at that time: it was a way of guarding the gospel in that church—his overarching concern in those letters—rather than a permanent injunction based on a supposed "hierarchical creation ordering" of gender relationships. Paul, then, does not require that we read the text as saying that temporal order establishes relational order.

But what about the Genesis text itself? Again, it seems to me that, read in its context, the order of events cannot be used to establish relational priority. In Gen 1:1-2:3 the last is first—that is, the creation of humanity is the last of God's creative acts—yet certainly we would not say that this means that humans are subordinate to other creatures. So too in Gen 2:4-25: while the man is created before the woman, the animals are created after the man but before the woman, and surely that cannot be taken as evidence that the woman is seen as subordinate to them. Rather, the delay in the creation of the woman in Gen 2:4-25 is for the purpose of dramatic effect. It retards the progress of events, creating tension and a sense of anticipation. It establishes the importance of community for God's creational purposes for humanity. This ordering of events is a matter of literary artistry, theologically emphasizing the importance of interpersonal relationships; it does not establish a hierarchical order of those relationships.

The third argument is that the woman was taken from the man and so is dependent on and subordinate to him (Gen 2:21-22). This notion is also partly driven by a particular interpretation of Paul, this time of his argument in 1 Cor 11:3-16, especially v. 8. Once again, however, it seems to me that this argument is based on a misreading of Paul, who is not concerned with whether men have authority over women but rather about how women's heads are to be adorned *when* they speak in church. Paul is appealing not to a hierarchical ordering of relationships but rather to the interdependence of men and women as the reason why it is inappropriate for women to act in a manner that asserts their independence of men. That concern for interdependence is apparent in 1 Cor 11:11-12. Paul's concern in 1 Cor 11:3-16 is with men and women in relationship; however, his concern is not who has authority over whom but rather that men and women belong together in the creative and redemptive purposes of God, and that this should be reflected in the way that cultural patterns play out in the public ministry of the church in Corinth. Paul is not saying that Genesis affirms a hierarchical ordering of gender relationships; his interests lie elsewhere.

Is this, then, the best understanding of Gen 2:4-25? True, the woman is taken from the flesh of the man, but what feature of the text suggests that this establishes hierarchical ordering? After all, the man's substance is taken from the ground, and obviously this doesn't indicate his subordination to it. Why should the fact that the woman's substance is taken from the man's indicate her subordination to him? The reason for this detail becomes clear in light of the creation of the animals and their inadequacy to the task of being a counterpart helper. The animals are fellow creatures: they are of like substance to the man (from the earth), but they are not the right kind of fellow creature. The woman is not of like substance to the man (her substance is not taken from the ground); rather, she is the self-same substance (her substance is taken from the man himself). Furthermore, this is not the man's work, but God's: the man is asleep through the whole process and is no more than the delighted beneficiary of God's gracious work. The woman is dependent for her existence on God, not the man (cf. 1 Cor 11:12: "all things are from God"). The fact that the woman's "raw material" was taken from the man does not indicate her relational subordination to him.

The fourth argument is that the man named the woman and thus has authority over her (Gen 2:23). This argument assumes that one of the key functions of one person naming another is the establishing of authority of the namer over the named. Granted, Gen 2:23 is an instance of the naming formula; the issue here is whether naming is intrinsically an act of authority or not. Naming can be associated with authority: in the OT parents name their children (e.g., Gen 5:3), kings name their subjects (e.g., 2 Kgs 24:17), and so on. Naming is, then, associated with authority, but this is only in contexts in which authority is already established on some other grounds, such as social order (parents) or conquest (kings and vassals); it does not in itself establish authority. That, I suggest, is clear from Gen 16:13, where Hagar names God. It is unimaginable that the author is asserting that Hagar took or had authority over God!

What, however, of the naming of the animals in Gen 2:19-20? Does that not establish the man's authority over them? No. Although the man does have authority over the animals, that authority is established in Gen 1:26-28, not in Gen 2:19-20. So what is the function of naming in Gen 2:4-25? It is an act not of dominion but of discernment: the end of the man's naming the animals is the realization that none of them is the matching counterpart that he needs. In naming them the man identifies them and their place in the world, including that they are not what completes the creation of community; he does not establish authority over them. Naming in Gen 2:23 has the same function as man's naming of the animals in Gen 2:19-20: it is an act of discernment, not dominion. The man discerns that the woman is indeed the long-awaited helper-as-counterpart that the animals failed to be, and he responds with a joyous song, delighting in the fulfillment of his need. Genesis 2:23, then, does not establish the subordination of women to men.

The fifth argument is that the woman is naturally weaker than the man and more susceptible to temptation, which explains why she is the (natural) target of the serpent's temptation in Gen 3:1-5. Once again it is claimed that this argument is required by Paul's use of the Genesis text in 1 Tim 2 (a point that I have already dismissed above). So what features of the text suggest that the woman is the weaker, more susceptible of the two? If anything the text suggests the contrary: the man passively goes along with her suggestion; hers is the sin of action, while his is the sin of acquiescence (just going with the crowd—the first instance in Scripture of someone succumbing to peer-group pressure). Further, the text makes it clear that he is equally culpable for the sin and equally liable to God's penalty; he was there all along (Gen 3:6: "and she gave also to her husband *who was with her*" [emphasis mine]). How does that establish that she is naturally weaker than the man and more susceptible to temptation, let alone that all women are? Why, then, does the serpent target her? The text doesn't say, and all explanations are guesses (for instance: it is due to women's predilection for fertility cults and the serpent's association with them; or the woman received the command not to eat of the tree second-hand rather than directly from God). Certainly it is slender (perhaps nonexistent) evidence on which to build a case for hierarchical ordering of gender relationships.

The final argument is that integral to the man's sin is that he listened to his wife, over whom he should have taken authority, and that integral to her sin was the subversion of the proper order between men and women; after the fall, in Gen 3:16, God's reestablishes that creation order. A number of points can be made here, the first being that the text does not in fact establish a creational subordination of the woman to the man that was broken in sin and needs to be reestablished by God after the fall. There is no such broken order to reestablish, so that is not what God is doing. True, part of the reason for the man's judgment in Gen 3:17 is that he obeyed the woman and ate from the tree; however, the salient point is not that he listened to her, but rather that he listened to someone other than God, the God whose authority in this matter is established in the command not to eat. Further, 3:16 is a judgment on sin, not a command for the good ordering of human community. It is no more an expression of God's positive will for human affairs than is the reality of pain in childbirth (which would make the use of painkillers in labor a flouting of God's will) or the presence of thorns and thistles in the ground (which would make weeding the garden and careful agriculture a flouting of God's will). Rather, it is a word of judgment that both ratifies the reality of sinful distortion of relationships and marks it out as a sign of God's punishment of human sin.

This judgment consists in the distortion of relationships occasioned by the "will to power." The woman's "desire" in Gen 3:16 is often understood as a sexual desire for her husband despite the pains of pregnancy and delivery. It is, however, best understood as a desire for control. The same word (*teshuqah*, rare in the OT) is used in Gen 4:7 in relation to sin's desire for Cain; there it cannot refer to sexual desire but rather is symbolic of sin's desire to control Cain. So too the statement in 3:16 that the man will rule over the woman is an expression not of God's intent for human community but rather of the sinful distortion of society. In general, men have more power than women and use it for their own advantage and women's detriment, and this is a consequence of sin's fracturing of relationships. This word of judgment does not reestablish an original hierarchical ordering of relationships, instituted in creation, but now disrupted by sin; there is no such hierarchy. Instead, it expresses God's punishment on sin in the form of sin's distortion of that original creation order, an order of mutuality, equality, and delight. So much for the subordinationist arguments.

So what does Gen 1–3 tell us about God's intentions for human community and about the relationship between women and men? First, we need to go back to 1:26–30, which clearly establishes the equality of women and men as created in the image of God, equally entrusted with fulfilling God's purposes in the world. The distinction between male and female is central to human existence, but it does not entail a hierarchical ordering of relationships. Second, we need to recognize that God's goal in creating humanity was the establishment of a community of intimacy, equality, and delight (2:25). This community was fractured as a result of human sin, leading to distortion of all relationships. Hierarchical ordering of relationships, especially the expressions of power and control that go along with them, is a mark of this distortion. God's intentions for human community, and for relationships between men and women within it, are otherwise.

Why, then, have so many people throughout Christian history read it otherwise (a subordinationist reading is the dominant one in Christian history and, I suspect, among evangelicals today)? One reason is a distorted reading of Paul, but that, in turn, is related to a deeper issue. As we saw in chapter 1, biblical interpretation, like all else that humans do, is affected by the distorting power of human sin. I'm not claiming that those who accept the traditional interpretation are more inherently sinful than their egalitarian counterparts, or that they consciously prefer one reading over another because they are influenced by patriarchal patterns that favor them and their interests—after all, some women accept the subordinationist tradition of interpretation. Nonetheless, I believe that the dominant patriarchal traditions in Christian theology and exegesis have veiled the meaning of the text. The vested interests and blindness, conscious or unconscious, of predominantly male interpreters and theologians led to distorted readings of the text. These readings, consciously or unconsciously, sought to justify established patterns of male power and control. Speaking as a male, and thus as one who would profit from this patriarchal tradition of interpretation, I nonetheless renounce such readings as distorted by sinful culture and not reflective of God's intentions for humanity. Recent social developments have enabled us to reassess our patriarchal assumptions, helping us to see the ways we have distorted the text and so to get a better grasp of the meaning of Genesis (and other texts). This is not a matter of our placing ourselves over Scripture (let alone claiming that we, unlike our subordinationist colleagues, are free from the taint of sin in this or any other matter). Rather it is an effort to faithfully read Scripture in a new light and thereby see what was always there. Genesis does not, then, tell us that a hierarchical ordering of human relationships is God's will for human community or for relationships between males and females–quite the contrary.

Given that Genesis does not establish a creational subordination of women to men, we need to come to terms with the fact that women tend not to be treated as men's equals in the rest of Scripture. This is evident throughout the OT, but it is equally evident in the NT (see, e.g., Eph 5:21–33). I suggest that, as we've already seen with slavery, this is an instance of divine accommodation and of God preserving existing institutions but replacing their oppressive content with content that more adequately expresses God's redemptive purposes. Galatians 3:28 tells us that in God's new creative purposes, as in God's original creative purposes, gender, slavery, and race do not count in terms of how we stand before God or each other. The reality is, however, that the societies that both Testaments address were clearly patriarchal, with structures and institutions that reflected such a mindset. So, for instance, in both Israel and the Roman Empire men were seen as the economic and social head of the household in that they were seen as the source of the economic well-being and proper social order of the extended household (much more extensive households, by the way, than the modern Western "nuclear family"). The normal pattern was for the senior male to be the ultimate authority over the affairs of those within his household. That ordering is not divinely ordained. Nonetheless, it is how they operated, and those who lived in them needed to know how to live as God's people in that social world. Hence, Paul gives instructions such as those in Eph 5:21–33. The one in authority in this particular social world, the husband, is to exercise authority in a manner reminiscent of

Christ's self-sacrificial love for the church–hardly the exercise of authoritarian power (see, e.g., Matt 20:20–28). Similarly, women are to submit to their husbands; however, they do so as a sign not of blind acquiescence to the social order but rather of reverence for Christ and his lordship. The same pattern is seen in Paul's call to slaves to submit to their masters, matched by the revolutionary idea that masters must respect their slaves (Eph 6:5–9).

It seems to me, then, that God establishes a pattern of relationships in Gen 1–2 in which the human community is to be characterized by relationships of equality, intimacy, mutuality, and delight. It is sin that disrupts that pattern and gives rise to the oppressive inequalities so familiar to us. Our call is to mirror God's original and new creative purposes in our lives and in our mission. In my view that means supporting and seeking to extend those equalities that women now enjoy (to an extent) in the modern West. This, it seems to me, has implications for the issue of women in ministry, a matter requiring urgent attention by evangelical churches and agencies (but I'll leave that to one side). It also means working for gender equality and to empower women wherever they do not enjoy those freedoms, especially in the majority ("developing") world. It means seeking to improve their lot as persons and mothers, ensuring that their health is supported and maintained and that social services and education are made equally available to them. It means ensuring that the overseas development aid that flows (be it ever such a trickle) from Western countries to the majority world has women (and children) as a focus. We are not called to foster patriarchal social systems as if they are the sovereign will of our Creator. They are not. Rather, they are signs of the brokenness of human sin and its disruptive effects, and we are called to combat that in all its manifestations.

THE DECALOGUE (TEN COMMANDMENTS): DEUTERONOMY 5:6-21

The Ten Commandments are among the most familiar texts in oⱦ ethics and have been used as the basis of innumerable ethical systems and law codes. No exploration of the oⱦ and its application to Christian ethics would be complete without some examination of the Decalogue ("Ten Words," from the Greek translation of the traditional Hebrew term for the Ten Commandments). But which version should be examined? The Decalogue is found, in slightly different forms, in Exod 20 and Deut 5. It is possible to take it out of its canonical contexts and look at it as an isolated, abstract set of religious and moral commands (and many books on ethics do exactly that), but to do so is a mistake. We will focus on Deut 5:6-21, where the Decalogue is located in Moses's recounting of the events at "Horeb" (the name that Deuteronomy uses for Mount Sinai) and is immersed in encouragements to obedience, something typical of Deuteronomy. It is also placed prominently at the start of Moses's second, and longest, speech in the book, which also contains Deuteronomy's "law code," or set of detailed instructions (Deut 12-26; the speech itself runs from 5:1 to 29:1).

Particular features become apparent as we read the Decalogue in comparison with other legal material in the Torah. It consists of bare commands (two positive, eight negative), with no details, no circumstances, and no punishments or penalties. Four of them (commandments two through five) come with clear "motive clauses," or reasons to obey. These are negative for commandments two and three (warning of [unspecified] divine judgment), and positive for commandments four and five (memory of grace and the promise of blessing respectively). The Decalogue contains commands that reflect values found in most human communities as well as some that don't: murder, adultery (however defined), property, and so on are concerns shared by all human cultures, whereas the proper worship of Yahweh and the keeping of the Sabbath are not. That has implications for how we think about the function of these commands, as does the fact that one of them, at least, is not a matter of law and is entirely unenforceable (the tenth commandment). This suggests that, like other key ot texts, the Decalogue's primary function is to shape a moral vision, to give us a picture of the character of God and God's people, rather than to give us a list of rules to live by. Therefore I won't focus on specific actions or policies that arise out of these commands or their application to the law and social policy, in part because there are many books that do that (and it would take too much time and space), but mainly because that is neither the primary way the commands operated in Israel nor how they function for us as Christians. I will say more about these and other matters as we go along. Let's turn, then, to the commandments.

The Decalogue opens in a way that proves my earlier point about the primacy of God's grace (and reinforces the importance of looking at the commandments in their canonical context rather than as an abstract list of rules). The first thing that it does is not to issue a command but rather to identify God, and it identifies God as Yahweh, the gracious God who rescued Israel from bondage. Once again we are reminded that this is a relationship of response; indeed, all biblical ethics is the ethics of response. The Decalogue, in fact, opens by reminding us of "the story so far," refreshing our memory of the character of God and of God's works on behalf of God's people. This God of power, love, and faithfulness now issues commands that shape the response of God's people to God's grace. The first command follows on naturally from this. It is a call to exclusive loyalty. This, in Israel's day, was a radical concept. True, commands were issued in the names of the gods of Egypt and Mesopotamia, but each god was almost always seen as one god among many, and so the commandments did not call for exclusive worship of a particular god. But Yahweh's commands do, and for two reasons: first, Yahweh is the one true and living God (e.g., Deut 32:12, 39); second, because Yahweh alone delivered Israel from bondage in Egypt. Israel owes its freedom to no one else. No other god has a role to play—indeed, Yahweh's deliverance is an act of victory over the gods of Egypt (Exod 12:12)—and so no other god deserves Israel's worship. In addition, guarding their worship of Yahweh alone ensures that their new and free community is shaped solely by Yahweh's character and the nature of Yahweh's grace.

Commandments two and three are clearly connected to the first one and once again show the distinctiveness of Israel and their God. The prohibition against idols in the second commandment, of course, refers to images of gods used for religious purposes; unlike Islamic tradition, this is not a prohibition of artistic representation of creatures per se but rather of images *used in worship*. The commandment does not, however, specify whom the images might replicate. Does it refer to images of Yahweh or of other gods? I suspect that the command is deliberately ambiguous, allowing it to cover both cases. In one sense worshipping images of other gods is already taken care of in the first commandment, for if it is an image of another god that is being used in worship, then a god other than Yahweh is being worshipped. That's quite obvious. But people are such that a bit of repetition is a good thing; it does us no harm to hear similar ideas in different words. So, the second commandment excludes images of other gods but also, I suggest, images of Yahweh as well.

Why would images of Yahweh be prohibited? Two reasons can be offered. First, it is inconsistent with the nature of Yahweh. As Deut 4 puts it, Yahweh is the God who is not seen but is heard; Israel's understanding of the nature of Yahweh (and what Yahweh requires) is to be governed by Yahweh's word alone and not by their own imaginings of what a god might be like. The second reason is equally important but requires some understanding of religion in that time and place. Images were used in worship both to shape people's understanding of the gods and to give them access to the gods. The idea seems to have been that an offering made to an idol has an almost magical effect; the right sacrifice offered by the right person in the right way gives the worshipper a "hold" on the god. Idols, in a sense, give us leverage on the gods, requiring that they come to our aid. Clearly, Yahweh is not like that. Not only is Yahweh the holy God who is beyond our manipulation, but also Yahweh is the one who has brought Israel out of Egypt, demonstrating that Yahweh does not need to be coerced into acting on behalf of his people. Idols are prohibited not only because Yahweh demands appropriate worship but also because idols introduce fundamental distortions into the picture of God that we develop and thus the kind of lives that we lead.

The concern for Yahweh's freedom is even clearer in the third commandment, which prohibits blasphemy, the misuse of the name of Yahweh. Most of us probably have the wrong idea of what blasphemy is; we see it as condemning people who say, "God, no!," or in a moment of exasperation yell out, "Jesus H. Christ!" My father was such a man. He was fairly profane, with a ratbag (roguish, for the uninitiated) sense of humor. Most cars come equipped with "grab bars" over the passenger doors, something to hang onto when your driver tears around a hairpin turn. My dad called them "Jesus bars" because when my mother went haring around a sharp curve, he'd grab it and say "Jesus, Avril!" That's not what the third commandment is about. It has in mind something a bit more significant than that (not that such "casual blasphemy" is a good thing—it's just not the point of the command). Nor does it prohibit taking oaths in the name of Yahweh (see Deut 6:13). In order to understand this command, we need to understand the theology and function of Yahweh's name.

Yahweh's name is more than a set of syllables: it is who Yahweh is, demonstrated in words and deeds. That is the context in which Israel is entrusted with the unique name of God in Exod 3 and 6. Yahweh's words and works of deliverance, in which Yahweh makes Israel the people of God, are, so to speak, the very things that "name" or identify Yahweh (as we just saw in relation to Deut 5:6). Yahweh's name is also a gift given to Israel. Israel is the people who, because of their covenant relationship with God, can call upon the name of Yahweh in worship and in prayer. "Yahweh" is both God's act of self-identification for Israel and how they identify themselves with God in relationship. It also functions in their social life, especially in their pursuit of justice—hence, the command to take oaths in the name of Yahweh in Deut 6:13. To misuse the name of Yahweh, then, is to use it in a way that distorts those purposes for which Yahweh has given it to Israel by engaging in false worship and false personal and social programs.

Such misuse attempts to ally Yahweh, the sovereign God of justice, grace, and faithfulness, with false (vain or empty) causes. This, of course, includes false testimony in Yahweh's name, but it includes much more than that. It includes allying Yahweh's name with any religious, political, social, or personal project that is not endorsed by Yahweh or is, indeed, contrary to Yahweh's name—that is, Yahweh's character as revealed in Yahweh's own words and works. Such misuse of God's name connects Yahweh with causes that are not Yahweh's own, with projects that defy rather than reflect God's will, and seeks to use God to justify them. It is no wonder that Yahweh holds no one guiltless for such misuse. When Jeremiah speaks against Israel's complacency, relying on Yahweh's temple for blessing despite their injustice and breaking of the covenant, he is invoking the third commandment (Jer 7). Perhaps we in the church need to be careful about saying that God backs any particular political program or social project. We should make such claims only when the project clearly is in line with Yahweh's name—for instance, working to alleviate poverty or to obtain justice for those excluded from the world economic system. As we have seen, the ot is fairly clear that projects such as this honor God's name, reflecting God's own character and expressing God's will in the world. It seems to me that we cannot claim that a given political party or social program (conservative or progressive) is granted such divine imprimatur. The third commandment, then, ties a vision of a moral community to Yahweh's own character, reminding us that Yahweh, and Yahweh alone, determines the nature of the "project" of being God's people in God's world and warns us against attempting to use Yahweh for our own ends.

The connection between Yahweh's character and the shape of Israel's community is abundantly clear in Deuteronomy's version of the Sabbath commandment (the fourth commandment), which differs from that found in Exod 20:8–11 in two ways. First, there are some differences of detail ("keep," not "remember"; the addition of cattle; the care taken to ensure that no one sees a "wife" as included in a man's property). Second, a different motivation is given for keeping Sabbath. In Exodus the Sabbath is grounded in creation; in Deuteronomy it is grounded in redemption. In both versions there is a clear concern that servants (or slaves) be given rest along with their masters, an interesting detail that, as we have seen, clearly distinguishes Israelite society from all ancient (and most modern) societies. But in Deuteronomy the reason they are to rest, and particularly to give rest to their servants or slaves, is in remembrance of their exodus from slavery in Egypt. This is more than a psychological motivation (they should be kind to slaves because they know what it's like to be in slavery); it is theological. In fact it is grounded in their very character as the rescued people of God and, more importantly, in the character of their God and God's action on their behalf. As we saw in a previous chapter, God is the kind of God who is kind to slaves, and God's action in rescuing them was an act of kindness to slaves; Israel, therefore, is to be that same kind of people. It is interesting that this command, so often seen as primarily religious in nature, has such clear social consequences.

This is evident not just in the broad shape and motivation of the command but also in the details of daily life that the commandment picks out. First, all work is forbidden, for all people (and animals). All the members of a standard Israelite rural household are identified: you (i.e., the adult head of the house), male and female children (who had important roles to play in the economy of the household, such as being field hands or herders), male and female slaves and sojourners (those who were bound to the household's labor by either bonded servitude in the case of slaves or economic necessity in the case of foreign "day laborers"), and animals. But why are animals included, and in Deuteronomy why is "your ox" and "your donkey" specified along with (the rest of) "your livestock"?

In order to grasp this, we must imagine ourselves into the ancient agricultural world. Oxen and donkeys were the archetypal "beasts of burden." We tend to think of cattle as sources of meat, milk, and hides rather than as a source of work; if we want power to do a job such as more easily and efficiently convey something from one place to another or plow a field, we look to machines such as trains, trucks, and tractors. Obviously that kind of machinery was unavailable prior to the Industrial Revolution. Prior to that if you wanted to take something somewhere, you either carried it yourself, got someone else (such as a slave) to carry it for you, put it on an animal, or, if it were a large burden and you were a rich person, loaded it on a cart pulled by draft animals. If you wanted to plow a field, you used your own team of oxen or borrowed or hired someone else's, or, if you were desperate and poor, you did it manually. In wealthier households—those that could afford to own and feed slaves or hire foreign day laborers—it was the slaves or sojourners who used the animals to do hard manual labor. Similar observations would apply to those few who made a living by trade, craft, and so on. When Deuteronomy commands that no animals will do work on the Sabbath, then, the primary focus is not on rest for animals (although that is a useful by-product reflecting God's concern for all creatures), but rather on rest for those who use the animals in their daily labor. This commandment includes a restriction on using the main tools of trade of an ancient household, thereby ensuring that there is no backdoor route to denying slaves their right to rest: if the animals are inactive, the slaves must rest. That is why, I suggest, the purpose of this portion of the command—"that your slaves might rest as well as you"—comes *after* the reference to animals. The focus is on shaping Israel to be a community that reflects

God's own character, as well as ensuring that everyone who so desires is free to worship God on the Sabbath. Once again, this "religious" command has clear social implications.

It is worthwhile to turn aside here to consider this. As we do so, a key feature of the ethical use of the OT will, I hope, become clear. We've already seen that the Sabbath command has clear social implications, that in fact it shapes a particular kind of community. That, I believe, is fundamental to the Decalogue as a whole. This is not merely a list of rules and regulations; rather, it is a way of creating, shaping, and maintaining a new kind of community. That is God's primary purpose, and it is reflected in the very nature of the texts. They are, if you recall, God's gift to a rescued people and God's call for them to live as God's people, reflecting God's character and purposes in the world. Israel is, indeed, a "restoration community," partially embodying in its national life God's intentions for all human relationships. So, then, when we come to a particular text of the OT, our primary question is, "What does this tell us of God's character and the character of God's people?" We are to look for theological and relational principles (better, functions) expressed in the text. Turning to ethics in particular, we are to ask, "What is the function of this text for Israel?" That is, how would a text such as this affect their lives, their relationships, how they conduct themselves as a community? We are then to ask how those same functions can be expressed in our lives as the people of God, for God has neither changed God's fundamental nature nor turned from God's expressed purposes. Of course, as we've seen, we are uniquely privileged, knowing as we do, God's fullest declaration of God's nature and will in the person of Jesus. We are also a different kind of community from Israel, one formed not along national-political lines but rather on the basis of faith. So what, then, of the function of the Sabbath command for Israel and for us?

Here we need to look at the broader picture in the Torah, for this is the only reference in Deuteronomy to keeping the Sabbath day. The pattern of six-plus-one, however, also appears in relation to the seventh year, the year for canceling debts in Deut 15. Not only are debts to be canceled, but also those who sold themselves into slavery (as we've seen, best understood as a period of bonded labor) are to be released with enough resources to establish themselves in their new lives. Clearly, it is not just a religious rule; it is part of a vision of life, a vision of liberality and freedom. Precisely the same picture is found in Exodus, where Sabbath and the seventh day (or year) feature a little more prominently. Many of the same concerns are found there, such as the seven-year pattern for both release of slaves in Exod 21:2-11 and rest for the land in Exod 23:10-11 (followed by another reference to the seventh as a rest day). There we see, again, the concern for liberty and justice: (debt) slaves are set free (Exod 21); the (landless) poor are free to forage in others' fields; slaves and foreigners (those on the margins of Israel's society) are given rest. We also see a concern for creation. The Sabbath year allows the land to lie fallow, to be replenished as well as to provide for others; the Sabbath also grants freedom for animals to rest. This, of course, in part is aimed at ensuring that Israelite farmers do not continue to work, but it also shows a concern for nonhuman creation. This fits in the context of Exodus, for not only is the Sabbath command grounded in God's creational blessing in Exod 20:11, but also the exodus itself. Israel's creation as a people and God's freeing them and bringing them into the land, is presented in many respects as a new creation.

The unique feature of the Sabbath in Exodus, however, is that it is presented as a sign of the covenant, with all its attendant seriousness. Exodus 31:12-17, which further outlines Sabbath law, is located just after the instructions for building the tabernacle, the place where Israel would come to worship their holy God. This naturally connects Sabbath and worship and, given that there are echoes of Eden in the construction of the tabernacle, connects both rest and worship with God's creational purposes (see also Exod 20:11). It is also presented as a sign, both of the covenant relationship that they enjoy with God and of their own holiness (Exod 21:13, 16). As such, breaking Sabbath is breaking covenant and breaching holiness and thus is treated with utmost seriousness: the penalty for breaking Sabbath is death—a point reiterated after the covenant is renewed following the episode of the golden calf (see Exod 35:2-3). Sabbath, then, is a mark of the holiness, the distinctiveness, the "set-apartness" of Israel.

This rhythm of work and rest is, along with a number of other features of Israel's life that we have already examined, an aspect of "visible holiness." The connection with God's work in creation means that keeping the Sabbath, and the holiness that it expresses, are a reflection of God's own character. This holiness was expressed by Israel in social practices tied to their distinctive national-political identity. That is, they were called as a nation to be the people of God and so to express their distinctiveness in the concrete conduct of their lives. Sabbath, food laws, and so on worked as "covenant indicators," public demonstrations of holiness. For Christians, this is not the case. The manner of our being the people of God is different, and so too is our holiness. Our distinctiveness is seen in the quality of our relationships, not in special food or in the meticulous observation of particular days (Rom 13-14). Furthermore, we are given a new mark of distinctiveness: John 13:34-35 shows us that love is the sign of being new-covenant people.

This does not mean, in my view, that we are now free to jettison the Sabbath as so much ot baggage. Jesus himself suggests the contrary in an incident that shows his concern for the underlying social and theological purpose of the Sabbath over against the pettifogging legalism of his opponents: "The Sabbath was made for humans, not humans for the Sabbath" (Mark 2:27). Indeed, the Sabbath reminds us that we are called to be imitators of God, and this not just in abstract ways but rather in the concrete conduct of our lives. We are called to be those who live lives of liberality and freedom, lives in which others come to enjoy something of the liberty of the children of God. Further, we need to remember that we are creatures and thus are designed for rest (and for worship). Although we ought not to slavishly adhere to any particular Sabbatarian program (seventh-day or otherwise), we need to remember that we have been designed to benefit from a rhythm of work and rest. More than that, it also reminds us that creation, and the blessings that we enjoy, are not ultimately our own attainment. The Sabbatical year program reminded Israel that they were to depend upon God and to share God's creational blessings with those normally excluded from the economic system. Sabbath undercuts both workaholism and the blinkered selfishness of much of our modern Western lifestyle. When we understand this command as a social and theological vision, we are once again confronted with the revolutionary nature of ot ethics.

The fifth commandment is, I expect, one with which we are both more familiar and comfortable than the Sabbath commandment. Jesus and Paul both clearly affirm it (Mark 7:9-13; Eph

6:1–3), and honoring parents is a basic element of most human moral systems. There are, however, a few things that we need to bear in mind as we look at the fifth commandment. First, we must note the reference to the land. This is both typical of Deuteronomy–this book is set on the threshold of the land, instructing Israel how to live as God's people in the land that God has given them to possess–and a key to our understanding the command. The land is of more than incidental significance: it provides the context of the obedience required by the command and also is tied very closely to Israel's particular identity as the people of God. Thus, although concern for parents is a common feature of human morality, it has particular import for Israel. Second, the social arrangements in ancient Israel throughout all of its long and complex history are vastly different from current Anglo-American (and Australian) "nuclear families." Most households included two or three generations living together, including adult children and their families. The commandment is directed not, in the first instance, at juveniles but rather at adults and calls them to respect the family relationships that are basic to society. In fact, the extended family would have played a much more significant role in Israel's social world than is true for most of us. Many important social decisions were made in the context of those extended families, which also formed the basis of larger social networks.

This relates to the third thing we need to consider. Families, and particularly their oldest generation, were crucial to the moral, social, economic, and theological fabric of Israel. The land, a key to Israel's social and economic life, was tied to particular family groups. This land was the basis of Israel's economy, and the particular portion of land allotted to the family was seen as inalienable (Lev 25; 1 Kgs 21). The "elders" of the community had an important role in legal disputes, representing particular families in the social and judicial affairs of the community. The family, furthermore, had primary responsibility for passing down the knowledge of God, God's word, and what it meant to live as God's covenant community (Deut 6). Adult children are here being called to a commitment that will ensure social cohesion, economic stability, moral continuity, and intergenerational covenantal commitment.

The command to honor one's parents, then, is not primarily focused on children obeying their parents (although, of course, that is a good and valuable thing, as I occasionally remind my daughters). It is a way of maintaining the social, economic, legal, moral, and religious fabric of Israel. Indeed, if it were undermined, Israel's relationships as the community of God, and even their very relationship with God, would be threatened. It should not be a surprise, then, that this command comes with a promise (as Paul notes [Eph 6:1-3]), for honoring parents is primarily a way of ensuring "covenantal longevity." That is, it ensures that the next generation is instructed in the ways of Yahweh; it ensures that a family's connection to the land, one of their key covenant blessings and the source of their livelihood, is maintained; it ensures that the social and moral fabric of society is held together. So when we think about how it relates to Christians, we need to think about how we can reinforce the fabric of the communities in which we live, how we can ensure that people and their families are adequately connected to the economic system, how we can ensure that people have good access to the knowledge of God—as well as, more narrowly, thinking about how we honor our parents. Once again, this command shapes a vision of life in community, and our goal is to do what we can under God to achieve God's purposes in our communities.

We can deal with commandments six through ten more briefly, in part because they are more familiar and more obviously of ethical significance, and in part because the way they shape the ethical vision of the OT is fairly obvious. These commands are often described as the "second table" (or "tablet") of the Decalogue, related to the "horizontal" dimension of human existence. There is an element of truth in that, so long as we recognize that all of the commandments shape Israel as a moral and "religious" community.

The sixth commandment—the prohibition of murder—is, of course, clearly horizontal. Nonetheless, we need to connect this with its theological rationale and also to note its breadth. First, we must recognize that this is a prohibition of murder, not just of killing (the Hebrew word has roughly the same meaning as our English word and is generally used in contexts that speak of "malice aforethought"). It does not prohibit warfare or the death penalty, nor does it prohibit what we call "manslaughter"—causing the death of another person by accident or neglect. It would be odd, would it not, to prohibit accidentally killing someone? We can guard against that, which the Torah clearly does (Exod 21:33–34; Deut 22:8), but we cannot prohibit it as such. Logically, no command can prohibit manslaughter, for if someone thinks about his or her actions and goes ahead anyway, the result is no longer an accident or misadventure but rather is a deliberate act, and if it knowingly and maliciously causes another person's death, then it counts as murder. Second, the sixth commandment is broadly applicable because it draws no distinctions between persons. It does not say, as ANE codes (and many modern legal systems) implicitly do, "Don't kill important people, but if you're high enough up the social ladder, you can act with impunity toward the insignificant people at the bottom." It says baldly, with no qualifications, "Don't murder."

That tells us something about Israel's moral vision: they were called to value human life. That moral vision is connected, as always, with a theological vision. The command arises out of God's valuing of human life and tells us that Israel is to be a community that shares that way of looking at the world and of acting in it. This command too is connected with their experience of exodus: God has rescued those who were considered dangerous nobodies in the Egyptian Empire and given them freedom, a freedom that they are to use to express the same respect to others that God has shown to them. There's not really a lot that I need to say here. As those who know God's valuing of humans and relationship, seen in the sacrifice of God's own dear Son in order that we might be rescued, I think that this is quite clear.

That is not to say, however, that we have automatic answers to a range of puzzling questions relating to the beginning and end of life. For instance, I have often heard Christians opposed to the practice of abortion or euthanasia talk about them as instances of murder. I think not. Don't get me wrong: abortion and (so-called active) euthanasia are generally wrong, in part because they are claiming the kind of sovereignty over human life and its beginning and end that properly belongs to God alone. But these actions are not murder. Euthanasia doesn't count as murder, because it is not a killing with malice aforethought but rather is done out of misguided compassion. Abortion doesn't count as murder, because neither those who perform it nor those who choose to go through the procedure believe that what they are killing is a human person.

They may be wrong about that, although the wrongness in general of abortion doesn't depend on saying that an embryo counts as a full-fledged human being from conception. But given that they do not count the fetus as a human person, their intention is not to kill a human being, with or without malice; thus, although what they do is, in general, wrong, it does not count as murder. Furthermore, there are instances—say, where the mother's life is at risk—when abortion, while deeply regrettable, may not be wrong. This is, of course, a difficult and controversial question, and one outside the scope of this book. Nonetheless, given that in both the OT and modern law malice aforethought consciously directed against another human being so as to will their death (or serious harm) is a key criterion for identifying a particular wrongful death as murder, the absence of malice aforethought makes abortion and euthanasia, generally speaking, cases of wrongful death rather than murder.

But all of that is an aside. The primary function of this command is to shape a moral vision in which, in response to God's liberating grace, the people of God show the same even-handed concern for human life that Yahweh shows. We need that vision and its world-changing force. This is a world in which the arms trade is a billion-dollar industry costing the lives of thousands of people—men, women, and children—mainly in impoverished and unstable countries. It is a world in which millions of children die each year from dirty water and easily preventable diseases, and little is done about it because that might disturb the comfort and economic growth of wealthy nations. I could go on, but I think it's clear that this moral vision is one that we desperately need.

The prohibition against adultery is also fairly clear and unambiguous, and it is no respecter of persons: men and women, rich and poor, the weak and the powerful—all are commanded not to commit adultery. It is important to realize, however, that this command is not primarily about putting limits on sex; it is about the integrity of marriage and the broader family unit. This is clear, I think, when we recognize that in the OT fornication (sex with an unmarried woman) and adultery (sex with another man's wife) are treated differently. Fornication is dealt with by forcing the man to pay the bride price, whether or not the woman's father accepts the (required) offer of marriage (Exod 22:16–17). Adultery is punishable by the death of both parties (Lev 20:10; Deut 22:22). There are, I think, a number of reasons for this distinction. First, the OT is not as obsessed with sex as is modern Western culture (whether that obsession takes a permissive or restrictive form), as is seen in the fact that adultery and other sexual sins get much less "air time" in the OT than in Christian moralizing. This is not to say that sexual integrity is of no account; it is to say that the OT is not obsessed with sex. The OT is obsessed with relationships. Indeed, it is concerned with faithfulness in relationship, which is the second reason for the distinction between adultery and fornication. One factor that distinguishes adultery from fornication is that adultery is an act of unfaithfulness. Marriage involves a commitment to another person; that commitment is broken in adultery.

This relates to the third reason: adultery damages a key social institution, particularly in a culture such as Israel's (as we've seen in the fifth commandment). Adultery both undermines the marriage relationship and calls into question the passing down of the land in the father's family—something of immense importance in the old covenant. If a man's wife has sex with another man, her husband has no idea whether or not the children that inherit his family's land are his, in other words a legitimate (pardon the pun) part of his family and so rightful inheritors of the land. That, in part, is why the focus in adultery is on it being with another man's wife. Another factor, of course, is that the OT arose out of and addresses a patriarchal society, one that focuses on men and in which men have more power and freedom than do women. That, in part, is why a woman can have only one husband while a man can also have concubines (or subordinate wives) and more than one wife (Exod 21:7-11; Deut 21:15). Nonetheless, although there is that clear, and unpalatable, difference between men and women in defining adultery, there is no distinction in the penalty for it. Both the man and the woman are to be executed (Lev 20:10). This is, interestingly, one of the few references to the penalty for adultery, and it is unclear whether this penalty was understood as mandatory or as the maximum allowable (as seems to be the case with murder). Nonetheless in Israel, unlike in many other male-dominated societies, men are not effectively immune from punishment (compare, for instance, modern Pakistan). There is no double standard in the prohibition of adultery. As an aside, such a double standard is seen, and condemned, in the incident in John 8:2-11: why is only the woman caught in adultery and brought to be stoned? She couldn't have been caught committing adultery alone!

Although it is expressed negatively, this command is another expression of the moral vision of the OT, which both praises and encourages faithfulness in relationships and is concerned with the good order of the community. It is a call to faithfulness, particularly in marriage. It reminds us, yes, of the importance of sexual integrity, but primarily it speaks of the overriding value of faithfulness in relationships, particularly the paradigmatic relationship of marriage. This call to radical faithfulness is seen also, of course, in Jesus' teaching on both lust (Matt 5:27–30) and divorce (Matt 5:31–32; 19:1–12). The lustful look is one in which neither the "object of desire" nor one's spouse is treated as a person. Whatever constitutes such a look, it mentally undermines the radical, single-minded, absolute commitment to another person that is constitutive of the marriage relationship (forsaking all others and cleaving to one's spouse, as traditional wedding liturgies put it). This is an act of infidelity toward one's spouse; hence, it is adultery. So too is divorce for the purpose of "upgrading spouses." I think that it would be profoundly ironic to treat Jesus' teaching on divorce in a legalistic manner (as has sometimes happened in the Christian tradition), as if what counts is whether this or that counts as adultery (or desertion in 1 Cor 7:15). Jesus' primary concern is not with divorce but rather with marriage. He sees marriage as something ordained by God in creation and thus granted a significance that goes beyond mere social arrangements. It is not, then, a disposable relationship. He calls us, again, to uphold fidelity and faithfulness in that relationship, as in all others (again, see Jesus' call to love, justice, and faithfulness in Matt 23:23). Faithfulness matters in the moral vision of this command. Once again, whenever marriage and other key relationships are seen as disposable commodities to be discarded or embraced according to our consumerist desires, this OT vision of fidelity is sorely needed.

The eighth commandment, prohibiting theft, shows that the OT also has a concern for property, but not at the same high level as its concern for people and relationships. In this, it clearly contrasts with many ANE law codes (and some modern Western ones, for that matter) in which some kinds of theft were subject to the death penalty. This has some prominence in my own nation's history, for penal transportation was a commuting of the death penalty; many convicts were transported to Australia as a punishment for petty theft, such as stealing food for their children. Those who weren't transported were hanged. Property offenses were capital crimes in eighteenth-century England. In the OT, crimes against property are never capital offenses. Rather, if caught, the thief is to restore the goods and pay a fine, or if the goods cannot be restored, the thief is to pay back fourfold (Exod 22:1–15). The case laws on property in the OT are all about restitution. The only exception to this is the theft of a person (kidnapping), which, as a crime against a person, is subject to the death penalty (Deut 24:7).

The existence of property laws is grounded, however, not in capitalist notions of private property as an inalienable right subject to divine protection (if there is a God) but rather in a particular vision of community. The command is driven by the "communitarian" recognition that property enables people to function in community. Property, especially land (which, we must remember, was central to Israel's life, economy, and society), gives people space in which to live and flourish and the means to enable them to do so. Property gives people access to the economic life of a community and thus makes it possible for them to be productive members of the community. Property also allows people to invest in the future of their families and their society, as is seen in the clear concern of the OT to safeguard a family's inheritance. Further, disregarding others' interests in one's property, especially one's land, distorts community and can only arise out of a belief that self-interests are more important than the interests of others. And in this regard it is worth noting that the powerful are not exempt from this command; they too are to respect property rights of others, even when it is inconvenient (see 1 Kgs 21; Isa 5:8; Amos 2:6–8). However, property rights are not, in one sense, inalienable, for the laws of gleaning tell us that in Israel property was in the service of persons. It was a matter not of purely private property but rather of property entrusted to particular members of the community for their benefit and the benefit of all in the community, even those temporarily or permanently deprived of property rights to the land.

More fundamentally, in a society such as Israel's, which was predominantly a marginal agrarian society, property may mean life. Theft of a draught animal might make it impossible to plow for next year's crop, threatening the very survival of the family. Theft even of a garment from a poor person might mean the risk of debilitating discomfort or even death. As a result, in Israel a garment taken from a poor person in pledge of a loan was to be returned at night lest the person be exposed to the cold (Exod 22:25-27; cf. Amos 2:8). I could go on, but I think you get the picture. In a society such as Israel's (and, for that matter, for the billion people today who live in absolute poverty) a theft that for us would mean inconvenience, the expense of replacement, or the sadness of a lost heirloom could mean the difference between life and death. Property matters. The Decalogue envisions a community in which the rights of all people to those things that enable them to function well in community, even to flourish, are safeguarded, for their benefit and for that of the community as a whole. I suspect that those of us who live in capitalist democracies don't need much of a reminder of the importance of property; what we do need to be reminded of is why it matters and for what purposes. We need to reenvision our communities and economies so that property is in the service of people and their communities, not vice versa. The economy exists to serve society, not society to serve the economy. Property is there to enrich and enable life in community, and people do not exist for the sake of accumulating property, which is a means to such ends, always and everywhere, and never an end in itself. This vision matters.

We are almost done. Now we are on to the ninth commandment, which you may well have learned in Sunday school as "Do not lie." I have nothing against Sunday school, and truth-telling is important; those who know and live by the truth of God's liberating good news need to be people of the truth. Nonetheless, that Sunday school summary is not quite right. The ninth commandment doesn't say, "Do not lie"; it says, "Do not bear false testimony against your neighbor." False testimony relates not to truth-telling per se but rather to being an honest witness. This is a matter not of personal morality or individual ethics but rather of social ethics.

Its function is to guard the administration of justice (the context and purpose of bearing witness). As we have seen, justice is central to Israel's life as the people of God; so is the proper administration of justice. And this was relevant to all adult (male) members of the community, for most legal proceedings took place in the chief public space in local communities, the "gate," which was the entry to the town or village–roughly speaking, the public square. This is seen in Amos 5:10, which literally says, "They hate the one who judges (or 'reproves') in the gate; they abhor the one who speaks integrity (or 'what is sound')." The normal legal procedure was for an aggrieved person to bring a case to the "elders" of the community, trusted and wise people (generally men) who had the job of gathering and weighing the evidence for and against and then making a decision. There were also "courts of appeal," so to speak, such as the judges appointed in major centers (Deut 16:18-20 [roughly speaking, district tribunals]) or, for serious and difficult cases, what we might call the "supreme court" in the tabernacle (Deut 17:8-13) and later Jerusalem where the priests (and later the king [2 Sam 15:1-4; 1 Kgs 3]) served as judges. All such decisions, however, at whatever level of the justice system, depend on reliable witnesses; the quality of the evidence is paramount in any trial, which is why, of course, no serious matter could be decided on the evidence of just one person–two or three corroborating witnesses are needed (Deut 19:15).

Truth is at the foundation of justice and proper legal proceedings; justice and its proper administration, in turn, guard the fabric of society. When relationships go wrong, or when wrong is done to people or groups and they cannot rectify it themselves, there must be some means of redress; there must be a system of justice. That is what this commandment protects: the right ordering of relationships in community and the means to establish, restore, and maintain those relationships. It is about justice, and justice matters. At times, it is, quite literally, a matter of life and death. There were, as we know, offenses in Israel for which the penalty was death; serious and life- or community-threatening breaches of their relationship with God or each other warranted the execution of the guilty party (see, e.g., Lev 20:1-10). In cases such as these it is possible that someone might be unjustly condemned to death because of the mendacious malice of enemies (see, again, 1 Kgs 21). That would be an instance of "judicial homicide." And for that, Deut 19:16-21 tells us, the penalty would be death: whatever harm the false witness intended to inflict on another is to be inflicted on the false witness–not just "an eye for an eye," but "life for life" (v. 21). What's more, that passion for justice would preserve the character of Israel's community of freedom. We can see in Exod 23:1-3, 7-8 and Deut 16:18-20 that such a system, if administered justly, would ensure that the rich don't profit from unjust control of the judicial system, nor the poor from misapplied pity. The law guards against the rich using their wealth to bribe judges (thus undermining their impartiality) or using their social standing to distort the truth. But equally, the poor cannot unjustly appeal to their poverty as a way of avoiding proper penalty; judges are to show no partiality. This command, then, serves to highlight the importance of justice in Israel and the responsibility of all to ensure that they play their role in maintaining it. In a world in which the rich enjoy relative impunity because they can afford the best lawyers and they use their knowledge of and influence on the legal system to get their own way at the expense of those with less money and power, this OT vision of community is, again, sorely needed.

And so we come to the last of the Ten Commandments. The commandment against coveting is, perhaps, the strangest one to find here—at least, it would be strange if our traditional understanding of the Decalogue as law code were true. For coveting—the illegitimate desire for what belongs or pertains to someone else—is by its very nature invisible to all but God and the person involved. That means, of course, that it cannot be subject to legislation. If it were to become visible, it would have had to have been acted upon, and actions can be legislated against (such as theft, most obviously, but also adultery). Why, then, a separate command? Because the Decalogue is not a law code per se; rather, it is an expression of a moral vision, a way of understanding those relationships that are to pertain in God's new community. This command tells us that actions are not the only things that matter in community; motivations and the character of persons also matter. After all, motivations drive actions and shape persons and thus relationships. This command aims at shaping the kind of persons we are. However, it goes much deeper than that, to the very values and vision of life that drive God's rescued people. For coveting is not just the motivation that underlies breaches of other commandments; it is fundamentally foreign to God and God's purposes for Israel. They are to be a people of trust, to whom commitment to God and the neighbor is the overriding concern—more important than personal property, let alone the profit motive and all other forms of acquisitiveness. Coveting, then, is a denial and essential distortion of that fundamental vision of life and relationships. It's no wonder, then, that Paul equates coveting with idolatry (Col 3:5). This, I suggest, speaks a sharp and revolutionary word to our materialistic culture and our churches, which are more often shaped by an acquisitive view of life than by God's vision of a new community. There is much more that I could say about this and the other commands, but I think I've done enough to show how these commands are more (and other) than a list of principles that good people should abide by; they express and shape a remarkable moral vision.

We have seen, then, that the Decalogue functions in the OT primarily to shape a moral vision—a view of God, the world, human society, and individual existence—and a way of living out that vision. That vision is truly revolutionary, a point that I have made from time to time in the reflections above, but one I want to look at a little more closely. In order to do this, we need some grasp of ANE culture and of Israel's historical location in it. The Canaanite culture that Israel encountered on entering the land was, in many crucial ways, typical of ANE culture in general. It was a highly stratified culture in which power was concentrated in the hands of the few at the expense of the many. The few—in Canaanite culture, the royal elite who controlled the individual city-states that existed in the land under the authority of the large Egyptian empire to the south—controlled the economic, judicial, and political systems. Their existence and rule were, in turn, justified by a religious system that mirrored this social reality: there was a hierarchy of gods, the most significant being Baal, their patron deity and the guarantor of natural and social order. Social order was both expressed in and justified by a divine order. The end was a system in which power belonged in the hands of the elite and the common people were both poor and powerless—doubly so, because resistance to the social order (if at all imaginable) was considered tantamount to rebellion against the gods. Israel's moral vision overturned that order—theirs were dangerous aspirations.

These dangerous aspirations were embodied in that alternative reality projected by Torah. Yahweh—the one, true, and living God; the God of Abraham, Isaac, and Jacob; the God of the exodus—is one. This God does not embody and ratify an existing social order but rather calls into being a radically new society that reflects God's own character and values. And although the society that received and was shaped by these "laws" was not perfect, created *de novo* consisting only of perfect people, it nonetheless was called to embody radically different values—values by which even slaves are cared for, trust reigns and respect for persons and their needs overrides selfish interests, and even motivations are called to the bar of God's will. The call, then, to worship Yahweh alone and to adhere to Yahweh's Torah is not just a "religious" matter. This faith—for faith it is—also calls into existence a new way of living in the world.

The question for Christians, of course, is how this vision and the way of life that it calls forth relate to their lives. What, to put it another way, is the relationship between Christians and the law? The first thing is that the "law" is not a matter of "works" in contrast to grace. Whatever Paul was opposing in Galatians and Romans, it was not the law per se, which is, he states, holy, just, and good (Rom 7:12). The law, he says, cannot be used to determine one's standing as a member of the people of God—but then, it never could. That relationship was always envisaged as being established by God's sovereign grace; the law was a means of shaping the "obedience of faith." The law's problem is that, on its own, it is powerless to bring about the transformation of persons that the obedience of faith requires. A new community can only be created and maintained by renewed people. That, among other things, is what Jesus achieves in his own person and in us by the work of his Spirit—he came not to abolish but rather to fulfill the law in himself and his new community (Matt 5:17-20; see also Rom 3:31; 13:9-10). The shape of that new community is still, however, informed by the "law" (Rom 8:1-4; Jas 2). The Torah reflects the character of Yahweh, the one who redeems us in the person of Jesus the Messiah, and it reflects Yahweh's purposes for human community in the world. Jesus came to fulfill, not abolish, the law, but also, when calling the Pharisees to account, he chastises those who neglect the weightier matters of the law: justice, mercy, and faithfulness (Matt 23:23).

Torah, then, functions to shape our moral vision. Of course, it is not the only thing that does so: for Christians, Jesus and the gospel are at the heart of that moral vision. Nonetheless, inasmuch as Torah functioned to shape a community that was a paradigm of God's purposes for humanity, it still plays a vital role in informing us and our moral perception of ourselves and our communities. It does not bind us in slavish obedience—in Christ we are set free for the obedience of faith (Gal 5)—but the obedience of faith is nourished and molded by God's loving will expressed in Torah. And as we have seen in the Decalogue (and elsewhere), this is a revolutionary vision of a community set free by the one true God and called to express God's love, justice, and faithfulness in the concrete realities of a shared life. This community, living the worship of the one true God, is a community concerned for its key institutions and the maintenance of obedience. It is a community in which the weak and vulnerable are protected and that in Sabbath celebration invites all people into the liberty of the children of God. It is a community that demonstrates God's loving concern for human life and for the integrity of marriage and the faithfulness that it evokes. It is a community that is passionate about the truthfulness that is the foundation for all human justice and the proper ordering of the social world. It is a community concerned about all that disrupts relationships and interferes with people's ability to live well together and so has a suitable (and suitably limited) concern that the property rights of others are preserved. It is a community in which who we are matters as well as what we do, and in which the attitudes that drive us to idolatrous and selfish acquisitiveness are challenged and called to account—at least by the one who calls the community into existence. It is a vision that challenges us, as it challenged Israel, to truly live as the people of God in God's world.

CHAPTER 5

BRINGING THE
OLD TESTAMENT HOME

IN 2006 I HAD THE privilege of visiting India again. I was away from my family for over two weeks and was under instructions to bring gifts home for Alison, Elanor, Laura, and Alexandra—as if I needed to be instructed to do that! Nonetheless, each of them had something that they wanted me to look out for and bring back: a moonstone for Alison, and wooden elephants for each of the girls. On my first trip, way back in the 1980s, when Alison and I had just started dating, I bought for her a matching moonstone pendant and bracelet. Shortly after I gave it to her, however, the pendant was stolen; I was now commissioned, over twenty years after its loss, to find a replacement. On my second trip, in the late 1990s, Alison and our daughters came along. The girls loved India (they are, after all, sensible girls), and while we were there, they saw and loved beautiful lacquered handicrafts—figures of elephants, trinket boxes, and so on—and they wanted additions for their little collections. So, while in India in 2006, I went looking for a moonstone pendant and three carved and decorated wooden elephants, which, to my relief and their delight, I found. Also, however, I found things that I wasn't looking for—earrings, shawls, a cute model auto-rickshaw— that I thought my wife and daughters (and others in the family) might like; what's more, the particular forms of the pendant and the elephants were different from what I had imagined I'd find. And that only served, I think, to heighten their pleasure in the gifts. That's what happens when we go to a strange land. We expect to find interesting and useful things to bring home. And generally we do. Some are things that we went looking to find; others surprise us but are, though we didn't know it until we saw them, exactly what we wanted.

So it is when we go to the strange land of the OT. We go expecting to find some things—we have particular ethical issues that we want to be instructed about—and often we find them. But we must bear two things in mind. First, we must look for the right things. It's no use looking for carved wooden elephants in Iceland (unless you're happy with overpriced imports from India). Second, we must be willing to be surprised at the forms things take when we do find them. After all, we go to the OT for instruction; if we knew exactly what the answers were and what they looked like, we wouldn't need to go looking at all. There is also a third thing we must bear in mind. We might find things that we weren't looking for at all, things that surprise us, both in their content (what they say) and in their presence (that they say it at all). That is part of the joy and excitement— and anxiety—of visiting a strange land. That is what I want to explore, or rather, begin to explore, in this chapter.

We will look at "bringing the Old Testament home" in two ways, from two directions. First, we will look at an issue that arises out of contemporary life and bring it to the OT to see what we find. There are a number of contemporary ethical issues that Christians want to address in light of Scripture. We have already covered many of them, including poverty, power, justice, violence, the environment, and gender relationships, as they arise naturally out of key OT texts. In this chapter I want to look at an issue that is totally alien to the OT but is of great concern to us in the twenty-first century: cloning. The treatment of this issue will be a significant departure from our previous procedure, where the discussions were driven by the text that we sought to read with an eye toward contemporary concerns; here, instead, the discussion will be driven by contemporary concerns that we will seek to elucidate with reference to the text. Previously we dealt with what we found in the strange land of the OT; now we will go looking for what interests us. We will, of course, need to ensure that we do not force the texts to fit our own agenda, "finding" things that aren't really there and bringing our manufactured answers home in triumph. Still, it's worth doing, I think, for we do want all of our thinking and living to be informed by Scripture, our final authority on all matters of faith and practice. The second way we will bring the OT home is more familiar to us now, even if the topic may not be. The chapter (and book) will close with an examination of Isa 46 and its critique of idolatry. I recognize that at first glance this seems to have little, if anything, to say about ethics. That is one of the reasons I chose it for our closing study. The OT has more to say on ethics than we might first think, some of it surprising and found in surprising places. But first let's turn to the topic of cloning.

CLONING

I've been an avid reader of science fiction for years. As a genre, it explores "what ifs." What if this particular technology were developed? What if this particular social change happened? One of the "what ifs" often explored is the cloning of humans, and often in nightmare scenarios, such as in the movie *The Island*, where clones are raised for the sole purpose of having their vital organs removed for transplantation into their "original." Or, in the more far-fetched, but equally abhorrent, "what if" of *The Boys from Brazil*, cells from Adolf Hitler are cloned by Nazi fanatics and used to create a new Hitler. The "what if" of human cloning is now close to reality (although not in any of the nightmare scenarios that writers of science fiction have dreamed up). Indeed, if the Raelians and Italian IVF (in vitro fertilization) doctor Severino Antinori are to be believed (highly unlikely, in my view), then it has already happened. What are we to make of such developments?

Some people passionately believe that if we can clone humans, we should. Ian Wilmut, the man who headed up the team that famously (or infamously) cloned Dolly the sheep, believes in the very great possibilities that such research offers for improving the lot of human beings. He wants to be able to work with cloned diseased cells so as to figure out effective ways of treating diseases. Alan Trounson, an Australian IVF pioneer, believes that cloning may help infertile couples have desperately wanted children. What can be wrong with that? A great deal, many others would say. Most conservative Christians and right-to-life groups see cloning as a horrendous prospect. They oppose it on the grounds that it either sacrifices the life of a human being for research or other purposes (research or therapeutic cloning as advocated by Wilmut) or it is an unnatural interference in the God-given process of procreation (reproductive cloning as advocated by Trounson). Such extremes are evident in all areas of biotechnology, ranging from IVF through to genetic therapies.

Others (including me), of course, argue for what they see as a cautious middle ground. Some technology may be both useful and ethically justified, but we need to be careful in what we do and do not accept. After all, what was "morally offensive" in the last decade may become "technologically imperative" in this decade, with technological and therapeutic concerns illegitimately overriding valid ethical concerns. This is evident in the case of Ian Wilmut. After the successful cloning of Dolly, the specter of human cloning was raised by a number of people. In interviews shortly after the announcement in 1996, he was explicit in his opposition to all forms of human cloning, for "all of us would find that offensive." By 2002, however, he was applying for a license to engage in cloning research for the investigation of diseases and their treatment. What was unthinkable six years earlier is now obligatory. One reason why we need to think carefully about such matters, and do so in light of Scripture, is that it is easy for ethical questions to be silenced by the cries of human need and technical possibilities—hence our discussion of cloning.

Obviously, there are many important issues that I cannot deal with here, some of them beyond my technical competence. For instance, there are a number of important issues raised in relation to animal cloning. It might become possible to replicate one particular animal with consequent reduction in genetic diversity to the detriment of the species as a whole (say, cloning a particularly successful bovine, thus flooding the gene pool with that animal's genes). Others have raised the prospect of the cloning of transgenic and rDNA animals (animals that have genetic material taken from another species or that has been artificially modified), with no clear understanding of what that would do to the animal, its progeny, or the species as a whole. These animals might, then, be used in the production of drugs or vaccines (such as genetically modified cows producing human insulin in their milk) or as sources of histo-compatible organs in xenotransplantation (i.e., organs might be taken from animals such as pigs that have been genetically modified so that those organs can be transplanted into a human being without the risk of rejection).

Interesting and important questions are raised by all of these prospects; however, my focus here will be on potential applications of the technology to humans, as that is where current developments are leading us, and where some of the most acute ethical questions lie. But before we can answer these questions, we need to know what we're talking about. So, let me say something briefly about the science of cloning. I will try to be as nontechnical as possible, but some knowledge of the biology is important if we're going to think clearly about the issues.

First, some background information is in order. Normal, or differentiated, cells in an (adult) organism are "programmed" to reproduce only a specific type of tissue, say, liver cells (i.e., the cells that do the actual processing of material within the liver, as opposed to bile duct cells or blood vessel cells or other cells that make up the "scaffolding" of the liver). Such cells cannot develop into another complete organism; if isolated in a laboratory and stimulated to grow, they would simply reproduce that kind of cell and no other. So, liver cells would just grow a mass of liver cells, not a complete liver, for they would develop without blood vessels, bile ducts, and all the other things that go to make up a normal liver.

In cloning, or more properly, "somatic cell nuclear transfer" (SCNT), scientists transfer genetic material (DNA) from the nucleus of a donor adult cell to an egg cell from which they have removed the nucleus and thus its genetic material. The reconstructed egg cell containing the DNA from a donor cell must be treated with chemicals or electric current in order to stimulate cell division. If cell division proceeds properly, the result is the development of a blastocyst (the early, multicell phase of the embryo) and then an embryo. If, in turn, that is successful and a satisfactory embryo is implanted in a host mother, the result is the birth of an organism with the same nuclear DNA as the donor.

It is important to recognize that the new organism differs from the host in two ways. First, it has different mitochondrial DNA from that of the donor. Mitochondria are essential components of cells, being, if you like, the primary energy factory for individual cells, and have their own DNA. They are located in the cytoplasm (the main body of the cell outside the nucleus), and so they and their DNA are derived from the host egg cell, not the original donor. Second, it is only genetically "identical" to the donor, and so in the case of humans it is not a copy of the original *person*. Personal identity, after all, is a product not only of our genes but also of our environment, our choices, thoughts, memories, and so on, which are unique to each person. *The Boys from Brazil* is a nightmare, not even a potential reality, for without the precise replication of all the events of Hitler's life, including the most trivial, the person that would develop from his DNA would not have the same experiences, memories, and so on and thus would not develop identically. He might have a predilection for odd-looking moustaches, but it's unlikely that he'd grow up to be the scourge of the free world and the embodiment of the Nazi dream.

So what are the potential uses of SCNT? The first is "reproductive" cloning. Suppose that a woman decides that she wants to have a child, and that, for whatever reason, she doesn't want to use sperm from her partner or a donor. She could be cloned and, by way of IVF technology, impregnated with her own cloned cells, giving birth to a daughter genetically identical to her. If she were to decide that she wanted a boy (a "copy" of her partner, say, if she has one, or some other male), a male's cell could be cloned and implanted, and she would give birth to a son genetically identical to the donor. A man could do likewise, presuming, of course, that he had a willing partner or surrogate to bear the child. Of course, a "third party" could also be cloned if, for whatever reason, a person wanted a child genetically identical to someone else. The aim, then, of reproductive cloning is the birth of a healthy child genetically identical to its donor (in contrast to "normal" reproduction, in which half the child's DNA is derived from the mother and half from the father).

The second prospect is what is called "therapeutic" cloning, a term that I will define as the cloning of individuals for another person's benefit—for instance, an organ donor. Suppose that I develop renal failure. I need a new kidney. Who better to get it from than me? So, rather than look for a compatible donor, live or cadaveric, I clone myself and, after a few years, "harvest" a kidney from the clone. There would be no need for immune suppressants, with all their side effects, including the risk of infection, or of transplant failure, for this kidney would be genetically identical to me; it would be, in effect, my own kidney grown in another body. I should note here that I have seen no one, outside some bioethicists (for instance, Peter Singer) and science fiction authors, proposing this as an actual prospect, either nightmarish (for its opponents) or desirable (for its proponents). The focus at the moment in therapeutic cloning is on cloning embryonic stem cells for possible therapeutic use; indeed, that is what is generally meant by the term. However, given that stem cell research, both adult and embryonic, raises its own set of complicated questions, both scientific and ethical, I will leave that to one side and deal with the more "science fiction" scenarios of "whole person" cloning.

The final prospect is "research" cloning, such as proposed by Ian Wilmut. This involves cloning a diseased cell and reproducing just that cell line as an experimental model. It does not envisage implanting those cells or using them directly for any person's benefit (as in therapeutic cloning of either the "science fiction" or stem cell therapy kind). Wilmut's proposal is for research into genetic diseases, but it could also be used with cancer cells or other abnormal cell lines. Scientists would use these cell lines to understand the nature of the disease, examining how the abnormal cells divide and grow as well as when and how the abnormalities develop. They could also be used to test drugs, chemotherapeutic agents, and so on to see their effectiveness on these particular cells. This is seen as a viable, and ethically preferable, alternative to animal research. The issues here are similar (if not identical) to those raised by stem cell research, and I will leave them to one side.

So, what are Christians to think about cloning? And how can the ᴏᴛ help? First, let me repeat: cloning could not be used to duplicate an individual person; it can only replicate one's genetic composition. In order to duplicate a person, we would need to duplicate that person's history, upbringing, and all of their important relationships (and who knows which unimportant ones?), or, as in the movie *The 6th Day,* record, store, and replace their memories. We know this already by looking at identical twins. They have the same genetic composition, but although they are identical twins, they are not identical persons. Furthermore, there are serious technical issues that still need to be addressed. Animal cloning has a very high "failure" rate; in mice it has less than a 2 percent success rate. "Successfully" cloned animals have a significant proportion of defective genes and, furthermore, seem to have a much higher "genetic" as opposed to "biological" age, resulting in rapid and abnormal aging of the cloned animals. So too, cloned animals appear to have defective immune systems and are prone to the phenomenon of sudden, inexplicable death. Before cloning could be applied to human beings, all of these technical problems would need to be solved. Even if they were, however, there are still significant questions that we must ask about the possible uses of human cloning.

In relation to reproductive cloning, a number of things seem to be at stake. The first, and the one most frequently neglected, is the nature of reproduction and the context in which it should take place, and in particular how cloning affects that. Related to that is how we should see infertility and the begetting of children. Are children a right to which we are entitled? Is infertility a "disease" that needs to be treated? Furthermore, what costs are appropriate for people and the community to pay? In relation to therapeutic cloning, what is the status of the clone produced for organs? What about organ transplantation? What justifies the use of resources in that way? We can't do everything that we would like to do for all people; sometimes people will suffer and die. When do we say we have done enough? Our understanding of these issues can and should be enriched and informed by engagement with the OT.

As we do so, however, the first and most obvious thing to note is that the OT has nothing directly to say about cloning. That observation is, of course, banal and obvious; it is worth stating, however, because it significantly alters how we approach the relevant texts and think about the ethical relevance of the OT (and, for that matter, of the Bible as a whole). Cloning, like many other issues we face, was not and could not have been envisaged by the biblical authors; no one at the time when the texts were written had the knowledge and technical skills required. This means that we cannot turn to particular key texts, examine them, consider their ethical and theological function, and then see how those functions can be achieved in our theological and cultural contexts. This means that the procedure we have used so far cannot be applied to this issue; we need to do otherwise. However, what we can and should do is examine the theological and ethical shape of the OT (and the Bible as a whole), seeking to understand how the biblical story informs our ethical vision and how that can be applied to the issue at hand.

The story begins in creation and with God's gift of life and the blessing of fertility. Life and the ability to bear children are seen as God's gifts and subject to God's control (Ps 127). Furthermore, sex and procreation in the biblical vision of life in community are essentially personal and relational. They are located in the context of relationships of a particular kind; in the case of sex and the begetting and rearing of children, the context of the committed covenantal relationship of marriage (Gen 1:26-28; 2:23-25). We are also, in creation, invited to explore and understand the world and to develop technologies that help us to live effectively in it (Gen 1:26-28). The fall, however, reminds us that both the relationships that give rise to children and the process of childbirth are now fractured (Gen 3:16). Infertility is a reality in the OT and, interestingly, is seen as subject to God's sovereign control (see, e.g., 1 Sam 1:5). Furthermore, although children and the continuity of the family are seen as "goods" (desirable and beneficial things) in God's world, they are not absolute goods. Indeed, they are relativized in God's eschatological purposes, as even eunuchs have an honored place in God's kingdom (see Isa 56:4-5). So too, the harmful consequences of disease on human life (including those that cause organ failure) are consequences of the fall, as is the death that inevitably comes upon us all (Gen 3:17-19). (This is true irrespective of our view of how the early chapters of Genesis relate to contemporary scientific accounts of the earth's age and history—a controversial matter that I won't go into here.) This is "not the way it's supposed to be," and so we are justified in seeking solutions to these problems.

The fall also reminds us, however, that questions can be raised about all human endeavors, for sin and self-interest affect our search for solutions and how we apply them. Whenever we look at technology and its promises, we need to remember Gen 11 as well as Gen 1:1-2:3. Babel reminds us that humans can and do turn their technical and cultural expertise against God and God's purposes and seek to establish their own security and permanence in defiance of human finitude. The fall also reminds us that we can be self-interested, tending, as we do, to use God's blessings for selfish ends. So the questions always need to be asked: Who benefits? Who pays? There are limits to what we can and should do, because of both creaturely finitude and sinful excess. The nature of redemption and of God's restoration of all things also places limits on what we can and should do. Although death is God's enemy and will be defeated (Isa 25:7-8; cf. 1 Cor 15), it will not be defeated until "that day"; until then, we long for its ending and fight its coming, but always recognizing that this is a fight that we will lose. So too, fertility and the begetting of children seem not to be part of God's final purposes; they are a creational good, but they appear not to be a new-creational one (Isa 56:4-5; cf. Matt 22:30). That suggests to me that although it is appropriate to seek solutions to infertility, we should not let too much ride on it–certainly not our identity or sense of meaning and value.

Let's return to the question of reproductive cloning. The major issue here relates to the nature and context of reproduction: normal childbearing is a relational process of procreation. In the normal course of events, in order to have children, we must enter into a relationship with another person. Sexual intercourse is a component of that relationship and is itself essentially relational. Children are the result of that relational process–hence the older term "procreation," which suggests that as persons in relationships, we share God's creative activity in the bringing of a child into the world. If cloning (and IVF) were to be used instead, the bearing of children would be entirely removed from the relational realm. Indeed, for a woman in particular, no relationships at all would be needed in order to produce a child, except for austere "technologized" relationships with IVF technicians. If such were to happen, a richly relational procreative act between people would become a merely biological act of reproduction. On many grounds this would be at the very least an undesirable state of affairs. There are also questions that can and should be raised about the equity of such a procedure. In the foreseeable future, at least, such procedures might come at a prohibitive cost. The personal and relational costs of IVF alone are significant. The economic costs, especially for a new (not yet devised) procedure such as cloning, would be exorbitant, particularly if development costs are included. It seems to me that the question of "who benefits and at what cost" raises an insuperable obstacle to reproductive cloning. It is a procedure that would cost the community a great deal to satisfy a particular person's desire for a particular (kind of) child. Given the pressures on the health-care system, let alone the reality of global economic injustice, this is indefensible. (Of course, this important set of questions is applicable to more than cloning and should be brought to bear on many issues in [bio]technology, but that must await another occasion.)

The position in relation to therapeutic cloning seems to me absolutely clear. Wherein lies the problem with producing an embryo for "spare parts"? In this: the organism so produced would be a human person. This, of course, is a controversial claim. Some bioethicists, such as Peter Singer, argue that a human organism does not become a person until it develops personal qualities such as rationality and the ability to communicate. However, most of us feel, I believe correctly, that a newborn infant is a human person who should be nurtured rather than used for someone else's benefit. If I were to clone someone for the purpose of using the clone's organs for transplantation, however, I would be producing an infant who would be allowed to develop only to the point where his or her organs were sufficiently mature to be "harvested" and used. That infant would then die (in the case of, say, a liver or heart or lung transplant) or be forced, without his or her consent, to live with only one kidney.

Clearly, this would be the production of a human person as a means to someone else's end. Such an act violates all our moral intuitions regarding the care of human infants and our treatment of human persons. It flies in the face of the creational value of human beings, who, as those created in the image of God, can never be treated merely as the means to some other person's ends—a point that needs to be more generally born in mind (see Lev 19:18). Indeed, cloning for spare parts seems to me to be the bioethical equivalent of Babel: an act of human power seeking to overwhelm the limitations of human existence. It seeks to realize the eschatological state of the new heaven and earth here and now, and this in violation of both our limits and others' interests. It is also clearly unjust, both in global terms (again, the costs of such a procedure would be very high) and in relation to the individual clone. Now, lest you think I'm being an alarmist or dealing with the kind of bizarre scenarios that could only be dreamt up by science fiction authors or bioethicists, witness the birth of "savior siblings," whose parents specifically chose to have another child in order to provide a compatible donor for their sick child. That is a sci-fi author's dream come true. In these cases, of course, only the child's cord blood and bone marrow are on the line; even so, the child so produced was brought into being as a means to someone else's end—an act that seems fundamentally inconsistent with treating the child as a person.

An alternative would be to "harvest" the organ from the fetus at a suitable stage and then grow it artificially to maturity. Some would have fewer qualms about this, but still it requires that we produce embryos specifically for their potential benefit for others, which seems contrary to the nature of procreation (and perhaps the value of the fetus). This, of course, raises difficult questions, especially about the beginning of life, when can we say that a person "begins." I'm not persuaded that the Bible gives us a clear answer to this question (the standard texts, such as Exod 21:22-25 and Ps 139:13-16, do not directly address the issue of the beginnings of life and are not compelling evidence for the full humanity of the fetus); besides, it is one we that can put to one side in this debate, for such a use of cloning is unacceptable on other grounds. Questions of justice and the distribution of resources again provide an insuperable barrier to such technology. Further, if it is legitimate to raise questions about the impersonal nature of reproductive cloning and its conflict with the personal and relational nature of procreation, how much more problematic is using such a reproductive process for nonprocreative purposes?

If it were possible to "clone" individual organs—say, a kidney or a liver—these problems would not arise. There is no person produced, so there is no problem of a person being created, and then destroyed or impaired, simply as a means to another person's end. That, in a sense, is one possible use for a combination of stem cell and cloning technologies that might avoid some of the problems inherent in each. However, whole-person cloning is, for all the reasons I've mentioned, morally repugnant. Even in relation to single organ "cloning," however, questions of the control of technology and the justification of research arise. In a world of limited resources and unlimited needs and wants, what are the grounds by which research such as this is justified? Who says? Such questions must await another occasion. For now, it is clear that these and other biotechnologies open doors to new possibilities, many of them subject to serious question in light of the OT. Of course, judgments on matters such as these (and even some of the questions, such as those relating to benefits, costs, and justice) are based on the shape of the OT story and its picture of God, the world, and human community–its moral vision–rather than particular "proof texts." We need to think carefully about these possibilities and resist some of them in light of the moral vision of the OT, lest we become slaves of "the possible."

Isaiah 46 and the Critique of Idolatry

In closing, let's look at a striking example of the prophetic critique of idolatry. This, I hope to show, is a dangerous critique, a far cry from our (dare I say?) domesticated views of idolatry as an individualistic matter between God and us. It is a critique that lays bare the roots of our society, the soul of our culture. But before we get to that, it's important to deal with questions about the date of Isaiah and introduce the notion of "context of address" and its significance for interpreting Isa 40–55. Isaiah is a theologically rich book, one that has been described as giving the clearest outline of "gospel" that we find in the OT. It certainly features prominently in the NT's use of Scripture (matched only by the book of Psalms) and is familiar to Christians because of the way it articulates the messianic hope of the OT.

Isaiah is a large and complex book, much of which seems to speak to different times and circumstances in Israel's life. For this and other reasons many OT scholars have divided it into three sections, each of which is seen to have been produced at different times and to speak to different contexts. Many scholars speak of Isa 1–39 as Proto-Isaiah (or First Isaiah), largely the work of Isaiah of Jerusalem of the eighth century B.C., who spoke to Judah and Jerusalem (as well as Israel and other nations) during a period of economic prosperity but spiritual complacency. They describe Isa 40–55 as Deutero-Isaiah (or Second Isaiah), the work of an unidentified prophet during the exile, possibly located in Babylon, who spoke of God's turn from judgment to hope and restoration. The final section of the book, Isa 56–66, they call Trito-Isaiah (or Third Isaiah), which they see as the work of a group of disciples of Deutero-Isaiah in the postexilic period (from late sixth century on).

This group, it is theorized, edited the works of Proto- and Deutero-Isaiah and produced the sayings at the end of the book to address their own circumstances after the exile. The arguments for and against this viewpoint are beyond the scope of this book and are discussed in introductions and commentaries; more importantly, conclusions on its dating and authorship do not, in my opinion, materially affect our reading of the book, so I won't go into the debate here. What matters for our purposes is that Isa 40-55 speaks to Israel in exile, promising God's forgiveness of their sin, the end of their exile, the fall of Babylon, the rebuilding of Jerusalem, and their return home (see Isa 40; 45; 47; 54-55). The exilic context of address in this section of Isaiah is what matters to our reading of the book and these chapters in it.

This means that we need to grasp something of the history of Israel leading up to and including the exile if we are to grasp the meaning of Isa 40-55. We briefly examined the period up to the eighth century in the discussion of Micah in chapter 2 (see p. 80). From then on, Judah and Israel experienced almost unremitting decline. In fact, by 721 b.c. Israel was conquered by the Assyrian Empire and in 701 b.c. Judah, and in particular Jerusalem, barely escaped destruction at the hands of that same superpower. Between Hezekiah and Josiah, the two great reforming kings in Judah, came Manasseh, whose reign was one of apostasy and injustice (until his late repentance recorded in 2 Chr 33:10-17). Josiah's reforms, though significant, seemed to touch only the surface of Judah's political and religious life and could not avert the coming crisis, especially in light of his successors' failure to reform the nation. The result was exile, as proclaimed by Jeremiah and Ezekiel (and earlier by Micah and Isaiah [see, for instance, the generally neglected content of Isaiah's commission in Isa 6:11-13]) at the hands of Babylon, first in 597 and then finally in 587/6 b.c. Babylon had, by that time, subdued Assyria, previously the main player on the stage of international politics. Now Babylon subdued Judah, as the result of both God's judgment and geopolitical necessity, and with violence. Jerusalem was sacked, the temple destroyed, and the religious and political elite were either executed or taken into captivity in Babylon (see 2 Kgs 18-25). That is the context being addressed in Isa 40-55 and hence in Isa 46.

So, having recognized that this section of Isaiah speaks to Israel in exile, let's look at Isa 46 (especially vv. 1-7) in light of the experience of exile. To do that, let's for a moment use our imaginations and try to get a feel for what it may have been like for a captive from Judah to confront the realities of idolatry in Babylon. Picture the scene of the Babylonian New Year festival, the greatest event on the Babylonian religious and political calendar. The year is 560 b.c., the scene Babylon, the capital of the greatest empire the world had seen for centuries, the center of wealth, power, and control. And this, the New Year festival, is the celebration of its splendor. The streets leading to the great ziggurat temple are lined with people. It is a time of festival and color as the people of Babylon celebrate their power and the gods who guarantee it. As you stand in the crowd, waiting for the festal procession to pass you by, a roar goes up: "Marduk is king! Marduk is king!" Here they come: the priests attired in gorgeous costumes, displaying on their bodies the glory of their gods. The king Amel Marduk (called Evil-merodach in the ot; e.g., 2 Kgs 25:27; Jer 52:31) leads the procession, the physical embodiment of the triumph of their gods. They wind their way past the thronging crowds toward the great stepped temple that towers over all other buildings in this mighty city. The climax, which most people never see but everyone knows about, sees Marduk, the chief god of the Babylonian pantheon and guarantor of its power, reenthroned in his ziggurat temple. The cosmic order is reestablished, the earthly order reaffirmed. The gods are in their heaven, all is right with the world.

The sheer opulence and majesty of a religious procession such as this is hard for us in the secular, industrialized modern West to grasp. We tend to confine the excesses of our "religious" festivals to the mall and the marketplace. But if you've seen religious festivals elsewhere, it may be a bit easier. Some years ago I visited India with my family. I co-taught an intensive course at a theological college in Bangalore, and it seemed like a great opportunity for my daughters, then ages five, seven, and nine, to see another culture and get a small grasp of some of the realities of the world in which we live. At the end of our time we played tourist in Mysore, a town a little to the south. On the way home we got stuck in the kind of traffic jam only found in India. There was a festival going on—I can't remember which one—and hundreds of people were in procession following the statues of their gods. There was noise, color, food, fireworks, and people everywhere. The idols themselves were so bedecked with flowers and offerings that I couldn't tell if it was Shiva or Ganesha being worshipped. That's the kind of scene that we're trying to envision, but with this crucial addition: you are an Israelite, an exile in Babylon.

Imagine, then, the pomp, power, and grandeur of this spectacle, imagery that lies behind the language of Isa 46:1. This celebration is not an abstract religious phenomenon divorced from the realities of life and power in Babylon. Theirs was not a secular society. Marduk's enthronement was an important *political* act, for Marduk, and the arrangement of the pantheon associated with his rule over the other gods, was the guarantor of Babylonian political power (similar to what we saw earlier with the gods of Canaan). The political and religious importance of the festival in Babylon is seen in the crisis that occurred during the reign of the last true king of Babylon, Nabonidus (556-539 B.C.). A foreign conqueror, Cyrus the Persian, conquered Babylon, though he was welcomed as something of a liberator in the capital city (or at least, so he claimed). The OT remembers Cyrus as the ruler who effectively ended Israel's exile (see the Cyrus Cylinder on p. 209). Nabonidus was unusual for his time, being something of a religious "free thinker." This did not mean abandoning the gods of his ancestors—skepticism, let alone atheism, was rare in the ancient world—but it did mean granting supremacy to a god other than Marduk and relocating his capital away from the city of Babylon, the religious and political heart of the empire. His devotion to Sin (a moon god) meant that he refused to leave his new capital Tema (an oasis in the Arabian desert) to return to Babylon for the New Year festival—after all, this festival celebrated the supremacy of Marduk over other gods. He did leave his son and regent Belshazzar to act in his stead, but that was inadequate, and so the festival was cancelled. Without the king, and the symbolic mutual reinforcement of dynasty and deity, it could not go on. The festival, then, was both a religious and a political act. It aimed to represent and reinforce the power of Babylon and its gods.

Excerpts from the Cyrus Cylinder

He scanned and looked (through) all the countries, searching for a righteous ruler willing to lead him (i.e. Marduk) (in the annual procession). (Then) he pronounced the name of Cyrus (*Ku-ra-as*), king of Anshan, declared him (lit.: pronounced [his] name) to be(come) the ruler of all the world.

Marduk, the great lord, a protector of his people/worshipers, beheld with pleasure his (i.e. Cyrus') good deeds and his upright mind (lit.: heart) (and therefore) ordered him to march against his city Babylon.

Without any battle, he made him enter his town Babylon, sparing Babylon any calamity. He delivered into his (i.e. Cyrus') hands Nabonidus, the king who did not worship him (i.e. Marduk). All the inhabitants of Babylon as well as of the entire country of Sumer and Akkad, princes and governors (included), bowed to him (Cyrus) and kissed his feet, jubilant that he (had received) the kingship, and with shining faces. Happily they greeted him as a master through whose help they had come (again) to life from death (and) had all been spared damage and disaster, and they worshiped his (very) name.[1]

But you, remember, are an exiled Israelite. It is important here to pause and think about the interplay of religious, military, and political ideologies in the ancient world: there was a direct connection in popular imagination between the strength of a nation, its fate, and its gods. One nation's defeat of another was seen as the work of its gods, particularly its chief god (most ancient societies were polytheistic, worshipping a number of gods with their own hierarchies, power plays, and so on). It was a kind of cosmic "My dad's bigger than your dad" game. Babylon's supremacy over the surrounding nations and their defeat and incorporation into the Babylonian Empire were taken to indicate the supremacy of

---

[1] A. Leo Oppenheim, "Babylonian and Assyrian Historical Texts," in *Ancient Near Eastern Texts Relating to the Old Testament* (ed. J. B. Pritchard; 2d ed.; Princeton, N.J.: Princeton University Press, 1955), 315-16.

Marduk over the gods of defeated nations. If those gods had any further role to play, it was like the role that their people played in the empire: the gods of defeated nations were seen as vassals, submitting to their overlord, Marduk. So the pomp and circumstance of the New Year's festival serves to reinforce the power of your new masters and their gods and thus to declare the weakness of Yahweh. Yahweh no longer has a temple from which to rule; Yahweh no longer has a land over which to rule; Yahweh may not even have a people to rule over. Yahweh has been, it was thought, defeated by Marduk, just as Jerusalem was defeated by Babylon. If Marduk is king and his people triumphant, then Yahweh and Yahweh's people are nothing.

The temptation facing Israel in exile is all too real. Babylonian gods both symbolize and endorse Babylonian power, in which the Israelites are immersed in exile. The glories of these gods and their festivals represent the wealth, comfort, and security of this great world power. This is not just a matter of rival gods; at stake is an alternative system of values, rival objects of trust. What's more, that system seemed to have won—Babylon triumphant, Israel in chains—and the exiled Israelites were confronted daily with the symbols and realities of that power. Those exiles living in Babylon itself were at the center of this world power, amid the wealth, luxury, and power of those who embraced that system and enjoyed its benefits. This is the all-too-visible allure of Marduk—a tangible god with tangible benefits. What did Yahweh have to offer? The promise of Yahweh's invisible presence, but a destroyed temple; the challenge and hope of Yahweh's universal reign, but no king on the throne in Jerusalem; the promise of a return home, but the reality of exile. Babylon's values seem to work; their gods seem successful. Israel in exile is faced with the temptation to trust in this visible, seemingly successful system of power and control in the face of the call to trust in the promises of Yahweh. The danger is that Israel in exile would come to trust Babylon and its gods and the system of power and control that those gods represent. Israel would then be shaped by Babylon's values, not the Torah's, by Marduk's values, not Yahweh's—values of domination, elitism, and control, not mercy, justice, and trust. Then, no matter what God does for them, they would be forever in exile; wherever history takes them, they would never be free.

Yahweh, the loving, sovereign lord of Israel, is not willing to have the people of God lost in bondage. But how can Yahweh combat the allure of the idols? Yahweh must do so, for the sake of Israel and their future. But how? By exposing these idols for what they are: useless fictions. That is the aim of Isa 46. Yahweh, through the prophet, reveals the nature of the idols: they are "handmade" objects; and as for the function of the idols: they are "no-thing," powerless. Verses 6–7 present a scathing description of the process of making an idol–similar, if briefer, to what is found earlier in Isa 44:9–20. Idols are "manmade" deities. This is both a literal and a symbolic truth. The literal truth is fairly obvious, for every physical image that people worship (or, to be a little more generous, use to clarify their understanding of the divine and focus their worship) has been fashioned by a human being. Clearly, they are human constructs. This is equally true at a symbolic level, for all the images that we make in likeness of humans, birds, animals, and reptiles represent our cultural values and aspirations. The objects that we choose–the particular kinds of human persons, or the type and form of animal–are chosen because they signify something we value. They depict particular aspects of human nature, or ways of living and acting in society or the world, or powers in the world or our projects, or characteristics of society that we value and want to claim for ourselves or others. There is a certain reality, a concreteness, so to speak, to the idols; they are tangible expressions of underlying social realities and associated systems of power and control. In their embodiment of those characteristics that we value–power, control, beauty, luck, success, fertility–they come to represent and justify our social structures and systems (as seen in the Babylonian New Year festival). Ludwig Feuerbach's famous claim about religion is true of idols: they are gods made in our own image.

These idols are, however, lifeless and powerless: for all their beauty, for all the power of the symbols and the social realities that they represent, the idols are in fact nothing, they do nothing. This is the force of the sarcastic portrait of idols in Isa 46, especially vv. 1–2 and the end of v. 7. When the systems that created the idols collapse, there is nothing left to hold them up; when the people cry out in the rubble of a fallen social order, there is no answer. Their prayer goes unheard, for the very system that created and validated the idols (and in turn was validated by them) has fallen, and so have the idols (v. 1). There is no one to answer; when the nation is in crisis, there is no rescue (v. 7b). The captives are led away with their idols in tow (v. 2)–a potent image for Israel in exile. Indeed, in the striking imagery of Isa 46, the very festal procession that symbolized the power of Babylon and its gods is scattered in confusion. The language of bowing and stooping is normally used to describe the kind of awe-filled obeisance offered by a worshipper to a god; here, however, it is used with devastating irony against the idols. Rather than being the objects of veneration, the idols totter and cower in powerlessness. The gods that they represent cannot save even their own images, let alone the worshippers who created and depended upon them. Idol and worshipper are equally helpless when their system falls. So it is when the gods fail.

All of this is in stark contrast to the reality of Yahweh, the one, true and living God, as the rest of the passage makes plain. This God, Yahweh, is an active God, as Israel knows from their own history. Yahweh acts, Yahweh answers. Isaiah 46:3, 8–10 prove this from their own past; vv. 4, 11–13 promise it for their present and their future. Verses 3–4 are particularly powerful, for they specifically reverse the language of vv. 1–2: what the people have to do for their gods is what Yahweh, the one true God, has done and will do for Yahweh's people. English translations don't quite capture this, for the same Hebrew verbs used of the people carting around (excuse the pun!) their idols are used of Yahweh carrying his people. This God has not ceased to be God just because God's people are in exile. Yahweh has not ceased his commitment to Israel. The one who made them is the one who will carry them. Yahweh is not to be compared to foreign gods, for they are nothing and can do nothing. But Yahweh is the sovereign lord, the God who hears, answers, and acts. The reversal of imagery goes further, as seen in Yahweh's claim in v. 4: "I have made." Note the contrast with the idols of Babylon: the people of Babylon construct their gods, but the God of Israel constructs the people of God.

That claim has been substantiated in their past, as God's people are called here to remember (Isa 46:3, 9)–Yahweh has carried them from birth. And remembering their past includes exile, for this text is addressed to the remnant of Israel (v. 3), those who lived through the failure of the Israelite system, who survived the fall of Jerusalem, the destruction of the temple, and the end of the monarchy. But the fall of Jerusalem is not the fall of Yahweh; the destruction of the temple does not demolish God's power, and the end of the monarchy does not diminish God's sovereignty. The exile of the people of God is not the failure of God's power but rather its demonstration, for unlike the idols, God is not the projection of Israelite hopes, values, and aspirations. Yahweh is the creator, not the creation, of Israel. And their failure to live out the reality of Yahweh's system of values, their failure to live as those who truly trusted the one true and living God, brought about their end. It was an act of judgment, not an accident of history; it was a demonstration of Yahweh's sovereign power, not the victory of Marduk; it is the achievement, not the frustration, of Yahweh's purposes. Yahweh has not been silent; but has acted in history, both for and against Israel. This God is no human cultural construct. Just as Yahweh acted as judge in the past, so Yahweh will act as savior in the future. Whatever Cyrus himself might say about Marduk, it is Yahweh who has called Cyrus to achieve Yahweh's own purpose, restoring Yahweh's own people to their land (v. 11; cf. 44:24-28; 45:1-13).

This polemic against idols—the demonstration that Yahweh is unlike any human god—has a clear and practical purpose: to call the people to trust Yahweh in the present and the future. The call to trust is real. It involves trusting God alone, embracing God's system of values, living as those created by God, in line with God's purposes. An essential element in that call is the claim that the idols and the cultural systems that they embody and represent are, in the end, nothing. The gods of Babylon are not real, except as human constructs. But how does this square with Paul's statement in 1 Cor 10:14-22 that worshipping idols is tantamount to worshipping demons? Space here allows only a few brief observations on Paul. The cultural values and systems of power and control that idols represent and substantiate are more than human; they are also "principalities and powers," as Paul describes them in Eph 6:12. It is also worth noting that Paul shares Isaiah's perspective: in 1 Cor 8:1-13 he acknowledges that an idol is nothing at all in the world. How, then, does this work? Idols are nothing but the concrete expression of a culture's values and aspirations. Inasmuch as these are truly idolatrous, an expression of values and aspirations contrary to God and God's purposes, they are truly demonic. There is a kind of supernatural ecology; these demonic social values are inscribed on images that, though empty themselves, come to represent and empower those demonic forces. An idol constructs a sort of spiritual vacuum around these idolized values. But both the natural and supernatural worlds abhor a vacuum; something always rushes in to fill it. And if the one true God is written out of the image, what is left but the demonic? Now let's return to Isa 46, where the emphasis is on the nothingness of the idols, not the spiritual forces that rush in to fill the vacuum.

The biting sarcasm of Isa 46, its proclamation to Israel in exile of the nothingness of the idols, has been vindicated by history. Babylon fell, and so did its gods; Yahweh did set Israel free. Outside of museums, the Babylonian cultural system and all that it represented is gone. So are the gods that represented and supported it–there are few devotees of Marduk now. Truly, the idols are nothing. That's easy for us to say about the challenges that Israel faced in exile, but what about us? We too face the temptation of idolatry, and this text speaks powerfully to us in that temptation. We often think of idolatry in personal, even individualistic terms: someone might idolize a car that takes up an exorbitant amount of time and money, or a relationship that becomes all-consuming and interferes with faith, or money that subverts God's rightful position as lord and arbiter of life. That counts as idolatry and is to be condemned. But this text challenges us to look at idolatry also from a corporate and social point of view. It calls us to examine the power of the cultural forces arrayed against us and to consider the temptations that we face. For we, like Israel, are confronted by a foreign social system; we face alternative systems of values, rival objects of trust, and they too have their spectacle. We need to be honest, to recognize the power that they represent. Some are obvious, such as social power, wealth, and the desire for control; others are less obvious, such as the idea that technology has a solution to every problem, from communication to conception, or the view that fame is what counts. These are powerful forces, and we feel our weakness in the face of their power.

These are the gods of our culture: alternative systems of values, rival objects of trust, and they are embodied in the idols of our culture. As much as we enjoy popular music and cinema, we need to realize that the idols of stage and screen, inasmuch as they are embodiments of idolatrous cultural values, are idols. They embody what we value: wealth, success, popularity, and control. These are seen as the ways to power, the guarantees that we will make it in the world. So too is technology, which is increasingly becoming a means of controlling not just our environment but also our societies and our selves. You may not agree, but it seems to me that in Western culture personal technologies, or techniques of control, are invading every realm of our personal lives. This is also embodied in our celebrity idols, with their therapists and personal trainers. As Radiohead put it in the song "Creep," "I want to have control. I want a perfect body, I want a perfect soul." The desire for control, prosperity, success, and wealth extends to a demand for a pristine psyche and a sculptured body. Pop psychology preaches the myth of "closure" for all our wounds; it promises to root out all the attitudes and behaviors that stop us being healthy, wealthy, and wise. Diet and exercise programs and cosmetics (and cosmetic surgery) augment (or reduce) what is counted as physical imperfection, all in search of beauty and control over the self, its appearance, its destiny. There is even now a "Botox on the go" clinic half a block from Bloomingdale's in Manhattan, allowing walk-ins to get a Botox treatment in an hour. Perhaps the perfect fusion of these values is seen in speculation about creating "designer babies," whereby technology would be used to impose parental reflection of these idolatrous cultural values on the very bodies and intellects of their chosen children—children designed or selected to match standards of beauty and success determined by a previous generation's culture, thus enshrining it in the next generation. If that seems too fanciful, think of other cultures where even now prenatal screening is being used for sex selection—always in favor of boys, precisely as a result of cultural values that see boys as preferable to girls.

These values seem to work; their gods seem successful. But these gods, too, will fail. Many of us remember the "dotcom" crash, when, at least for a while, the idols of wealth and technological control tumbled. And they will fail in the end, as will our "personal technologies": plastic surgery, for all its advances, cannot forestall aging forever. As Radiohead put it in the song "Fake Plastic Trees": "He used to do surgery for girls in the eighties, but gravity always wins." So does death. Even the fittest, best product of psychotherapy, plastic surgery, and "body sculpting" will end up a corpse, no more than a sculptured *body.* Our technologies, our myths of control, cannot stand in the face of death and economic collapse. We may turn to them in our crises, but they cannot save, for our crises are the failure of the systems of value that we construct, the failure of the objects of our trust. And just as there was no true reality behind the gods of Babylon, so too there is no reality behind the gods of our culture. But still the myths persist, and they have a semblance of power, a surface appeal.

This is the context in which we live. We too live, so to speak, in the heart of imperial power, in the midst of the "success of the gods." We have wealth, we have control. We have technologies that can control our world, information, even ourselves. This is our festival of technology. There may be no parades as such, but there is real allure. It is easy for us to point the finger at the world outside the church, but we need to remember that Isa 46 addresses the people of God. And so we must ask ourselves, "What are our idolatries? What social values have led to the cultural captivity of Christians and the church?" We are immersed in an "alien cultural system." It is easy to become saturated with false values, and all too often we do. We too trust in wealth (if only we had more money, we could really do great things for God), in technology (if only we had a multimedia projector), and so on. None of these things are inherently bad, but still they are human cultural constructs. And when we take these human constructs and place our trust in them, we have created an idol. We construct such gods, but in the end they are silent. They are nothing, they do nothing. They answer no prayer, they cannot save. They are as empty and impotent as Marduk.

We need to face ourselves and, painful as it is, identify our idols and turn from them. We must confess and repent. But repentance doesn't mean just turning *from* the gods of this age; it involves turning *to* the one true and living God. We must look to the one true and living God, the one who made us, who shaped the people of God from the beginning, re-created them in Christ, and who draws us into God's future. We need to remember who this God is, what this God's values are and how those values are to shape us. In Yahweh we trust, and Yahweh's values we adopt. These values are seen most clearly in the person of Jesus, God the Son made flesh (there, if you like, is the true image of God; in that man's flesh, not in wood or stone). These are values not of wealth, power, technology, and control but rather of love and justice, of faithfulness no matter what. These are values in which the least and the lost are rescued and granted dignity and significance. This is the trust in which we work and wait. And when we do so, we trust the one, true, and living God, the God who is there, the God who is and who acts, the one who hears, who answers, who saves. Then we will come to see that, even when all systems fail, when the gods are silenced and fall, our God and our God's purposes stand.

LAST WORDS: ON FINDING A HOME IN A STRANGE LAND

Well, that's it. We're at the end of our journey—certainly a long journey, but I hope also a fruitful one. Let me remind you of where we've been. After an introduction to some of the issues that confront us as we approach the OT for moral guidance, we began in chapter 1 by looking at some of the theological and interpretive issues that underlie and inform our reading the Bible as God's word. I suggested that the OT is God's authoritative word and must be understood as human and divine communication, requiring that we understand each part of the Bible in light of it being a part of the whole. Christian ethics, in turn, needs to be governed by the narrative shape of Scripture and the relational perspective that arises out of it. We then turned, in chapter 2, to some of the basic skills required for biblical exegesis and their application to some of the kinds of texts that we find in the OT, using Lev 19:9-10; 2 Sam 11-12; Ps 24; Mic 6:6-8; and Eccl 11 as examples of how to understand the OT and bring it to bear on our lives and values. In chapter 3 we rehearsed the problematic practices of slavery, ritual cleanness, and holy war, noting that although problems and issues remain, we can see how these practices can be "rehabilitated" for Christians in light of their theological and social contexts. Chapter 4 returned to two key texts in the OT and Christian thought, Gen 1-3 (the creation story) and Deut 5:6-21 (the Ten Commandments), and sought to understand ways in which they shape Christian moral vision. Finally, in the present chapter, we used cloning and idolatry as examples of how we can "bring the Old Testament home."

I'm all too aware of the flaws, failings, and absences in this book. It contains nothing on Esther, a puzzlingly "godless" book that speaks profoundly to us and our circumstances; nothing on Chronicles, thus perpetuating its neglect in OT studies and the church; little on Proverbs, which has guided so many in the church with its practical wisdom and thought-provoking aphorisms; and frustratingly little on ethical theory, biblical theology, the grand sweep of Scripture, and how the Testaments relate to each other. Such flaws are, perhaps, inevitable. Christian ethics is too rich and complex and has too many interesting traditions and perspectives to be covered by one person and in one book; and the OT is more rich, complex, and diverse than any other body of literature that I know. For the sake of not making an already long book longer, I have deliberately set these, and many other matters, aside. For these sins of omission and, no doubt, many other errors and weaknesses that I have not confessed, I beg your pardon.

There are two emphases, however, for which I will not apologize, even though this may surprise and even irritate some people. The first is the emphasis on moral vision rather than specific rules or principles of behavior. As I have said repeatedly, the reason for my emphasizing this is that this is how I understand the OT. It is instruction (and other things) given to the people of God who have been saved by God's sovereign grace, in order that their lives might be shaped by God's character in response to God's grace. Such a vision informs our living as the people of God as well as theirs. The second is that the issues of justice and society have come up frequently in the discussion. You may have been surprised at the prominence of justice; we tend to see it as an ancillary concern, one to be addressed when the important "spiritual" issues have been resolved (which effectively means "never"). Micah and his greater successor Jesus tell us that justice, along with mercy and faithfulness, do indeed comprise an important spiritual issue. This is "core business" for Christians, not a peripheral matter. That is reflected in the prominence that such concerns have in the OT itself: OT ethics is much more about "social" ethics and justice than "personal" ethics. Thus, the OT serves to challenge our tendency to focus on the individual, personal, and "spiritual" over against the corporate, social, and "physical." Indeed, it challenges that dichotomy, forcing us to recognize that

God's vision for life in community is one that embraces all aspects of individual and corporate life.

I'll now end this apology and leave you to get on with the business of living as one of the people of God. But before I do, let me have one last word. My aim in all of this was not just to tell you a bunch of things about the OT and how we can use it as Christians in our ethical reflection. That is a good and valid aim, but mine is much broader. Indeed, all of this has been primarily a means to an end: to encourage, enable, and equip you to use the OT for yourself in your ethical reflection and to shape your Christian living. The point is that you should indeed "try this at home"; this book is more like a cooking or a craft workshop than a TV show such as *MythBusters*.

My daughters and I are fascinated with shows such as *MythBusters* and the way they put the most bizarre ideas to the test. I think that their favorite episode featured Jamie and Adam's attempt to see whether a ceiling fan could, in fact, decapitate someone. Nice work if you can get it. But, of course, at some point in the program they inevitably say, "Don't try this at home." Sure, Jamie, we were going to jump into a high-speed ceiling fan to see whether it will slit our throats! That's clearly one to leave alone. Other of their tests aren't quite so dangerous but are equally worth avoiding. I happened to see on one of these morning shows that so blight the television landscape a Scandinavian contortionist called Captain Frodo. His trick was to push a tennis racket—minus its strings, of course—over his head and then push the rest of his body through it. And the commentator said, "Don't try this at home." Sure, of course I'd try it—if they made tennis rackets with heads the size of hula hoops (but, given my luck and lack of limberness, even then I'd probably get stuck). Well, this book is altogether unlike the antics of *MythBusters* and Captain Frodo: the whole point of this exercise is so that you *can* try this at home. So, by all means, leave the whirring ceiling fans and unstrung tennis rackets alone. But please don't neglect the OT. For I hope and pray that this book has helped you start to find yourself at home in the strange land of the OT.

Appendix A

The Geek Zone
(a.k.a. Annotated Bibliography)

In the two appendices, we have sought to provide opportunities for additional exploration. In this first one, we have provided information about general works on the subject of OT ethics, listed in order of value (the most useful and accessible things first, followed by more technical works or those expressing alternative points of view. I will make some comments about the relative strengths and weaknesses of the sources, but I will not give detailed references to particular points or arguments unless I think that they are especially important, nor will I seek to be exhaustive. The aim of this "Geek Zone" is to give you some idea of where to go if you want to find out more about OT ethics in general; it is designed to be neither a detailed bibliography nor a series of endnotes.

General Works on the Old Testament and Ethics

The most obvious place to turn to find out more about the OT and Christian ethics is works focused on OT ethics. There are some excellent resources. Some, however, are quite technical and clearly aimed at a specialist audience of OT scholars or ethicists. As important as they are, and although many of them have shaped my thinking on these issues, I won't list them here and will only refer to them if they have bearing on a particular topic in a particular chapter.

Christopher J. H. Wright, *Living as the People of God: The Relevance of Old Testament Ethics* **(Leicester: Inter-Varsity Press, 1983)**

Wright's is the best, most accessible treatment of OT ethics that I have found. He deals with issues relating to how we should approach the OT, the ethical and theological shape of the OT (and the Bible) as a whole, and he covers most of the key themes of OT ethics. As I noted in the body of the book, I find his ethical/theological "triangle" very helpful for understanding the shape of the OT, and his idea of Israel as a paradigm to be a particularly fruitful notion. The main problems with the book are it doesn't demonstrate sustained engagement with particular texts, it is aimed at a (theological) college-level audience, and it is out of print, having been superseded by a much larger (and less accessible) work.

 Christopher J. H. Wright, *Old Testament Ethics for the People of God* **(Downers Grove, Ill.: InterVarsity Press, 2004)**

This is the newer, more detailed and in-depth version of his original, more accessible book. It is an excellent book, but the extra material makes it a much larger and less generally accessible work. Parts 1 and 2 largely correspond to *Living as the People of God*. Wright's work is one of the most obvious and important influences on my thinking on ethics; indeed, *Living as the People of God* first inspired and shaped my passion for OT ethics and its relevance for Christians. Parallels and reflections of his ideas are found throughout my book in relation both to the shape of OT ethics and Israel as a paradigm of God's purposes for the world (and the church), as well as specific topics such as economics, the land, and justice.

 Hetty Lalleman, *Celebrating the Law? Rethinking Old Testament Ethics* **(Milton Keynes: Paternoster, 2004)**

Lalleman aims to give a popular-level introduction to OT ethics. She surveys approaches to OT scholarship and OT ethics and presents her own framework, largely drawn (as is mine) from the work of Christopher Wright, before applying it to particular cases, such as food laws, warfare, and so on. Although she covers territory similar to what I cover, her approach is more theme- than text-driven, and her argument, in my view, isn't as accessible or focused as it could be. Nevertheless, it is a useful book.

Bruce Birch, *Let Justice Roll Down: The Old Testament, Ethics, and Christian Life* (Louisville: Westminster John Knox, 1991)

Birch gives a very good outline of the ethical witness of the OT from a moderately critical point of view. That is, he does not adopt a classically evangelical perspective on the authority of the Bible, and so he criticizes some OT texts and traditions (such as those dealing with the Canaanite conquest) as falling short of an independently determined theological and ethical ideal in a manner alien to the evangelical tradition. Nonetheless, it is well worth exploring his canonically driven reading of the OT and its relevance to Christian living and critically appropriating insights from it.

Waldemar Janzen, *Old Testament Ethics: A Paradigmatic Approach* (Louisville: Westminster John Knox, 1994)

Janzen is a North American Mennonite OT scholar, so he brings an interesting and valuable perspective to OT ethics. His understanding of "paradigm" is quite different from Wright's, and I'm not persuaded that all of his paradigms and their related stories work in the way or as well he thinks they do. Nonetheless, his is an important voice calling us to recognize the value of narrative in OT ethics.

Walter Kaiser Jr., *Toward Old Testament Ethics* (Grand Rapids: Zondervan, 1983)

Kaiser, I must confess, is not my favorite evangelical OT scholar, nor is this, in my view, the most useful book on OT ethics. He does have a sustained focus on the OT in its historical context, but his exegesis tends to be conservative, and his ethics is strongly principle-driven and naively absolutist. Although I don't find his writing style engaging, he does present a fairly comprehensive treatment of OT ethics from a particular conservative perspective.

John Barton, *Ethics and the Old Testament* (2d ed.; London: SCM, 2002)

Barton is a leading OT scholar who has had a sustained interest in ethics and the OT. He is clearly not an evangelical scholar, seeing much in the OT to criticize theologically and ethically. In his view, the OT is valuable but limited in its application to our circumstances, in part because much of it is flawed or deeply alien to us. In this respect, I find both his exegesis and his hermeneutics unpersuasive. Nonetheless, he raises thought-provoking questions and offers many useful insights, especially in relation to the importance of narrative as a moral resource.

 Cyril Rodd, *Glimpses of a Strange Land: Studies in Old Testament Ethics* (Edinburgh: T&T Clark, 2001)

This is the least helpful of all the books listed here, because of its intended academic audience and its perspective. Rodd, in fact, spends most of the book explaining why there is no such thing as *an* ethics of the OT, and that where an ethics can be determined it must be considered largely irrelevant or even counterproductive for Christians. He believes that there are numerous contradictions and inconsistencies in the ethical teaching of the OT, and that the most we can say is that it speaks with many voices. Moreover, OT ethics is so deeply imbued with ideas of purity, patriarchal values, and ancient ideas of honor that it is almost entirely alien to us and our circumstances. You might notice, however, the echoes of his title in mine. I specifically chose the title *At Home in a Strange Land* in contrast to his unnecessarily (and unjustifiably) negative view of the OT and its ethical value for Christians. His book is of value, however, inasmuch as it expresses from an academic perspective many of the common negative attitudes toward the OT that I've found among Christians.

General Introductions to the Old Testament

If you want to understand the OT and its relevance for Christians, it is useful to do a bit of background reading in the OT and its historical and cultural context. This is where surveys and introductions to the OT come in handy. These works deal with issues of genre, background, and so on, relevant to the specific texts and topics that I cover in chapter 3 onward. Once again, I will list them in order of accessibility and general usefulness and make some general comments about them.

John H. Hill and Andrew E. Walton, *Old Testament Today: A Journey from Original Meaning to Contemporary Significance* (Grand Rapids: Eerdmans, 2004)

This is an excellent popular-level introduction to the ᴏᴛ, its context, contents, and significance, dealing with both the main storyline and many of the details of the ᴏᴛ. It does as its title says: each major section of the book (Pentateuch, Historical Books, Prophets, Wisdom literature, and Psalms) deals with original meaning (including some background in ANE history where relevant), building contexts and contemporary significance. Of course, I do not agree with the authors on all points of hermeneutics, exegesis, or application, but this is a fine volume and a good place to start. It will give you a good feel for the ᴏᴛ as literature as well as many of the historical and cultural background issues that will enrich your understanding of the ᴏᴛ and enable you to make connections with your faith and life. It is also an attractive volume, with numerous charts and color illustrations.

 John Drane, *Introducing the Old Testament* (Oxford: Lion, 1987)

This too is a good popular-level introduction to the ᴏᴛ. It is arranged in two main sections, one dealing with the main historical periods of the ᴏᴛ, the other with its main themes. This has the virtue of a clear and coherent structure, but it means that you won't be given as clear and consistent an introduction to a particular book or body of literature as you will find in other introductions.

 Gordon D. Fee and Douglas Stuart, *How to Read the Bible Book by Book: A Guided Tour* (Grand Rapids: Zondervan, 2002)

As its title suggests, this book is more about orienting you to each biblical book as literature than providing a classical introduction such as the others in this section. It covers the whole Bible, not just the ᴏᴛ, and so it is more general in its treatment and much briefer than the other books listed here. As is generally the case, I don't agree with the authors on every point (for instance, their particular take on the theological structure of the Psalter). Nonetheless, this is a very helpful book.

Raymond B. Dillard and Tremper Longman III, *An Introduction to the Old Testament* (Leicester: Apollos, 1995)

This is an excellent college-level introduction. It focuses on literary and theological analysis but also deals with major lines of ot scholarship and makes some contemporary connections. After a brief general introduction it goes through the ot book by book in its (English, Protestant) canonical order.

 Andrew E. Hill and John H. Walton, *A Survey of the Old Testament* (2d ed.; Grand Rapids: Zondervan, 2000)

This book (by the same authors as *Old Testament Today*) is a more classical ot survey aimed at entrance-level theological students. It articulates an evangelical point of view and covers the main elements of such a survey, including historical background, organization of contents, and themes, and it does so with respect to each book of the ot (again, in order of the English, Protestant Bible).

 William LaSor, David Hubbard, and Frederic Bush, *Old Testament Survey* (2d ed.; Grand Rapids: Eerdmans, 1996)

This is another good evangelical introduction to the ot, which focuses on historical issues but also gives a good orientation to the content and ideas of each book.

 Gordon Wenham, *Exploring the Old Testament, Volume 1: A Guide to the Pentateuch* (Exploring the Bible; Downers Grove, Ill.: InterVarsity Press, 2002)

Philip Satterthwaite and Gordon McConville, *Exploring the Old Testament, Volume 2: A Guide to the Historical Books* (Exploring the Bible; Downers Grove, Ill.: InterVarsity Press, 2007)

Ernest Lucas, *Exploring the Old Testament, Volume 3: A Guide to the Psalms and Wisdom Literature* (Exploring the Bible; Downers Grove, Ill.: InterVarsity Press, 2003)

Gordon McConville, *Exploring the Old Testament, Volume 4: A Guide to the Prophets* (Exploring the Bible; Downers Grove, Ill.: InterVarsity Press, 2002)

This series of four books is the best and most comprehensive introduction to the OT and its diverse literature currently available. It is aimed at entrance-level theological students, and part of its purpose is to orient students to the disciplines, tools, and traditions of OT scholarship. This means that some of the discussion in these volumes will be of less interest and value than that in, say, *Old Testament Today*. Nonetheless, these volumes give an excellent guide to issues of genre, context, interpretation, and theological themes. They comprise a very helpful reference tool.

 William Dumbrell, *The Faith of Israel: A Theological Survey of the Old Testament* (2d ed.; Grand Rapids: Baker, 2002)

This is, as its title states, a theological introduction to the OT. As such, it is aimed primarily at theological students and deals with content and themes rather than background issues. With that in mind, you will find this to be a very good and relatively brief guide to major theological themes of the OT from a (Reformed) evangelical perspective.

 Bruce Birch, Walter Brueggemann, Terence Fretheim, and David Petersen, *A Theological Introduction to the Old Testament* (Nashville: Abingdon, 1999)

This, as the title states, is another theological introduction to the OT. This one is more detailed than Dumbrell's and also deals with the OT from a looser, canonical-narrative point of view. It also does not present a consistently evangelical perspective on the texts, but it is quite interesting for its insights in the connection between sociological, canonical, and theological readings of the text.

GENERAL WORKS ON CHRISTIAN ETHICS

I haven't come across many introductions to Christian ethics that I find to be outstanding.

 Arthur F. Holmes, *Ethics: Approaching Moral Decisions* (Downers Grove, Ill.: InterVarsity Press, 1984)

Holmes deals primarily with philosophical ethics and a Christian take on it. This is probably the most accessible introduction to philosophical ethics that I have found, and it provides some good reflections on a few practical issues.

Kyle Fedler, *Exploring Christian Ethics: Biblical Foundations for Morality* (Louisville: Westminster John Knox, 2006)

This is an excellent general introduction to different theories of ethics and the general shape of biblical ethics. He deals with some basic interpretive issues and discusses Genesis, Torah, and the prophets as well as Jesus and Paul. His discussion is, in general, clear and accessible, and he makes some interesting points of application.

 Stanley Grenz, *The Moral Quest: Foundations of Christian Ethics* (Leicester: Apollos, 1997)

Grenz was an interesting and fruitful evangelical theologian and ethicist. This book, as the title suggests, looks at theoretical and methodological issues in Christian ethics more than particular issues. It is also pitched at a relatively well-informed audience. He sees love as at the heart of Christian ethics, and though I agree, I believe that there are other key elements (as I note in chapter 2). Nonetheless, this is a good general account of a Christian ethical theory.

 John Stott and John Wyatt, *Issues Facing Christians Today* (ed. Roy McCloughry; 4th ed.; Grand Rapids: Baker, 2006)

This is predominantly issues-driven rather than dealing with the biblical and theological framework of Christian ethics. Nonetheless, it is a useful resource.

 Michael Hill, *The How and Why of Love: An Introduction to Evangelical Ethics* (Kingsford, New South Wales: Matthias Media, 2002)

Hill outlines Christian ethics from the perspective of a gospel-centered biblical worldview. As the title suggests, he sees the center of Christian ethics as love. I agree, but as I argue in chapter 2, this needs to be supplemented by justice and faithfulness. I also disagree with his conclusions on some issues. Still, this is a good general introduction to ethics.

 Mark Worthing, *When Choice Matters: An Introduction to Christian Ethics* (Millswood, South Australia: Pantaenus, 2004)

Worthing is an Australian Lutheran theologian whose ethical theory reflects a Lutheran dichotomy between law and gospel and a corresponding disparagement of the OT's ethical significance that I find theoretically flawed and practically unhelpful. Even so, he is a clear thinker, his book is accessible, and he covers an interesting range of topics.

David Atkinson and David Field, eds., *New Dictionary of Christian Ethics and Pastoral Theology* (Leicester: Inter-Varsity Press, 1995)

This is, strictly speaking, a resource for academics and theological students. Consequently, some of the articles are quite technical and heavy going. However, it does have some excellent general survey essays at the start, and many of the treatments of particular topics provide insightful introductions to key ethical issues. It's worth encouraging your pastor to buy it (and then borrowing it freely!).

Norman L. Geisler, *Christian Ethics: Options and Issues* (Grand Rapids: Baker, 1989)

Geisler is not my favorite thinker in this or any other area. His view of Christian ethics is absolutist and focuses on rules for behavior. He does recognize that there are higher rules that take precedence over the lower; nonetheless, his view is strongly rule-driven in a way that I don't believe does justice to the nature of Christian ethics. His exegesis and application of the biblical text is often flawed. He adopts a conservative viewpoint on most disputed matters. Nonetheless, he does survey a range of viewpoints and discuss a number of important ethical issues.

Kerby Anderson, *Christian Ethics in Plain Language* (Nashville: Nelson, 2005)

Anderson takes a line similar to Geisler's on the substantive issues. His moral theory is driven more by principles than by rules, but in practice his views are very similar to Geisler's.

Appendix B

Further Travels in the Geek Zone (a.k.a. For Further Reading)

In this second appendix, I provide references for specific topics covered in each chapter. Where I refer to a work that I have previously mentioned, I simply note the author (and title if necessary) rather than listing the details again.

Chapter 1: Equipment for the Journey

 Marcion

A brief and helpful outline of Marcion's views is given in Bruce Shelley, *Church History in Plain Language* (2d ed.; Dallas: Word, 1995), 62-64.

 Theonomism (or the Christian Restoration Movement)

For an outline and defense of the theonomist position, see Greg L. Bahnsen, "The Theonomic Reformed Approach to Law and Gospel," in *The Law, the Gospel, and the Modern Christian: Five Views* (ed. Wayne G. Strickland; Grand Rapids: Zondervan, 1993), 93-143. For a much more detailed account, see Greg L. Bahnsen, *Theonomy in Christian Ethics* (2d ed.; Phillipsburg, N.J.: Presbyterian & Reformed, 1984). For criticisms and alternatives, see the other essays in Strickland, ed., *The Law, the Gospel, and the Modern Christian;* and Christopher J. H. Wright, *Old Testament Ethics for the People of God* (Leicester: Inter-Varsity Press, 2004), ch. 12 (esp. 403-8).

HERMENEUTICS

There is no one book that gives a good, accessible introduction to hermeneutics. A good starting place, however, is Elmer Dyck, ed., *The Act of Bible Reading* (Downers Grove, Ill.: InterVarsity Press, 1996). Also useful, though a more technical collection of essays on the theory of interpretation, is Roger Lundin, ed., *Disciplining Hermeneutics: Interpretation in Christian Perspective* (Leicester: Apollos, 1997). Helpful discussions of the theory and practice of interpretation are found in William Klein, Craig Blomberg, and Robert Hubbard, *Introduction to Biblical Interpretation* (Dallas: Word, 1993); and, more technically, Grant Osborne, *The Hermeneutical Spiral: A Comprehensive Guide to Biblical Interpretation* (Downers Grove, Ill.: InterVarsity Press, 2006).

 THE BIBLE AND GOD SPEAKING TO US

What I have presented is a version of what is called a "speech-act" approach to texts, with interpretations drawn, as I've noted, from the work of Nicholas Wolterstorff. He discusses these ideas in a number of places, the briefest and most accessible being his essay in Roger Lundin, ed., *Disciplining Hermeneutics: Interpretation in Christian Perspective* (Leicester: Apollos, 1997). The most complete is found in a book-length treatment of the issue. It is written by a philosopher for philosophers and theologians and so is at times quite dense and closely argued, and I disagree with his conclusions on a few matters, including the canonical function of the psalms. Nonetheless, it is the best treatment of these issues that I have found. See Nicholas Wolterstorff, *Divine Discourse: Philosophical Reflections on the Claim That God Speaks* (Cambridge: Cambridge University Press, 1993).

 THE BIBLE AND THE STORY OF GOD AND THE WORLD

For a good outline of the "grand narrative" of Scripture, see Craig Bartholomew and Michael Goheen, *The Drama of Scripture: Finding Our Place in the Biblical Story* (Grand Rapids: Baker, 2004).

One idea central to the story—namely, that the world is "not the way it's supposed to be"—is brilliantly explored by Cornelius Plantinga in the book of the same name. See Cornelius Plantinga

Jr., *Not the Way It's Supposed to Be: A Breviary of Sin* (Grand Rapids: Eerdmans, 1995).

The role of the story of God's community in Christian theology is discussed from the point of view of systematic theology in Stanley Grenz, *Theology for the Community of God* (2d ed.; Grand Rapids: Eerdmans, 2000).

The questions of particularity, election, and God's missional purposes for the world are explored in Christopher J. H. Wright, *Old Testament Ethics for the People of God* (Leicester: Inter-Varsity Press, 2004); and Richard Bauckham, *The Bible and Mission: Christian Witness in a Postmodern World* (Carlisle: Paternoster, 2003).

The idea of *shalom* in the Bible and contemporary church life and is explored in Walter Brueggemann, *Living Toward a Vision: Biblical Reflections on Shalom* (2d ed.; New York: United Church Press, 1982). Although some of his reflections on culture are dated (by over twenty years), and I don't agree with all of his methods or conclusions, much of his discussion is both challenging and insightful. The best brief articulation of *shalom* that I have found is in Nicholas Wolterstorff, *Until Justice and Peace Embrace* (Grand Rapids: Eerdmans, 1983; esp. 69–72), which also deals nicely with its connections with Christian engagement with the world.

The three dimensions of ethics that I mentioned–principles, character, and consequences–are the focus of deontological, virtue, and teleological ethical theories respectively. Good discussions of these matters can be found in any decent textbook on Christian ethics, such as Arthur F. Holmes, *Ethics: Approaching Moral Decisions* (Downers Grove, Ill.: InterVarsity Press, 1984). I have taken the AAA and CCC frameworks from Gordon Preece and Graham Cole, former colleagues of mine at Ridley.

CHAPTER 2: GETTING GOING

 ### GENRE AND BIBLICAL INTERPRETATION

Good general discussions of genre in the Bible can be found in the OT introductions and the books on hermeneutics listed above. Another useful book on genre and biblical exegesis in general is Gordon D. Fee and Douglas Stuart, *How to Read the Bible for All*

Its Worth (3d ed.; Grand Rapids: Zondervan, 2003). I find their approach rather mechanical at times, giving the impression that following the right method or principles will give assured and definitive conclusions. I also strongly disagree with their claim that narrative has no normative value (as discussed in chapter 3 and below).

🌳 LAW (TORAH): LEVITICUS 19:9-10

Good discussions of Torah (law) can be found in the OT introductions listed above, particularly in Christopher J. H. Wright, *Living as the People of God: The Relevance of Old Testament Ethics* (Leicester: Inter-Varsity Press, 1983), ch. 7; idem, *Old Testament Ethics for the People of God* (Leicester: Inter-Varsity Press, 2004); and Bruce Birch, *Let Justice Roll Down: The Old Testament, Ethics, and Christian Life* (Louisville: Westminster John Knox, 1991), ch. 5. Once again, my view of OT law as shaping a community relies heavily on the detailed work of Wright.

For further information on ANE law codes, see John Walton, *Ancient Israelite Literature in Its Cultural Context* (Grand Rapids: Zondervan: 1989), chs. 3-4; and the classical reference work J. B. Pritchard, ed., *Ancient Near Eastern Texts Relating to the Old Testament* (2d ed.; Princeton, N.J.: Princeton University Press: 1955), 159-206.

Wright, Birch, and Barton argue for the distinctiveness of OT legal material and its shaping of a unique community compared with ANE law codes and the societies that produced them. Rodd disagrees with this analysis, seeing that there is nothing particularly unique about OT law compared to ANE codes (see, e.g., Cyril Rodd, *Glimpses of a Strange Land: Studies in Old Testament Ethics* [Edinburgh: T&T Clark, 2001], ch. 14 [on the poor]). The evidence and the discussions by the aforementioned authors fairly plainly prove him wrong. The relationship between Israel and surrounding culture is explored in J. P. M. Walsh, *The Mighty from Their Thrones: Power in the Biblical Tradition* (Philadelphia: Fortress, 1987). His analysis arises, in part, from a particular, and controversial, reconstruction of the development of Israel and of OT literature, and his practical conclusions are rather too quietistic to adequately account for the biblical literature. Nonetheless, his discussion of the revolutionary significance of Israel's religious and political vision is stimulating and instructive.

For more on the book of Leviticus, see the general introductions listed above. An excellent, if now somewhat older, commentary that presents a helpful outline of the theology of Leviticus is Gordon Wenham, *The Book of Leviticus* (New International Commentary on the Old Testament; Grand Rapids: Eerdmans, 1979). Also good is John Hartley, *Leviticus* (Word Biblical Commentary; Dallas: Word, 1992); as is Derek Tidball, *The Message of Leviticus* (Leicester: Inter-Varsity Press, 2005), which, though brief, has good discussions of the law and its role in Christian ethics. A technical but fascinating treatment from a leading Jewish scholar is Jacob Milgrom, *Leviticus 17–22* (Anchor Bible; New York: Doubleday, 2000) (see esp. 1623–30). Milgrom offers an interesting discussion of gleaning in Jewish tradition that mandates one-sixtieth as the minimum that should be left in the field for the poor.

The land and its significance for OT theology, politics, and ethics are discussed in Christopher J. H. Wright, *Living as the People of God: The Relevance of Old Testament Ethics* (Leicester: Inter-Varsity Press, 1983), chs. 3–4; idem, *Old Testament Ethics for the People of God* (Leicester: Inter-Varsity Press, 2004), chs. 3–6; and in the classic study by Walter Brueggemann, *The Land: Place as Gift, Promise and Challenge in Biblical Faith* (Philadelphia: Fortress, 1977).

For a biblical theology framework on issues of wealth and poverty, see Craig Blomberg, *Neither Poverty nor Riches: A Biblical Theology of Material Possessions* (Leicester: Apollos, 1999). He makes some good points and certainly combats the rampant materialism of Western culture; however, he presents little by way of a structural analysis of our societies and their values.

For a more general justification of Christian engagement on behalf of the poor, as well as practical suggestions for action, see Dewi Hughes with Matthew Bennett, *God of the Poor: A Biblical Vision of God's Present Rule* (Carlisle: OM Publishing, 1998); Graham Gordon, *What If You Got Involved? Taking a Stand against Social Injustice* (Carlisle: Paternoster, 2003); Tim Chester, *Good News to the Poor: Sharing the Gospel through Social Involvement* (Leicester: Inter-Varsity Press, 2004); or visit the Micah Challenge website (http://www.micahchallenge.org).

NARRATIVE: 2 SAMUEL 11-12

Gordon Fee and Douglas Stuart's understanding of narrative is found in their chapters on OT narrative and Acts in *How to Read the Bible for All Its Worth* (3d ed.; Grand Rapids: Zondervan, 2003). In the first edition of their book (1982) they state that their driving assumption in reading narrative is that "*unless Scripture explicitly tells us we must do something, what is merely narrated or described can never function in a normative way*" (97, italics in the original). They qualify this in the third edition: "*Unless Scripture explicitly tells us we must do something, what is only narrated or described does not function in a normative (i.e. obligatory) way–unless it can be demonstrated on other grounds that the author intended it to function in this way*" (118-19, italics in the original). Nonetheless, this is a minimal qualification, as they repeat the principles for interpreting OT narrative from the first edition, including "An Old Testament narrative usually does not directly teach a doctrine" and "An Old Testament narrative usually illustrates a doctrine or doctrines taught propositionally elsewhere" (78 [1982]; 108 [2003]). As they acknowledge elsewhere, narrative is in fact crucial for both the theological and ethical shape of the Bible–think, for a moment, of Exodus and the Gospels. I understand the motive for their claims about narrative, but I think that it needs to be reframed. A much more helpful, if less accessible, approach to ethics and narrative is Gordon Wenham, *Story as Torah: Reading the Old Testament Ethically* (Edinburgh: T&T Clark, 2000).

For a more detailed outline and defense of the history of Israel, see Iain Provan, V. Philips Long, and Tremper Longman III, *A Biblical History of Israel* (Louisville: Westminster John Knox, 2003). They specifically outline and counter more recent negative depictions of the historical value of the OT and its narrative.

The most interesting and engaging work on the books of Samuel is John Goldingay, *Men Behaving Badly* (Carlisle: Paternoster, 2000). I don't agree with all of his interpretations, but this book is probably the single best work available at a more popular level. Other useful commentaries are Joyce Baldwin, *1 and 2 Samuel* (Leicester: Inter-Varsity Press, 1989); Mary Evans, *1 and 2 Samuel* (New International Biblical Commentary; Peabody, Mass.: Hendrickson, 2000); idem, *The Message of Samuel* (Leicester: Inter-Varsity, 2004); Robert Gordon, *I & II Samuel* (Grand Rapids: Zondervan, 1986);

Walter Brueggemann, *First and Second Samuel* (Interpretation; Louisville: John Knox, 1990).

For an interesting reading of David's story from the perspective of "virtue ethics" (i.e., looking at the Bible, especially narratives, for what they tell us about moral character and its formation and deformation), see Richard Bowman, "The Complexity of Character and the Ethics of Complexity: The Case of King David," in *Character and Scripture: Moral Formation, Community, and Biblical Interpretation* (ed. William P. Brown; Grand Rapids: Eerdmans, 2002), 73-97. I find it interesting that he states that David, in "taking" Bathsheba, "sexually assaults" her, a crime that is then precisely mirrored in Amnon's rape of Tamar (73-74). He also nicely engages with the realities of human complexity as shown in David's story and shows us both the realism of biblical narratives and their portrayal of characters such as David and their ethical value for us.

🌳 POETRY: PSALM 24

For more on the book of Psalms, see Walter Brueggemann, *Worship in Ancient Israel: An Essential Guide* (Nashville: Abingdon, 2005); Tremper Longman III, *How to Read the Psalms* (Downers Grove, Ill.: InterVarsity Press, 1988); J. Clinton McCann Jr., *A Theological Introduction to the Book of Psalms: The Psalms as Torah* (Nashville: Abingdon, 1993); James Mays, *The Lord Reigns: A Theological Handbook to the Psalms* (Louisville: Westminster John Knox, 1994); and Philip Johnston and David Firth, *Interpreting the Psalms: Issues and Approaches* (Leicester: Apollos, 2005). The best entry-level commentary is Craig Broyles, *Psalms* (New International Biblical Commentary; Peabody, Mass.: Hendrickson, 1999). Other good commentaries include James Luther Mays, *Psalms* (Interpretation; Louisville: John Knox, 1994); J. Clinton McCann, "Psalms," in *The New Interpreter's Bible* (ed. Leander Keck; 12 vols.; Nashville: Abingdon, 1996), 4:639-1280; and Gerald Wilson, *Psalms Volume 1* (The NIV Application Commentary; Grand Rapids: Zondervan, 2002). See also J. Clinton McCann Jr., "'The Way of Righteous' in the Psalms: Character Formation and Cultural Crisis," in *Character and Scripture: Moral Formation, Community, and Biblical Interpretation* (ed. William P. Brown; Grand Rapids: Eerdmans, 2002), 135-49.

PROPHETS: MICAH 6:6-8

The best entry-level commentary on Micah is Elizabeth Achtemeier, *Minor Prophets I* (New International Biblical Commentary; Peabody, Mass.: Hendrickson, 1996). Also quite good are David Prior, *The Message of Joel, Micah and Habakkuk* (Leicester: Inter-Varsity Press, 1988); and David Baker, T. Desmond Alexander, and Bruce Waltke, *Obadiah, Jonah and Micah* (Leicester: Inter-Varsity Press, 1988). Other useful but more technical commentaries include Leslie Allen, *The Books of Joel, Obadiah, Jonah, and Micah* (New International Commentary on the Old Testament; Grand Rapids: Eerdmans, 1976); William Brown, *Obadiah through Malachi* (Westminster Bible Companion; Louisville: Westminster John Knox, 1996); Bruce Waltke, "Micah," in *The Minor Prophets* (ed. Thomas E. McComiskey; Grand Rapids: Baker, 1993), 2:591–764; and James Luther Mays, *Micah* (Old Testament Library; London: SCM, 1976).

For information on the Micah Network and the Micah challenge, see

http://www.micahchallenge.org.au

http://www.micahchallenge.org

http://www.micahnetwork.org

For more on the UN Millennium Development Goals, see

http://www.un.org/millenniumgoals

http://www.makepovertyhistory.com.au

http://www.makepovertyhistory.org

 WISDOM: ECCLESIASTES 11

Good general introductions to wisdom are found in Graeme Goldsworthy, *Gospel and Wisdom* (Exeter: Paternoster, 1987); Roland Murphy, *The Tree of Life: An Exploration of Biblical Wisdom Literature* (2d ed.; Grand Rapids: Eerdmans, 1990).

The best entry-level work on Ecclesiastes is found in an excellent volume on five neglected OT books: Barry Webb, *Five Festal Garments: Christian Reflections on The Song of Songs, Ruth, Lamentations, Ecclesiastes and Esther* (Leicester: Apollos, 2000). Other useful commentaries include Roland Murphy and Elizabeth Huwiler, *Proverbs, Ecclesiastes, Song of Songs* (New International Biblical Commentary; Peabody, Mass.: Hendrickson, 1999); Ellen F. Davis, *Proverbs, Ecclesiastes, and the Song of Songs* (Westminster Bible Companion; Louisville: Westminster John Knox, 2000); Kathleen Farmer, *Who Knows What Is Good? A Commentary on the Books of Proverbs and Ecclesiastes* (The International Theological Commentary on the Old Testament; Grand Rapids: Eerdmans, 1991); and J. A. Loader, *Ecclesiastes: A Practical Commentary* (Text and Interpretation; Grand Rapids: Eerdmans, 1986).

The Crenshaw quotation is from James Crenshaw, *Ecclesiastes* (Old Testament Library; London: SCM, 1988), 53. Longman's thesis is outlined in Raymond B. Dillard and Tremper Longman III, *An Introduction to the Old Testament* (Leicester: Apollos, 1995), ch. 18; and in Tremper Longman III, *The Book of Ecclesiastes* (New International Commentary on the Old Testament; Grand Rapids: Eerdmans, 1998).

For an interesting discussion of the traditional cardinal virtues—wisdom, discipline, prudence, temperance—in the book of Proverbs in contrast to our selfish, acquisitive, destructive, market-driven consumerist culture, see Ellen F. Davis, "Preserving Virtues: Renewing the Tradition of the Sages," in *Character and Scripture: Moral Formation, Community, and Biblical Interpretation* (ed. William P. Brown; Grand Rapids: Eerdmans, 2002), 183-201.

CHAPTER 3: AVOIDING PITFALLS, HACKING THROUGH THE JUNGLE

 SLAVERY

General discussions of slavery can be found in the books on OT ethics noted above.

For information on slavery and how you can take action, see

http://www.freetheslaves.net

http://www.notforsalecampaign.org

Many organizations, such as World Vision, run programs aimed at supporting children at risk of being trafficked as slaves or into the "sex industry." For details of one such program, see

http://www.worldvision.com.au/childrescue

Let me indulge here in a brief technical discussion on Exod 21:21. The translation of this verse is a tricky matter, and one with some significance. If the NRSV is correct, the slave may still die, but because he lives for a day or two, the owner is not punished, other than by the loss of his property (literally, silver or money). This is the majority view of the commentators, who see that this is either an example of the persistence of unjust social structures in the OT (so, e.g., Walter Brueggemann, "The Book of Exodus," in *The New Interpreter's Bible* [12 vols.; ed. Leander Keck; Nashville: Abingdon, 1994], 1:675–981), or of the relative violence of the owner's action, or the lack of murderous intent (so, e.g., Martin Noth, *Exodus: A Commentary* [Old Testament Library; London: SCM, 1962]). In support of that translation and interpretation is the absence of a preposition (*'ahar*, "after") and the fact that the verb in question (*'amad*, "stand") can mean "endure, persist." Where it has this meaning, however, it refers either to God, a structure, an abstract noun such as a covenant, or to God's righteousness, not a human person. With reference to a person it means "remain, stand" or "stand up," not "live" or "survive." Furthermore, Hebrew often fails to use prepositions (such as "on," "to," "for," or "after") where we might expect them.

Thus, given the normal meaning of the verb, it seems to me that the NIV gives a better translation. The text, then, speaks not of the slave living a day or two (then dying), indicating that the owner did not use murderous force or have murderous intent, but rather of the slave being able to stand after a day or two, indicating that the owner did not use such excessive force that the slave was permanently incapacitated. That, it seems to me, is important and indicates that, contrary to the view of most commentators, slaves might be property, but they are still persons (so too G. H. Haas, "Slave, Slavery," in *Dictionary of the Old Testament: Pentateuch* [ed. T. D. Alexander and D. W. Baker; Downers Grove, Ill.: InterVarsity Press, 2003], 779–83). Even so, the text is clear that the slave is his (or her) master's property, his silver or money, which is the main point in question.

John Calvin's idea of accommodation is found throughout his work, but is clearly expressed in the *Institutes of the Christian Religion* (trans. F. L. Battles; Philadelphia: Westminster, 1960), I.xiii.1, where he speaks of God "lisping" to us as a nurse does to children.

 ### CLEAN AND UNCLEAN

The issues relating to Leviticus and the role of cleanness, uncleanness, and holiness are discussed in the Leviticus commentaries listed above. As I noted, my discussion depends heavily on the work of Gordon Wenham. There is also a useful (if somewhat technical) discussion of the cleanliness system and its rationale in Joe Sprinkle, "The Rationale of the Laws of Clean and Unclean in the Old Testament," *Journal of the Evangelical Theological Society* 43 (2000): 637-57.

For the claim that true leprosy (Hansen's disease) was unknown in ancient Israel, see Richard Heller, "Mold: 'Tsara'at,' Leviticus, and the History of a Confusion," *Perspectives in Biology and Medicine* 46 (2003): 588-91.

 ### HOLY WAR

The book *Show Them No Mercy: Four Views on God and Canaanite Genocide* (Grand Rapids: Zondervan, 2003), by C. S. Cowles, Eugene Merrill, Daniel Gard, and Tremper Longman III, does as it says and presents four evangelical views on the issue. I find Cowles's position the least satisfactory, and although I see value in all the pieces, in the end I found none of them entirely satisfactory, largely because they deal with the issue, at least in part, as one of ethics rather than theology. Nonetheless, this book is a good place to start.

Useful discussions of Deut 7 and the general issues it raises are found also in the major commentaries on Deuteronomy. For more "negative" perspectives, see Walter Brueggemann, *Deuteronomy* (Abingdon Old Testament Commentaries; Nashville: Abingdon, 2001); Thomas Mann, *Deuteronomy* (Westminster Bible Companion; Louisville: Westminster John Knox, 1995); and Patrick Miller, *Deuteronomy* (Interpretation; Louisville: John Knox, 1990). For views approximating those outlined in chapter 4, see

Christopher J. H. Wright, *Deuteronomy* (New International Biblical Commentary; Peabody, Mass.: Hendrickson, 1996); J. Gordon McConville, *Deuteronomy* (Leicester: Apollos, 2002); Peter Craigie, *Deuteronomy* (New International Commentary on the Old Testament; Grand Rapids: Eerdmans, 1976); and J. Gary Millar, *Now Choose Life: Theology and Ethics in Deuteronomy* (Leicester: Apollos, 1998). Also helpful, though brief, is the appendix in Christopher J. H. Wright, *Old Testament Ethics for the People of God* (Leicester: Inter-Varsity Press, 2004). The larger issues of war in the OT and God's role as a warrior, are addressed in Peter Craigie, *The Problem of War in the Old Testament* (Grand Rapids: Eerdmans, 1978); and Tremper Longman III and Daniel Reid, *God Is a Warrior* (Grand Rapids: Zondervan, 1995). Wright outlines his alternative view of the ban in his Deuteronomy commentary.

Chapter 4: Exploring the Territory

 ### Genesis 1–3 and the Environment

For the nature of our environmental crisis and Christian responses to it, see R. J. Berry, ed., *The Care of Creation: Focusing Our Concern and Action* (Leicester: Inter-Varsity Press, 2000); Lawrence Osborn, *Guardians of Creation: Nature in Theology and the Christian Life* (Leicester: Apollos, 1993); Wesley Granberg-Michaelson, ed., *Tending the Garden: Essays on the Gospel and the Earth* (Grand Rapids: Eerdmans, 1987); and Alister McGrath, *The Re-Enchantment of Nature: Science, Religion and the Human Sense of Wonder* (London: Hodder & Stoughton, 2002).

The best commentaries on Genesis are, in my view, Gordon Wenham, *Genesis 1-15* (Word Biblical Commentary; Waco, Tex.: Word, 1987); Terence Fretheim, "Genesis," in *The New Interpreter's Bible* (12 vols.; ed. Leander Keck; Nashville: Abingdon, 1994), 1:319-674. Both of these are, however, fairly technical works. Probably the best entry-level commentary is John Hartley, *Genesis* (New International Biblical Commentary; Peabody, Mass.: Hendrickson, 2000). Other useful commentaries include Laurence Turner, *Genesis* (Sheffield: Sheffield Academic Press, 2000), which takes an interesting literary-theological approach to the text; Victor Hamilton,

The Book of Genesis: Chapters 1-17 (New International Commentary on the Old Testament; Grand Rapids: Eerdmans, 1990); and Walter Brueggemann, *Genesis* (Interpretation; Louisville: John Knox, 1982), whose views, though misguided on several important matters, are stimulating.

GENESIS 1-3 AND GENDER RELATIONSHIPS

For statistics and so on relating to women, development, and the UN Millennium Development Goals, see the Micah Challenge and Make Poverty History websites listed above.

There is an enormous body of literature on the Bible and gender issues, much of it from an explicitly evangelical perspective. Two key evangelical works are John Piper and Wayne Grudem, eds., *Recovering Biblical Manhood and Womanhood: A Response to Evangelical Feminism* (Wheaton, Ill.: Crossway, 1991); and Ronald Pierce, Rebecca Merrill Groothuis, and Gordon Fee, eds., *Discovering Biblical Equality: Complementarity without Hierarchy* (Leicester: Apollos, 2004). Both deal with the key texts and with theological and social issues but present diametrically opposite points of view: the Piper and Grudem volume is subordinationist or complementarian (to use their confusing, but preferred, term); the Pierce, Groothuis, and Fee volume is, obviously, egalitarian. Wayne Grudem, *Biblical Foundations for Manhood and Womanhood* (Wheaton, Ill.: Crossway, 2002), attempts–unsuccessfully, in my view–to counter the egalitarian biblical arguments and present "feminism" as a threat to true evangelical faith. Mary Stewart van Leeuwen, ed., *After Eden: Facing the Challenge of Gender Reconciliation* (Grand Rapids: Eerdmans, 1993), is an interesting multidisciplinary volume exploring gender equality from a Reformed and evangelical point of view.

My arguments have been very much influenced by Phyllis Trible, *God and the Rhetoric of Sexuality* (Philadelphia: Fortress, 1978), although I part company with her on a few points, such as whether Gen 2:23 is an instance of the naming formula, and the sexuality of the man prior to the advent of the woman. Wenham's Genesis commentary takes a subordinationist line on gender issues in Gen 1-3, while those of Fretheim, Hartley, and Hamilton take an egalitarian line similar to mine.

The Decalogue (Ten Commandments): Deuteronomy 5:6-21

I adopt the standard Reformed Protestant numbering of the commandments. For a discussion of this matter and others, see the Deuteronomy commentaries listed above.

There are many studies on ethics and the Ten Commandments, more or less useful. An interesting example is Walter Harrelson, *The Ten Commandments and Human Rights* (Philadelphia: Fortress, 1980), a moderately technical treatment of the Decalogue and its development in the OT. Although I disagree with him on the development and role of the Ten Commandments in Israel's moral vision, and I think that he is fundamentally wrong about the Sabbath in particular, he has a number of interesting insights.

For an interesting treatment of the Decalogue as shaping a vision of a moral community in terms of a "good neighborhood," see Patrick D. Miller, "The Good Neighborhood: Identity and Community through the Commandments," in *Character and Scripture: Moral Formation, Community, and Biblical Interpretation* (ed. William P. Brown; Grand Rapids: Eerdmans, 2002), 55-72.

The question of adultery and whether it is an instance of property law has been much discussed in OT exegesis and ethics. The arguments for wives being treated as a kind of property are rehearsed and refuted in the fairly technical work by Christopher J. H. Wright, *God's People in God's Land: Family, Land, and Property in the Old Testament* (Grand Rapids: Eerdmans, 1990).

Chapter 5: Bringing the Old Testament Home

 ## Cloning

A number of the introductions to Christian ethics listed above deal briefly with issues of bioethics. The best general discussion of bioethics from a Christian point of view is Gilbert Meilaender, *Bioethics: A Primer for Christians* (2d ed.; Grand Rapids: Eerdmans, 2005). Another good, if more technical treatment, is Edwin Hui, *At the Beginning of Life: Dilemmas in Theological Bioethics* (Downers Grove, Ill.: InterVarsity Press, 2002), which also has a useful discussion of cloning, including stem cell research.

For an alternative, clearly non-Christian (perhaps even anti-Christian), viewpoint, see Peter Singer, *Rethinking Life and Death: The Collapse of Our Traditional Ethics* (Melbourne: Text, 1994); or, his much more philosophically focused *Practical Ethics* (2d ed.; Cambridge: Cambridge University Press, 1993). Singer specifically states that using (say, anencephalic) infants for organ donation is ethically preferable to xenotransplantation (see, e.g., *Rethinking Life and Death*, 38-56). For a Christian response to Singer's views, see Gordon Preece, ed., *Rethinking Peter Singer: A Christian Critique* (Downers Grove, Ill.: InterVarsity, 2002).

 ## Isaiah 46 and the Critique of Idolatry

The OT introductions listed above discuss issues relating to Isa 40-55 and the book of Isaiah, as do the commentaries. The most helpful commentaries on Isa 40-55 are John Goldingay, *Isaiah* (New International Biblical Commentary; Peabody, Mass.: Hendrickson, 2001), a good, one-volume commentary that reads Isa 40-55 clearly in the context of exile; Barry Webb, *Isaiah* (Leicester: Inter-Varsity, 1996), is another good one-volume commentary that takes the whole book as written by Isaiah of Jerusalem in the eighth century B.C.; John Oswalt, *The Book of Isaiah: Chapters 40-66* (New International Commentary on the Old Testament; Grand Rapids: Eerdmans, 1998), is much more technical but is a useful conservative commentary; Walter Brueggemann, *Isaiah 40-66* (Westminster Bible Companion; Louisville: Westminster John Knox, 1998) is fairly detailed, often anything but conservative, but stimulating; Christopher Seitz, "The Book of Isaiah 40-66," in *The New Interpreter's Bible* (12 vols.; ed. Leander Keck; Nashville: Abingdon, 2001), 6:307-552, provides very interesting reflections on the text. Christopher Wright has an interesting discussion of idolatry in the Bible and contemporary society in his recent book, *The Mission of God: Unlocking the Bible's Grand Narrative* (Downers Grove: InterVarsity Press, 2006)—see chapter 5, "The Living God Confronts Idolatry."

Interesting, if at times dense, reflections on the exile and Christian faith are found in Erskine Clarke, ed., *Exilic Preaching: Testimony for Christian Exiles in an Increasingly Hostile Culture* (Harrisburg,

Penn.: Trinity, 1998); and Michael Frost, *Exiles: Living Missionally in a Post-Christian Culture* (Peabody, Mass.: Hendrickson, 2006).

Jacques Ellul, a twentieth-century French sociologist and theologian, presents a brilliant and devastating critique of the cultural idol of technique. See, for instance, *What I Believe* (Grand Rapids: Eerdmans, 1989).

INDEX OF MODERN AUTHORS

INDEX OF SUBJECTS

Index of Scripture References